Quod scriptura, non iubet vetat

The Latin translates, "What is not commanded in scripture, is forbidden:'

On the Cover: Baptists rejoice to hold in common with other evangelicals the main principles of the orthodox Christian faith. However, there are points of difference and these differences are significant. In fact, because these differences arise out of God's revealed will, they are of vital importance. Hence, the barriers of separation between Baptists and others can hardly be considered a trifling matter. To suppose that Baptists are kept apart solely by their views on Baptism or the Lord's Supper is a regrettable misunderstanding. Baptists hold views which distinguish them from Catholics, Congregationalists, Episcopalians, Lutherans, Methodists, Pentecostals, and Presbyterians, and the differences are so great as not only to justify, but to demand, the separate denominational existence of Baptists. Some people think Baptists ought not teach and emphasize their differences but as E.J. Forrester stated in 1893, "Any denomination that has views which justify its separate existence, is bound to promulgate those views. If those views are of sufficient importance to justify a separate existence, they are important enough to create a duty for their promulgation ... the very same reasons which justify the separate existence of any denomination make it the duty of that denomination to teach the distinctive doctrines upon which its separate existence rests." If Baptists have a right to a separate denominational life, it is their duty to propagate their distinctive principles, without which their separate life cannot be justified or maintained.

Many among today's professing Baptists have an agenda to revise the Baptist distinctives and redefine what it means to be a Baptist. Others don't understand why it even matters. The books being reproduced in the *Baptist Distinctives Series* are republished in order that Baptists from the past may state, explain and defend the primary Baptist distinctives as they understood them. It is hoped that this Series will provide a more thorough historical perspective on what it means to be distinctively Baptist.

The Lord Jesus Christ asked, *"And why call ye me, Lord, Lord, and do not the things which I say?"* (Luke 6:46). The immediate context surrounding this question explains what it means to be a true disciple of Christ. Addressing the same issue, Christ's question is meant to show that a confession of discipleship to the Lord Jesus Christ is inconsistent and untrue if it is not accompanied with a corresponding submission to His authoritative commands. Christ's question teaches us that a true recognition of His authority as Lord inevitably includes a submission to the authority of His Word. Hence, with this question Christ has made it forever impossible to separate His authority as King from the authority of His Word. These two principles—the authority of Christ as King and the authority of His Word—are the two most fundamental Baptist distinctives. The first gives rise to the second and out of these two all the other Baptist distinctives emanate. As F.M. Iams wrote in 1894, "Loyalty to Christ as King, manifesting itself in a constant and unswerving obedience to His will as revealed in His written Word, is the real source of all the Baptist distinctives:' In the search for the *primary* Baptist distinctive many have settled on the Lordship of Christ as the most basic distinctive. Strangely, in doing this, some have attempted to separate Christ's Lordship from the authority of Scripture, as if you could embrace Christ's authority without submitting to what He commanded. However, while Christ's Lordship and Kingly authority can be isolated and considered essentially for discussion's sake, we see from Christ's own words in Luke 6:46 that His Lordship is really inseparable from His Word and, with regard to real Christian discipleship, there can be no practical submission to the one without a practical submission to the other.

In the symbol above the Kingly Crown and the Open Bible represent the inseparable truths of Christ's Kingly and Biblical authority. The Crown and Bible graphics are supplemented by three Bible verses (Ecclesiastes 8:4, Matthew 28:18-20, and Luke 6:46) that reiterate and reinforce the inextricable connection between the authority of Christ as King and the authority of His Word. The truths symbolized by these components are further emphasized by the Latin quotation - *quod scriptura, non iubet vetat*— *i.e.,* "What is not commanded in scripture, is forbidden:' This Latin quote has been considered historically as a summary statement of the regulative principle of Scripture. Together these various symbolic components converge to exhibit the two most foundational Baptist Distinctives out of which all the other Baptist Distinctives arise. Consequently, we have chosen this composite symbol as a logo to represent the primary truths set forth in the *Baptist Distinctives Series.*

A TREATISE ON
CHURCH ORDER

JOHN L. DAGG
1794-1884

Photo courtesy of:
Southern Baptist Historical Library and Archives,
Nashville, Tennessee

A TREATISE ON
CHURCH ORDER.

BY

JOHN LEADLEY DAGG

That thou shouldst set in order the things that are wanting, and ordain elders in every city.—Titus i. 5.

The rest will I set in order when I come.—1 Cor. xi. 34.

With a Biographical Sketch of the Author by John Franklin Jones

Charleston, South Carolina
THE SOUTHERN BAPTIST PUBLICATION SOCIETY
1858.

he Baptist Standard Bearer, Inc.
NUMBER ONE IRON OAKS DRIVE • PARIS, ARKANSAS 72855

Thou hast given a *standard* to them that fear thee;
that it may be displayed because of the truth.
– Psalm 60:4

Reprinted 2006

by

THE BAPTIST STANDARD BEARER, INC.
No. 1 Iron Oaks Drive
Paris, Arkansas 72855
(479) 963-3831

THE WALDENSIAN EMBLEM
lux lucet in tenebris
"The Light Shineth in the Darkness"

ISBN# 1579784984

PREFACE.

In the Preface to the "Manual of Theology," published last year, it was said :—" This volume contains nothing respecting the externals of religion. The form of godliness is important, as well as its power, and the doctrine respecting it is a component part of the Christian system; but I have been unable to include it in the present work." The defect here acknowledged, the following treatise on Church Order, including the ceremonies of Christianity, is intended in part to supply.

In all religious investigations, the Holy Scriptures are our chief source of knowledge. This is especially true in regard to positive institutes, which derive all their obligation from the revealed will of the lawgiver. The present work, therefore, relies wholly on the Bible for proof of its positions, so far as they relate to subjects on which the Bible professes to give instruction. But the volume of inspiration was not given to teach us the meaning of words, or the facts of ecclesiastical history after the times of the apostles. When these subjects come under investigation, I have made such reference to human authority as the case seemed to require. It has been my aim, however, so to lay the facts before the mind of the reader, as to give full scope for the exercise of private judgment, and a consciousness that he is not bowing to the decisions of any fallible master.

In most of the investigations attempted in these pages, the sacred volume sheds its light on our path, and enables us to tread the way with confidence; but, at a few points, the light seems to shine with less clearness. Here, the inquiry becomes appropriate, whether the very silence of Scripture is not instructive? We may infer that whatever is not clearly revealed, must be of less importance; and that difference of judgment respecting it ought not to divide the people of God.

The objections and opposing arguments which this work encounters, are such as appear to me most likely to embarrass an inquirer. They are generally expressed in my own language; but, in the discussions on baptism, I am in a few instances indebted for the language, as well as the thoughts, to the Lectures of Dr. Woods. In controverting the opinions of Baptist authors, I have, in some instances, thought it best to present these opinions in the form of direct quotation.

The preparation of this treatise has yielded less religious enjoyment to the Author, than was experienced in writing the "Manual." The subject has less to do with the heart, and furnished fewer occasions for those emotions in which religious enjoyment consists. But the work has been prosecuted under a calm conviction of duty; and if it shall tend to produce, in those who read it, a scrupulous adherence to the precepts of Christ, with expansive love to all who bear his image, the Author's labor will not be in vain. With a hope that it may contribute somewhat to this result, it is commended to the blessing of him whose will it attempts to unfold.

Gratitude requires that I should acknowledge my obligations to the Rev. G. W. Samson, of Washington City, and the Rev. A. M. Poindexter, of Richmond, Va. These brethren have kindly made suggestions, from which the work has received valuable improvements; and Mr. Samson has directly contributed the chief article in the Appendix.

July 31, 1858.

CONTENTS.

INTRODUCTION.

	PAGE
Obedience to Christ	9

CHAPTER I.

	PAGE
Baptism	13
Sec. 1. Perpetuity of Baptism	13
2. Meaning of *Baptize*	21
Tables of Examples	23
Remarks on Table I.	31
Relation between βαπτω and βαπτιζω	32
Deduction from Table II.	34
Confirmation of the Result	36
Burial in Baptism	38
Arguments for another meaning	44

            1. For partial immersion, 44; 2. 3. For purification, 46, 50; 4. For a peculiar sense in Scripture, 51; 5. For a peculiar sense in religious ceremony, 54; 6. 7. From circumstantial evidence, 58, 60; 8. From Baptism of the Spirit, 65.

	PAGE
Arguments against the requirement of literal obedience	66

            1. From feet-washing, 66; 2. From the command by which the Supper was instituted, 67; 3. Unsuitableness of Immersion, 67.

(v)

CONTENTS.

	PAGE
Sec. 3. Subjects of Baptism	68
4. Design of Baptism	70
5. Connection of Baptism with Church Order	73

CHAPTER II.

Local Churches	74
Sec. 1. Moral Characteristics	74
Assembly	74
Members	79
Organization	80
Independence	83
Divine Rule	84
Design	93
2. Ceremonial Qualification for Membership	95
3. False Professors	97

CHAPTER III.

The Church Universal	100
Sec. 1. Membership	100
The generic church	101
2. Visibility	121
3. Unity	125
4. Organization	128
The Visible Church Catholic, 130; The Baptized Church, 136.	
5. Progress and Duration	137
6. Relation to Christ's Kingdom	139
7. Relation to Local Churches	142

CHAPTER IV.

Infant Membership	144
Sec. 1. Direct Arguments for Infant Membership	144
1. The Epistles, 144; 2. Matt. xix. 14, 146; 3. 1 Cor. vii. 14, 155; 4. Congregation of the Lord, 156; 5. Abrahamic Covenant, 164.	

CONTENTS. vii

Sec. 2. Arguments for Infant Baptism 183
    1. Faith required of adults only, 184; 2. On the same ground as female Communion and the Christian Sabbath, 184; 3. Infants included in all nations, 186; 4. Infants may be disciples, 187; 5. Commission to proselyte, 190; 6. Baptism takes the place of circumcision, 191; 7. Baptism is analogous to circumcision, 194; 8. Baptism of households, 195; 9. Ecclesiastical history, 199.

CHAPTER V.

Communion 203
  Sec. 1. Perpetuity of the Lord's Supper 203
    2. Design 209
    3. Communicants 212
    4. Open Communion 214
    Arguments.—1. First Communicants, 214; 2. Commission, 215; 3. Primitive example, 216; 4. Order of the things signified, 217; 5. Brotherly love, 217; 6. The true Church, 218; 7. Exclusion a punishment, 219; 8. Toleration, 219; 9. Pulpit Communion, 223; 10. The Lord's Table, 224.

CHAPTER VI.

Washing of Feet 226

CHAPTER VII.

Public Worship 232
  Sec. 1. Time.—Christian Sabbath . . . 232
    2. Mode 238

CHAPTER VIII.

Ministry 241
  Sec. 1. Ministry of the Word 241
    A distinct class 241
    Their Work 243
    Their Call 245
    Objections 252

CONTENTS.

	PAGE
SEC. 2. Administration of Baptism	254
3. Apostolic Succession	257
4. Church Officers	263
Bishops	263
Deacons	266

CHAPTER IX.

Discipline	268
SEC. 1. Admission of Members	268
2. Spiritual Improvement	270
3. Excommunication	273

CHAPTER X.

Miscellaneous Topics	275
SEC. 1. Expedience of the Scriptural Order	275
2. Fellowship between Churches	279
3. Imposition of Hands	281
4. Rebaptism	282
May be necessary	282
Who must decide	282
First Case	283
Second Case	284
5. Treatment of Unbaptized Ministers	286

CONCLUSION.

Duty of Baptists	299

APPENDIX.

Situation of Enon	305
Place of the Eunuch's Baptism	306
Immersion in Cold Climates	308

CHURCH ORDER.

INTRODUCTION.

OBEDIENCE TO CHRIST.

To love God with all the heart is the sum of all duty. Love must be exercised according to the relations which we bear. When a parent loves his child, he feels bound to exercise parental authority over it for its benefit; but the love of a child towards a parent requires obedience. So love to God produces obedience; for it is impossible to love God supremely without a supreme desire to please him in all things. Hence this one principle contains, involved in it, perfect obedience to every divine requirement.

The loveliness of the divine character is not abated, by being exhibited in the humble nature of man, in the person of Jesus Christ. In him the glory of the Father appears, claiming our supreme affections; and he is invested with the Father's authority, to which perfect obedience is due. The divine perfections are rendered more intelligible to us by his mediation; and, in proportion to the clearness of the discovery, the obligation to love and obey becomes increased.

A powerful motive, to love and obey Christ, is drawn from the love which he has manifested in dying for us. Paul felt this in an overpowering degree, when he said, "I am crucified with Christ, nevertheless I live; yet not I, but Christ liveth in me; and the life which I now live in the flesh, I live by the faith of the Son of God, who loved me, and gave himself for me."[1] The same overpowering impulse to love and obedience, is brought to view in another declaration of this apostle: "The love of Christ constraineth us; because we thus judge, that if one died for all, then were all dead; and that he died for all, that they which live should not henceforth live unto themselves, but unto him which died for them, and rose again."[2] When our love to the Saviour grows cold, we should repair to his cross, and fix our thoughts on the exhibition of love there presented. And when we feel our hearts melt, the recollection that the suffering Saviour is God over all, must produce a full purpose to yield to him the obedience of all our powers during our whole existence. From the cross we come forth to be Christ's, resolved to glorify him with our bodies and our spirits, which are his.

Jesus said to his disciples, "If ye love me, keep my commandments." This claim of obedience is cordially admitted by every true disciple. When the first emotion of love to Christ throbbed in the heart of the persecuting Saul, he inquired, "Lord, what wilt thou have me to do?"

The first disciples were required to serve their Lord and Master by strenuous efforts to spread his religion through the world; and the same obligation devolves on us. He came to be the Saviour of the world; and, notwithstanding the humility of his appearance, and the feebleness of the instrumentality which he chose, the religion of the despised Nazarene must prevail over the earth, and bless every nation of mankind. The conquest of the world has not yet been achieved, but the work is before us; and, if we are loyal subjects of Zion's King, we must give ourselves to its accomplishment.

The means which our King employs, for diffusing the blessings of his reign, are not such as human wisdom would have adopted. It has pleased the Lord, "by the foolishness of preaching, to save them that believe." It has seemed good to infinite wisdom, that the religion which is to bless mankind, should be propagated by the simple instrumentality of the Christian ministry and the Christian churches. If we seek military force, or legislative enactments, to accomplish the work, we turn away from the simplicity of Christ,

---

[1] Gal. ii. 20.   [2] 2 Cor. v. 14, 15.

and convert his kingdom into one of this world; and, whenever human wisdom has attempted, in any particular, to improve the simple means that Christ ordained, the progress of truth and righteousness has been impeded.

Much that has existed, and that now exists, among the professed followers of Christ, cannot be contemplated by one who sincerely loves him, without deep distress. Different creeds, and different ecclesiastical organizations, have divided those who bear his name into hostile parties, and Christianity has been disgraced, and its progress retarded. The world has seen hatred and persecution where brotherly love ought to have been exhibited; and Christ has been crucified afresh, and put to open shame, by those who claim to be his disciples.

For these evils, what shall be the remedy? Shall we look to the wisdom of this world, to devise the cure? Human wisdom did not originate the institutions of Christianity; and it is now unable to give them efficiency. We must return to the feet of our divine Master, and again receive his instructions. Let us, in the spirit of obedient disciples, inquire for the good old paths, that we may walk therein. No individual can accomplish everything; but it is his duty to do what he can. Let each one show that he possesses the spirit of Christ, and carefully obey all the commands of Christ. If he cannot cure the existing evils, he will, at least, not increase them; and the influence of his example may produce salutary effects beyond his most sanguine hopes.

The true spirit of obedience is willing to receive the slightest intimations of the divine will. All the truths of Revelation are not equally clear; yet none of them may be disregarded because of difficulty in their investigation. If some most needful to be known, are presented prominently on the inspired pages, and written in characters so large that he who runs may read; there are others which are discoverable only by diligent search. Yet the truths, thus discovered, are precious gems dug from an exhaustless mine; and even the very labor of discovery brings its own reward in the mental and spiritual discipline which it furnishes. The diligent student of the Scriptures derives an abundant recompense for his toil, not only from the enlarged and clearer views of divine truth to which he attains, but also from that constant exercise of humility and faith, for which he finds occasion at every step of his progress.

As the truths of revelation differ in the clearness with which they are exhibited, so our faith embraces them with different degrees of strength. A man who does not investigate for himself, may receive, with unwavering confidence, and maintain, with obstinate pertinacity, every dogma of his party: but he who uses his own powers in the search after truth, will find some things to be received as undoubted articles of faith, others as opinions to be held with various degrees of confidence, according to the strength of evidence with which they have been severally presented to the mind. By not furnishing overpowering evidence on every question of faith and practice, the divine wisdom has given scope for the moral dispositions of men to exert their influence. A careful inquiry respecting the minutest portions of duty, and a fixed determination to observe the will of God in every particular, may exhibit proofs of obedience more strong and decisive, than would be possible, if all truth and duty were discovered by intuition.

Our obedience to Christ should be universal. The tithing of mint, anise, and cummin, is of less moment than the weightier matters of law, judgment, mercy, and faith; but it is not therefore to be disregarded. Christ taught that both were to be observed. "These ought ye to have done, and not to leave the other undone."[1] Church order and the ceremonials of religion, are less important than a new heart; and in the view of some, any laborious investigation of questions respecting them may appear to be needless and unprofitable. But we know, from the Holy Scriptures, that Christ gave commands on these subjects, and we cannot refuse to obey. Love prompts our obedience; and love prompts also the search which may be necessary to ascertain his will. Let us, therefore, prosecute the investigations which are before us, with a fervent prayer, that the Holy Spirit, who guides into all truth, may assist us to learn the will of him whom we supremely love and adore.

---

[1] Matt. xxiii. 23.

CHAPTER I.

BAPTISM.

SECTION I.—PERPETUITY OF BAPTISM.

WATER BAPTISM IS A CHRISTIAN ORDINANCE OF PERPETUAL OBLIGATION.

The commission of Christ to his apostles reads thus: " Go, teach all nations, baptizing them in the name of the Father, and of the Son, and of the Holy Ghost; teaching them to observe all things whatsoever I have commanded you; and lo, I am with you alway, even unto the end of the world."[1] It is not expressly stated in these words that water must be used in the baptizing which is enjoined; but so common is the use of water, that a command to immerse, wash, or sprinkle, naturally implies the use of it, unless something in the circumstances of the case, or connection of the word, suggests the use of some other liquid. The word baptize is often used in Scripture where water is implied without being expressly mentioned. The apostles had been accustomed to the administration of water baptism. They had been chosen to be Christ's attendants and witnesses, from the baptism of John;[2] and, in all probability, many of them saw their Master baptized in the Jordan. They had witnessed John's baptism in other cases; and some, if not all of them, had been baptized by him. After Jesus entered on his ministry, it was said that he "made and baptized more disciples than John."[3] Water baptism must be intended here; and we are expressly informed that the disciples, and not Jesus himself, administered it. This they did while they were under the imme-

---

[1] Matt. xxviii. 19, 20.   [2] Acts i. 22.   [3] John iv. 1.

diate direction of their Master, and were his personal attendants. His ministry, and their baptisms, were confined to the nation of Israel. The commission quoted above enlarged the field of their operation. The presence of their Master was promised, though his body was about to be removed from them; and the command to teach or make disciples, and to baptize, would naturally be interpreted by them according to the use of terms to which they had been accustomed. In their subsequent ministry, they preached and baptized; and the record, called the Acts of the Apostles, contains frequent mention of baptisms. In these, no reasonable doubt can exist that water was used: and sometimes it is expressly mentioned.

The commission was given, just before Christ ascended to heaven, and was designed for the dispensation which was to follow. The apostles, before proceeding to execute it, were commanded to tarry in Jerusalem until they should be endued with power from on high. This promised power was given when the Holy Spirit was poured out upon them on the day of Pentecost. It is clear, therefore, that, in the view of the Lord Jesus, water baptism was not inconsistent with the spiritual dispensation which the day of Pentecost introduced.

Besides its literal use, the word baptize is sometimes employed figuratively, when spiritual influence, or overwhelming sufferings, are intended. In such instances there is always something in the context, or circumstances of the case, directing to the proper interpretation. When there is nothing that directs to a figurative interpretation, we are required, by a well known law of criticism, to take the word in its literal sense. According to this law, we are bound to interpret literally the language of plain command used in the commission; and, if "baptizing" must be taken literally, no doubt can exist that the use of water was intended in the command.

Since the ascension of Christ, no change of dispensation has occurred by which the commission could be revoked. The promise which it contains, of Christ's presence until the end of the world, implies its perpetuity. Under this commission the ministers of Christ now act, and by it they are bound, according to the manifest intention of his words, to administer water baptism.

In different ages of Christianity some persons have denied the obligation of water baptism. The modern sect, called Quakers, are of this number. The objections which they urge deserve our attention.

Objection 1.—The proper rendering of the commission, is, "baptizing into the name of," &c. The name of God signifies his power, or some influence proceeding from him. The baptism *into* spiritual influence cannot be water baptism.

We admit the correction of the translation, but not the inference drawn from it. The same Greek preposition is used in other passages which forbid the inference now drawn. John said, "I baptize you unto [into] repentance." Repentance is a spiritual duty: but baptism into repentance is not, therefore, a spiritual baptism; for the words of John fully quoted, are: "I baptize you *with water* into repentance." In another passage it is said, "John preached the baptism of repentance for [into] the remission of sins:" and Peter, on the day of Pentecost, commanded, "Repent and be baptized for [into] the remission of sins." The remission of sins is a spiritual blessing, but it does not follow that baptism into the remission of sins must be a spiritual baptism. John's we know was water baptism; and when those who received Peter's command are said to have been baptized, the sacred historian employs the simple language of plain history: "Then they that gladly received his word were baptized."[1] These examples prove that the use of the preposition *into*, is not inconsistent with the literal interpretation of the commission.

Objection 2.—The baptism of John is, in the Scriptures, carefully distinguished from the baptism of Christ; the former being with water, the latter with the Spirit. The apostles were to act for Christ, and the commission authorized them to administer *his* baptism. Parallel texts may be found, in which the apostles are said to impart spiritual gifts.

Although John had predicted, that Christ would baptize with the Holy Spirit; yet the disciples made by Christ during his personal ministry, were baptized with water. This was administered by his disciples, and doubtless with his sanction. The careful mention by the evangelist that Jesus did not himself baptize, shows that baptism with the Holy Spirit is not in this case intended. John's words, "He shall baptize you with the Holy Ghost," describe spiritual baptism as Christ's peculiar personal work, and we do not

---

[1] Acts ii. 41.

find any passage of Scripture which speaks of the apostles, or any other ministers of Christ, *baptizing* with the Holy Spirit. Such baptism as they had been accustomed to administer, in the presence, and by the authority of Christ, the commission required them to administer.

It is true that Paul was sent to the Gentiles, to open their eyes, and to turn them from darkness to light, and from the power of Satan unto God; but these things are mentioned as the effects of his mission, and not as things directly commanded. The duty commanded, was to preach the gospel. The blessing of God on his ministry rendered his mission effectual to open the eyes of the Gentiles, and to confer the spiritual benefits mentioned in the special commission which he received. But the baptizing mentioned in the commission given to the other apostles, is a commanded duty, and the command must be understood according to the literal import of the words.

Objection 3.—Paul teaches that there is one baptism. Now, there is a baptism of the Spirit; and if water baptism is a perpetual ordinance of Christianity, there are two baptisms, instead of one.

Paul says, "One Lord, one faith, and one baptism." As he uses the words Lord and faith in their literal senses, so he uses the word baptism in its literal sense. In this sense there is but one baptism. John the Baptist foretold that Christ would baptize with the Holy Spirit: and Jesus said to his disciples, "Ye shall be baptized with the baptism that I am baptized with." Both these baptisms were known to Paul. These figurative baptisms were two in number; while the literal baptism was but one. He must, therefore, have intended the latter.

Objection 4.—Peter has defined the true Christian baptism, both negatively and positively. It is ("not the putting away of the filth of the flesh, but the answer of a good conscience toward God), by the resurrection of Jesus Christ."[1] The first clause denies that it is water baptism; and the second affirms that it is spiritual baptism. This is confirmed by the fact that it is said to *save*, which water baptism cannot do. Moreover, the words "the like figure," should be rendered *the antitype*. When spiritual things are compared to literal, the literal are the type, and the spiritual the antitype. Hence, as baptism is called the antitype, spiritual baptism must be intended.

---

[1] 1 Peter iii. 21.

Water baptism, as a Christian rite, is not administered to cleanse the flesh, either literally or ceremonially. It figuratively represents the burial and resurrection of Christ, on which the believer relies for salvation. The answer of a good conscience is obtained by faith in the finished work of Christ, represented in the rite. In the language of Scripture, a thing is said *to be* that which it represents: thus, "The field *is* the world." "This *is* my body." "This cup *is* the new testament." So Paul was said to wash away his sins in baptism, because it represented their being washed away: and so in this passage, baptism is said to save, because it represents our salvation, which is effected by the burial and resurrection of Christ; not by the removing of any corporeal defilement.

The criticism on the word antitype is inaccurate. The antitype is that which corresponds to the type; but it is not necessarily spiritual. The earthly sanctuary is, in one place, called the antitype of the heavenly, "which are the figures [antitypes] of the true."[1] In this passage "the holy places made with hands" are the antitype; and heaven is the type to which the antitype corresponds. This relation between the type and antitype, reverses the order which the objection assumes to be universal.

Objection 5.—The Jews had divers baptisms, which Paul calls "carnal ordinances imposed on them till the time of reformation."[2] An ordinance is not rendered carnal by the time when it is observed; but by its own nature. The Jewish baptisms were commanded by God, and were significant of spiritual things. Water baptism cannot have higher authority, or be more significant; and is, therefore, a carnal ordinance in its own nature, and not suited to Christ's spiritual dispensation. It belonged properly to John's dispensation, and was designed to be superseded by Christ's spiritual baptism, according to the words of John, "He must increase, but I must decrease."[3]

In speaking of the Jewish ceremonies, Paul says, "Which stood in meats and drinks, and divers baptisms, and carnal ordinances." This passage does not confound baptisms, with carnal ordinances, but seems rather to distinguish between them. Nevertheless, as the Jewish baptisms sanctified to the purifying of the flesh, there may be a propriety in denominating them carnal. Christian baptism is not administered for this purpose; and, therefore, is not

---

[1] Heb. ix. 24.   [2] Heb. ix. 10.   [3] John iii. 30.

carnal in the same sense. But, whatever it may be called, if Christ instituted it for the observance of his followers, we dare not account it unsuitable to his dispensation. The Jewish dispensation abounded with ceremonies; but amidst them all, a spiritual service was required; for even then the sacrifices of God were a broken spirit.[1] The ceremonies were wisely adapted to promote spirituality, rather than to hinder it. Our more spiritual dispensation needs fewer helps of this kind: but we are yet in the body, and God has judged it fit to assist our faith by visible representations. To reject their use, is to be wiser than God.

Water baptism was not superseded by the baptism of the Spirit. While Peter was preaching to Cornelius, and those who were in his house, the Holy Ghost fell on them. The apostle did not consider this a reason for omitting water baptism; but, on the contrary, argued the propriety of administering it, from this very fact: "Can any man forbid water, that these should not be baptized which have received the Holy Ghost, as well as we?"[2] Contrary to all his previous views, the Holy Spirit had guided the apostle to preach the gospel to these uncircumcised gentiles, and to admit them to Christian baptism. If this rite had been designed for Jews only, or to be superseded by the baptism of the Spirit, Peter committed a mistake in commanding these first Gentile converts to be baptized with water. It is true that he had been mistaken before, in confining his ministry to the circumcised; and it may be argued, that he may have been again mistaken in commanding water baptism to the uncircumcised. But the Holy Ghost was now correcting the first error, and it is wholly improbable that in doing this, he should have led him into a second. The propriety of admitting gentile converts had not been determined, as it afterwards was, by a council of the apostles; but Peter followed the teaching of the Holy Spirit, and the subsequent council justified his act. Now, if he had again mistaken the mind of the Spirit in commanding the use of water baptism, it is unaccountable, and inconsistent with the perfection of the Scriptures, that neither he nor the council, in reviewing the transaction under the influence of the Holy Spirit, discovered the mistake; and that no

---

[1] Ps. li. 17.   [2] Acts x. 47.

correction, such as was made of the former error, is anywhere to be found in the inspired writings.

When John spoke the words, "He must increase, but I must decrease," the Jews had said to him, "Rabbi, he that was with thee beyond Jordan, behold the same baptizeth, and all men come to him."[1] The baptism which they reported must have been water baptism, and so far as John's words applied to it, they must denote that water baptism, instead of ceasing under Christ's dispensation, would be greatly extended.

Objection 6.—Paul states in 1st. epistle to the Corinthians, "Christ sent me not to baptize, but to preach the gospel;" and he thanked God that he had baptized so few of them. Now, as he was not a whit behind the chief of the apostles, water baptism would not have been omitted in his commission, if it had been designed to be a perpetual ordinance; and if it was as much his duty to baptize as to preach, he would not have thanked God that he had baptized so few. He would as soon have thanked God that he had preached so little. He baptized some, as he circumcised Timothy, accommodating himself to the weakness of men; but he was thankful that such acts of accommodation had been seldom needed. As he was the chief opponent of the prevailing judaizing tendency, he was thankful that, in the matter of baptizing, he had yielded to it in so few instances.

In this quotation from Paul, the word baptize stands alone, without the mention of water. The objection very properly assumes that water baptism is meant; but, in so doing, it confirms our rule, that the word baptize, when alone, implies the use of water. If the word, when standing alone in such a sentence, could mean the baptism of the Spirit, and if Paul and the other apostles had been commissioned to administer this baptism, he could not have declared with truth, "Christ sent me not to baptize."

Paul claimed to be an apostle, not of men, neither by man, but by Jesus Christ. An apostle is one sent, and Paul was sent by Jesus, who said "to whom I now send thee." He claimed to be an apostle in the highest sense, because he had received his commission directly from Christ: "Am I not an apostle? have I not seen Jesus Christ?"[2] Now, in the commission which he received directly from Christ, he was not commanded, either to be baptized himself or to baptize others. He received the gospel which he

---

[1] John iii. 26.   [2] 1 Cor. ix. 1

preached without human instrumentality; but he did not so receive baptism. He submitted to it, at the command of Ananias, who was not himself one of those originally commissioned to administer it. In this act, Paul acknowledged the obligation to perpetuate the ordinance, and the right of Ananias to administer it by authority derived from the other apostles. At Antioch he was set apart with fasting, prayer, and imposition of hands, for ministerial labor; and, whether this was done with reference to the missionary service on which he immediately entered, or whether it was his first ceremonial investiture with the ministerial office, we learn, from what was done, that his direct commission from Christ, was not designed to set aside the Church order which had been previously established by the other apostles. Both in receiving his own baptism, and in being set apart to the work to which the Holy Ghost had called him, Paul acted as an ordinary Christian. His apostleship for preaching the gospel was directly from Christ, and not by man; but his baptism, and his authority to baptize, were received by man, and in a way which respected and honored the established order of things among the disciples of Christ. While he said with truth, "Christ sent me not to baptize," it was nevertheless true, that the baptisms which he did administer were not unauthorized. He considered the administration of the ordinance not his proper apostolic work; and since the Corinthians had divided themselves into parties, claiming Paul, Apollos, and Cephas, for their leaders, he was thankful that so few of them could claim him as their leader on the ground of having received baptism from him.

Paul did not baptize out of mere accommodation to the weakness of others. Because of the Jews who were in that quarter, he circumcised Timothy, whose mother was a Jewess; but when the judaizers desired to have Titus also circumcised, who was a Greek, he steadfastly and successfully opposed them. As a minister of the uncircumcision, he watchfully and zealously defended the gentile converts in the enjoyment of liberty from the Jewish yoke of bondage. But not a word can be found in all that he said or wrote, claiming for them freedom from the obligation of Christian baptism. On the contrary, he uses considerations derived from their baptism, to urge them to walk in newness of life. The rule of interpretation, confirmed by the very objection which we are considering, requires us to understand literal baptism to be meant, when it is said, "So many of us as were baptized into Jesus Christ, were baptized into his death;"[1] and again, when it is said, "As many of you as have been baptized into Christ, have put on Christ."[2] A public profession of Christ was, in the view of Paul, the design of this ceremony, involving an acknowledged obligation to be his, and to walk in newness of life. All that Paul taught, like his own example, tends to establish the perpetuity of Christian baptism.

SECTION II.—MEANING OF BAPTIZE.

TO BAPTIZE IS TO IMMERSE.

We have seen that the commission which Christ gave to his apostles, instituted baptism as an ordinance to be observed by his disciples to the end of the world. It becomes important, therefore, to ascertain the meaning of the word "baptizing," by which this duty is enjoined.

The commission has come down to us in the Greek language; and the word translated "baptizing" is a participle of the Greek verb βαπτιζω. Our present inquiry is, what does this Greek verb mean?

In the ordinary process of translating the writings of a Greek author, when we wish to ascertain the meaning of some word that he uses, we satisfy ourselves, for the most part, by consulting a Greek lexicon.[3]

The laws of interpretation require us to take the primary signification of words, unless there be something in the context, or nature of the subject, inconsistent with this signification. As there

---

[1] Rom. vi. 3.   [2] Gal. iii. 27.

[3] The Lexicons of Donnegan, and of Liddell and Scott, are in common use and high repute. They give the meaning of the word as follows:—

Donnegan.—"To immerse repeatedly into a liquid; to submerge, to soak thoroughly, to saturate; *hence* to drench with wine *Met.*, to confound totally; to dip in a vessel and draw.—Pass. Perf. βεβαπτισμαι, to be immersed, &c."

Liddell and Scott.—"To dip repeatedly, to dip under. *Mid.* to bathe; *hence* to steep, wet; *metaph.* οι βεβαπτισμενοι, soaked in wine; to pour upon, drench, εισφοραις οφλημασι βεβ. over head and ears in debt. Plut. μειρακιον Βαπτιζομενον, a boy overwhelmed with questions. Heind. Plat. Euthyd.—to dip a vessel, draw water—to baptize. N. T."

is no such difficulty in the present instance, our first decision, if we follow the lexicons, must be in favor of the sense *to immerse.*

When, from any cause, the decision of lexicons is unsatisfactory, the ultimate recourse is to Greek authors who have used the word in question. We search out the various examples of its use; and, by an examination of these, we learn in what sense the authors used the word. Since use is the law of language, the sense in which Greek authors used a word is its true meaning. The lexicons themselves yield deference to this law, and cite examples from authors in proof of the significations which they assign to words.

Our search of Greek authors, for the use of βαπτίζω, is greatly facilitated by the labors of learned men who have preceded us in the investigation.

Professor Stuart[1] has collected, from different Greek writers, a number of examples in which βαπτίζω, and its primitive, βάπτω, occur, with a view to determine the meaning of the words. To his collection, which he considered sufficiently copious for the purpose, I have added many other examples, from a similar collection by Dr. Carson, and a few others, from a smaller collection by Dr. Ryland. All these are included in the following tables, which may, therefore, be regarded as a fair exhibition of the use made of these words in Greek literature. The examples are so classified as to render the examination of them easy. In rendering the words in question, I have not closely followed the learned men of whose labors I have availed myself, but have aimed at a more literal and uniform translation. This is always put in italics; and the reader may consider the spaces, occupied by the italicized words, as so many blanks which he may fill with any other rendering that he may think better fitted to express the author's meaning. Let it be regarded as a problem to be solved, how these several blanks shall be filled, so that the supply may fit every example, and, at the same time, be consistent, throughout the table, as the meaning of the same word.

In a few of the examples the italicized words are marked with an asterisk. In these cases they are renderings, not of the verbs

---

[1] Dissertation on the question, "Is the mode of Christian Baptism prescribed in the New Testament?"

themselves, which are placed at the head of the tables, but of substantives or adjectives derived from them, and involving the same signification. In the English prepositions which are construed with the verbs, I have sometimes followed Professor Stuart, when, without his authority, I should have been inclined to adopt other renderings. This remark applies especially to the use of "with," in Class III. of Table II. A different rendering would correspond more exactly with the idea of immersion; but it has been my wish to give immersion no advantage to which it is not clearly entitled.

TABLES OF EXAMPLES.

TABLE I.

EXAMPLES OF ΒΑΠΤΩ.

CLASS I.

TO DIP LITERALLY AND STRICTLY.

§ 1. *For the purpose of imbuing or covering.*—1. He took a thick cloth and *dipped* it in water.[1] 2. *Dipping* sponges in warm water.[2] 3. And a clean person shall take hyssop, and *dip* it in the water, and sprinkle it upon the house.[3] 4. Send Lazarus, that he may *dip* the tip of his finger in water.[4] 5. Cakes *dipped* in sour wine.[5] 6. *Dip* thy morsel in the vinegar.[6] 7. One of the twelve that *dippeth* with me in the dish.[7] 8. Who *dippeth* his hand in the dish.[8] 9. And when he had *dipped* the sop.[9] 10. *Dipping* hay

---

[1] 2 Kings viii. 15. [2] Hippocrates. [3] Num. xix. 18.
[4] Luke xvi. 24. [5] Hippocrates. [6] Ruth ii. 14.
[7] Mark xiv. 20. [8] Matt. xxvi. 23. [9] John xiii. 26.

into honey, they give it them to eat.¹ 11. Venus *dipped* the arrows in sweet honey.² 12. He put forth the end of the rod that was in his hand, and *dipped* it in a honeycomb.³ 13. Ye shall take a bunch of hyssop, and *dip* it in the blood which is in the basin.⁴ 14. The priest shall *dip* his finger in the blood, and sprinkle of the blood.⁵ 15. The priest shall *dip* his finger in the blood of the bullock, and sprinkle it.⁶ 16. He *dipped* his finger into the blood.⁷ 17. And shall *dip* them and the living bird in the blood.⁸ 18. And he shall *dip* it into the blood.⁹ 19. The Greeks *dipping* the sword and the Barbarians the spear-head [in blood.¹⁰] 20. Having *dipped* a crown into ointment.¹¹ 21. The priest shall *dip* his right finger in the oil that is in his left hand.¹² 22. *Dip* the probes in some emollient.¹³ 23. *Dipping* the rag in white sweet-smelling Egyptian ointment.¹⁴ 24. *Dipping* the rags in ointment.¹⁴ 25. By reason of heat and moisture, the colors enter into the pores of things *dipped* into them.¹⁵ 26. They *dip* it [into the dye-stuff.¹⁶]

§ 2d. *For the purpose of filling, or of drawing out, the verb sometimes taking the sense to dip out.*—27. The youth held the capacious urn over the water, hasting to *dip* it.¹⁷ 28. Take a vessel, ancient servant, and having *dipped* it into the sea, bring it hither.¹⁸ 29. The bucket must be first *dipped* and then be drawn up again.¹⁹ 30. The lad directed his large pitcher towards the water, hastening to *dip* it.²⁰ 31. He *dipped* his pitcher in the water.²¹ 32. Instead of water, let my maid *dip* her pitcher into honeycombs.²² 33. Bubbling water *dipped* up with pitchers.²³ 34. To-day, ye bearers of water, *dip* not [from the river Inachus].²⁴ 35. *Dip up* the sea-water itself.²⁵

§ 3. *For the purpose of cleansing.*—36. The Egyptians consider the swine so polluted a beast, that if any one in passing touch a swine, he will go away and *dip* himself with his very garments,

---

[1] Aristotle.   [2] Anacreon.   [3] 1 Sam. xiv. 27.
[4] Ex. xii. 22.   [5] Lev. iv. 6.   [6] Lev. iv. 17.
[7] Lev. ix. 9.   [8] Lev. xiv. 6.   [9] Lev. xiv. 51.
[10] Xenophon.   [11] Ælian.   [12] Lev. xiv. 16.
[13] Hippocrates.   [14] Hippocrates.   [15] Aristotle.
[16] Plato.   [17] Theocritus.   [18] Euripides.
[19] Aristotle.   [20] Theocritus.   [21] Hermolaus.
[22] Theocritus.   [23] Euripides.   [24] Callimachus.
[25] Nicander.

going into the river.[1] 37. It shall be *dipped* into water: so shall it be cleansed.[2] 38. First they *dip* the wool in warm water, according to ancient custom.[3]

§ 4. *For the purpose of hardening.*—39. The smith *dips* a hatchet into cold water.[4] 40. Iron *dipped*.[5]

§ 5. *For other purposes.*—41. Bring the torch, that I may take and *dip* it.[6] 42. They cannot endure great changes, such as that, in the summer time; they should *dip* into cold water.[7] 43. If the crow has *dipped* his head into the river.[8] 44. The feet of the priests that bare the ark were *dipped* in the brim of the water.[9] 45. Of which the remedy is said to be a certain stone which they take from the sepulchre of a king of ancient times, and having *dipped* it in wine, drink.[10] 46. If any one *dips* anything into wax, it is moved as far as he *dips*.[11] 47. Having melted the wax, he took the flea, and *dipped* its feet into the wax.[12] 48. With his own hand, he shall *dip* his sword into the viper's bowels.[13] 49. He *dipped* his whole chin into the belly of the ram.[14] 50. The one *dipped* his spear between the other's ribs, who at the same moment [dipped his] into his belly.[15] 51. Taking his sounding scimitar from the dead, he *dipped* it into the flesh.[16]

CLASS II.

TO DIP IN A LESS STRICT SENSE.

§ 1. *In appearance.*—52. If the sun *dip* himself cloudless into the western flood.[17] 53. Cepheus *dipping* his head or upper part into the sea.[18]

§ 2. *In effect.*—54. From the dew of heaven, his body was *dipped* [as wet as if it had been dipped.][19] 55. Having *dipped* [wetted or filled as if he had dipped] the hollow of his hand, he sprinkles the tribunal.[20] 56. He was clothed with a vesture *dipped* [colored as if it had been dipped] in blood.[21]

---

[1] Herodotus. [2] Lev. xi. 32. [3] Aristophanes.
[4] Homer. [5] Plutarch. [6] Aristophanes.
[7] Aristotle. [8] Aratus. [9] Josh. iii. 15.
[10] Aristotle. [11] Aristotle. [12] Aristophanes.
[13] Lycophron. [14] Philippus. [15] Dionysius of Halicarnassus.
[16] Euripides. [17] Aratus. [18] Aratus.
[19] Dan. iv. 33, v. 21. [20] Suidas. [21] Rev. xix. 13.

CLASS III.

TO COLOR.

§ 1. *By dipping.*—57. The color of things *dyed* is changed by the aforesaid causes.¹ 58. The *dyers*,* when they are desirous to *dye* wool so as to make it purple; . . . and whatever may be *dyed* in this manner, the thing *dyed* becomes strongly tinctured. If any one *dye* other colors. That they may receive the laws in the best manner, as a *dye*,* that their opinion may be durable. And those streams cannot wash out the *dye*,* although they are very efficient to wash out.² 59. Some *dyed* with hyacinth, and some with purple.³ 60. Thou hast well *dyed* thy sword against [in close conflict with] the Grecian army.⁴ 61. For the wife has deprived each husband of life, *dyeing* the sword by slaughter.⁵

§ 2. *Without regard to mode.*—62. When it drops upon the garments, they are *colored*.⁶ 63. Nearchus relates that the Indians *color* their beards.⁷ 64. He endeavored to conceal the hoariness of his hair by *coloring* * it. 65. The old man with the *colored* hair,⁸ 66. Does a patron affect to be younger than he is? Or does he even *color* his hair?⁹ 67. This garment, *colored* by the sword of Ægisthus, is a witness to me.¹⁰ 68. He fell, without even looking upward, and the lake was *colored* with blood.¹¹ 69. Garments of variegated appearance, *colored** at great expense. 70. A *colored** bird.¹² 71. Lest I *color* you with a Sardinian hue.¹² 72. Then perceiving that his beard was *colored*, and his head.¹³ 73. The physiologists, reasoning from these things, show that native warmth has *colored* the above variety of the growth of the things before mentioned.¹⁴ 74. Using the Lydian music or measure, and making plays, and *coloring* himself with frog-colored [paints.]¹⁵

---

¹ Aristotle.   ² Plato.   ³ Josephus.
⁴ Sophocles.   ⁵ Æschylus.   ⁶ Hippocrates.
⁷ Arrian.   ⁸ Ælian.   ⁹ Nicolas of Damascus.
¹⁰ Æschylus.   ¹¹ Homer.   ¹² Aristophanes.
¹³ Plutarch.   ¹⁴ Diodorus Siculus.   ¹⁵ Aristophanes.

CLASS IV.

METAPHORICAL USE.

§ 1. *Allusion to dipping.*—75. Let him *dip* his foot in oil.¹ 76. Thy foot may be *dipped* in the blood of thine enemies.² 77. Thou hast *dipped* me deeply in filth.³ 78. They are all *dipped* in fire.⁴ 79. *Dipping up* pleasure with foreign buckets.⁵

§ 2. *Allusion to coloring.*—80. Dyer, who *dyest* all things, and dost change them by thy colors; thou hast *dyed* poverty also, and now appearest to be rich.⁶ 81. For the soul is *colored* by the thought: *color* it then by accustoming yourself to such thoughts.⁷

TABLE II.

EXAMPLES OF ΒΑΠΤΙΖΩ.

CLASS I.

TO IMMERSE LITERALLY AND STRICTLY.

§ 1. *Sinking ships.*—1. Shall I not laugh at the man who *immerses* his ship by overlading it?⁸ 2. Such a storm suddenly pervaded all the country, that the ships that were in the Tiber were *immersed.*⁹ 3. When the ship was about to be *immersed.*¹⁰ 4. For our ship having been *immersed* in the midst of the Adriatic Sea.¹¹ 5. The wave high-raised *immersed* them.¹² 6. They were *immersed* with the ships themselves. 7. How would not his ship be *immersed* by the multitude of our rowers.¹³ 8. They were either *immersed*, their ships being bored through.¹⁴ 9. Those from above *immersing* them [ships] with stones and engines.¹⁵ 10. They *im-*

---

[1] Deut. xxxiii. 24.   [2] Psalms lxviii. 23.   [3] Job ix. 31.
[4] Moschus.   [5] Lycophron.   [6] Helladius.
[7] Marcus Antoninus.   [8] Hippocrates.   [9] Dion Cassius.
[10] Josephus.   [11] Josephus.   [12] Josephus.
[13] Dion Cassius.   [14] Dion Cassius.   [15] Dion Cassius.

mersed many of the vessels of the Romans.¹ 11. The ships being in danger of being *immersed*.² 12. Many of the Jews of distinction left the city, as people swim away from an *immersing* [sinking] ship.³ 13. Whose ship being *immersed*.⁴ 14. As you would not wish, sailing in a large ship adorned and abounding with gold, to be *immersed*.⁵

§ 2. *Drowning.*—15. He would drive him from the bank, and *immerse* him headlong, so that he would not be able again to lift up his head above water.⁶ 16. He may save one in the voyage that had better be *immersed* in the sea.⁷ 17. The boy was sent to Jericho by night, and there by command, having been *immersed* in a pond by the Galatians, he perished.⁸ 18. Pressing him down always as he was swimming, and *immersing* him as in sport, they did not give over till they entirely drowned him.⁹ 19. The river being borne on with a more violent stream, *immersed* many.¹⁰ 20. Killing some on the land, and *immersing* others into the lake with their boats and their little huts.¹¹ 21. The dolphin, vexed at such a falsehood, *immersing* him killed him.¹² 22. Many of the land animals *immersed* in the river perished.¹³

§ 3. *For purification.*—23. Naaman *immersed* himself seven times in Jordan.¹⁴ 24. He that *immerseth* himself because of a dead body.¹⁵ 25. He marveled that he had not first *immersed* before dinner.¹⁶ 26. Except they *immerse*, they eat not.¹⁷ 27. Divers *immersions*.¹⁸* 28. She went out by night into the valley of Bethulia, and *immersed* herself in the camp at the fountain of water.¹⁹ 29. He who is *immersed* from a dead [carcass] and toucheth it again, what does he profit by his washing?²⁰ 30. The *immersion** of cups and pots, &c.²¹

§ 4. *Other cases.*—31. The person that has been a sinner, having gone a little way in it [the river Styx], is *immersed* up to the head.²² 32. He breathed as persons breathe after being

---

¹ Polybius. ² Æsop. ³ Josephus.
⁴ Diod. Siculus. ⁵ Epictetus. ⁶ Lucian.
⁷ Themistius. ⁸ Josephus. ⁹ Josephus.
¹⁰ Diodorus Siculus. ¹¹ Heliodorus. ¹² Æsop.
¹³ Diodorus Siculus. ¹⁴ 2 Kings v. 14. ¹⁵ Ecclus. xxxiv. 30
¹⁶ Luke xi. 38. ¹⁷ Mark vii. 4. ¹⁸ Heb. ix. 10.
¹⁹ Judith xii. 7. ²⁰ Ecclus. xxxiv. 25. ²¹ Mark vii. 8.
²² Porphyry.

immersed.¹ 33. Then *immersing* himself into the Lake Copais.² 34. *Immerse* yourself into the sea.³ 35. They marched a whole day through the water, *immersed* up to the waist.⁴ 36. The bitumen floats on the top, because of the nature of the water, which admits of no diving; nor can any one who enters it *immerse* himself, but is borne up.⁵ 37. But the lakes near Agrigentum have indeed the taste of sea water, but a very different nature, for it does not befall the things which cannot swim to be *immersed*, but they swim on the surface like wood.⁶ 38. If an arrow be thrown in, it would scarcely be *immersed*.⁷ 39. As when a net is cast into the sea, the cork swims above, so am I *unimmersed*.⁸* 40. When a piece of iron is taken red hot out of the fire and *immersed* in water, the heat is repelled.⁹ 41. Thou mayest be *immersed*, O bladder! but thou art not fated to sink.¹⁰ 42. Having *immersed* some of the ashes into spring water, they sprinkled.¹¹ 43. I found Cupid among the roses; taking hold of him by the wings I *immersed* him into wine.¹² 44. The sword was so *immersed* in blood that it was even heated by it.¹³ 45. He set up a trophy, on which, *immersing* his hand into blood, he wrote this inscription.¹⁴ 46. They are of themselves *immersed* and sunk in the marshes.¹⁵ 47. He *immersed* his sword up to the hilt into his own bowels.¹⁶

CLASS II.

TO IMMERSE IN A LESS STRICT SENSE.

§ 1. *In appearance.*—48. But when the sun *immerses* himself in the water of the ocean.¹⁷

§ 2. *In effect.*—49. Certain uninhabited lands which at the ebb are used not to be *immersed* [covered over as if they had been immersed], but when the tide is at the full, the coast is quite inundated.¹⁸ 50. And were all *immersed* [surrounded on all sides as if they had been immersed] unto Moses in the cloud and in the sea.¹⁹

---

¹ Hippocrates. ² Plutarch. ³ Plutarch.
⁴ Strabo. ⁵ Strabo. ⁶ Strabo.
⁷ Strabo. ⁸ Pindar. ⁹ Heraclides Ponticus.
¹⁰ Plutarch. ¹¹ Josephus. ¹² Anacreon.
¹³ Dionysius. ¹⁴ Plutarch. ¹⁵ Polybius.
¹⁶ Josephus. ¹⁷ Orpheus. ¹⁸ Aristotle.
¹⁹ 1 Cor. x. 2.

30   BAPTISM.

CLASS III.

METAPHORICAL USE.

§ 1. *For drunkenness.*—51. I am one of those who *immersed* yesterday [who drank wine freely].¹ 52. Having *immersed* Alexander with much wine.² 53. Seeing him in this condition, and *immersed* by excessive drinking into shamelessness and sleep.³ 54.. They easily become intoxicated before they are entirely *immersed*.⁴ 55. *Immersed* with wine.⁵ 56. *Immersed* by drunkenness.⁶ 57. He is like one dizzy and *immersed*.⁷

§ 2. *For afflictions.*—58. Perceiving that he was altogether abandoned to grief and *immersed* in calamity.⁸ 59. Since the things you have met with have *immersed* you.⁹ 60. Iniquity *immerses* me.¹⁰ 61. I have an *immersion** to be *immersed* with.¹¹ 62. *Immersed* by misfortune.¹² 63. Else what shall they do who are *immersed* for the dead?¹³ 64. Are you able to be *immersed* with the *immersion** that I am *immersed* with?¹⁴

§ 3. *Other uses.*—65. The mind is *immersed* [drowned like plants by excessive watering] by excessive labor.¹⁵ 66. *Immersed* with business.¹⁶ 67. *Immersed* with innumerable cares—having the mind *immersed* on all sides by the many waves of business, *immersed* in malignity.¹⁷ 68. *Immersed* into sleep.¹⁸ 69. He [Bacchus] *immerses* with a sleep near to death.¹⁹ 70. When midnight has *immersed* the city with sleep.²⁰ 71. *Immersed* with sins.²¹ 72. But the common people they do not *immerse* with taxes.²² 73. They *immersed* [sunk as a ship] the city.²³ 74. This as the last storm *immersed* [sunk as a ship] the tempest-tossed young men.²⁴ 75. Being *immersed* in debts of fifty millions

---

[1] Aristophanes.   [2] Plato.   [3] Josephus.
[4] Philo Judæus.   [5] Chrysostom.   [6] Justin Martyr.
[7] Lucian.   [8] Heliodorus.   [9] Heliodorus.
[10] Isa. xxi. 4.   [11] Luke xii. 50.   [12] Heliodorus.
[13] 1 Cor. xv. 29.   [14] Mark x. 38.   [15] Plutarch.
[16] Plutarch.   [17] Chrysostom.   [18] Clemens Alexandrinus.
[19] Evenus.   [20] Heliodorus.   [21] Justin Martyr.
[22] Diod. Siculus.   [23] Josephus.   [24] Josephus.

of drachmæ.[1] 76. He shall *immerse* you in the Holy Spirit.[2] 77. In one spirit have we been *immersed* into one body.[3]

REMARKS ON TABLE I.

The chief difficulty in classifying Table I., respects Class III. Under it I have placed all the examples in which the sense *to color* is given to the word, either by Professor Stuart, or Dr. Carson. Many of these examples might have been placed in Class I., § 1; and others in Class II., § 2.

To color.—Some learned men have maintained that the verb never signifies *to color, without regard to mode*. It is possible to explain the examples in which it appears to have this signification, like Ex. 56. Here the translators of the English Bible supposed the word, though denoting color, to be used with a reference to its primary meaning. But when we consider how many words from the root BAP were used for things pertaining to the dyer's art; and how frequently the verb βαπτω was used to denote *to color;* it seems most probable, that when employed for this purpose, it suggested to the minds of the Greeks in their familiar use of it, the idea of color directly, without that process of thought which was necessary to deduce this meaning from its primary sense *to dip*.

To smear.—Professor Stuart has assigned *smear*, as a secondary sense of the verb, and cites in proof from the Greek classic writers, Ex. 60, 61, 74. To the first two of these the rendering to *smear* is quite inappropriate. The warrior in battle does not redden his sword by *smearing* over it the blood of his enemies, but by *plunging* it into their bodies. In the other example, the rendering is less objectionable; but even here caution is necessary lest it mislead us. The verbs dip, plunge, immerse, wash, wet, pour, sprinkle, and smear, are construed with reference to two substances: one a solid, and the other a liquid. The first five have the solid for their direct object: *to pour* has the liquid for its direct object. We say to dip the hand in water, and to pour water on the hand; but not to dip water on the hand, or to pour the hand with water. The last two verbs, to sprinkle and to smear, admit both constructions. We say, to sprinkle the floor with

---

[1] Plutarch. [2] Matt. iii. 11; Acts i. 5. [3] 1 Cor. xii. 13.

water, and to sprinkle water on the floor; to smear the body with paint, and to smear paint over the body. In both these constructions, they always denote an application of the liquid to the solid, agreeing in this particular with the verb *to pour*. The verb βαπτω is always construed with the solid as its direct object. Throughout the table of examples, there can be found but one exception, which will be noticed hereafter. Even when it signifies *to color*, the verb takes for its object the solid, and does not signify that the color is produced by applying the coloring matter, as is done in the process of smearing. Hence, the rendering *to smear* is liable to mislead us into the belief that βαπτω, like *to smear*, may signify an application of the liquid to the solid. The verb never signifies this process. It may signify the effect of it, but never the process itself.

To dip out.—The exception above referred to, is Ex 35. In this, which is Nicander's comment on the preceding example, the verb takes the liquid for its direct object, and assumes the sense *to dip out*. In the metaphoric use of the word, Ex. 79 conforms to this construction. It is worthy of remark that the English verb *to dip* is used in the same way, taking the liquid for its direct object, contrary to its usual construction; thus: He dips water from the pool. We never say, He plunges, or immerses water from the pool. In this sense of abstracting a part of the liquid from the rest, the verb βαπτω, when it takes the solid for its direct object, may be construed with the genitive of the liquid, either with, or without the preposition απω. This remark will explain Ex. 13, 15, 21; to which Professor Stuart has given the sense *to smear*, because the verb is construed with απω. They do not signify *to smear* with *blood* or oil by applying it; but to dip into it so as to bring away a part of it from the rest.

RELATION BETWEEN Βαπτω AND Βαπτιζω.

Our search is for the meaning of βαπτιζω. This is a derivative from βαπτω; and because some aid in ascertaining its meaning, has been expected from the primitive word, examples in which this occurs, have been introduced in the preceding collection. Some lexicographers have regarded βαπτιζω as a frequentative, and have rendered it *to immerse repeatedly*. Robinson says it "is frequentative in form, but not in fact." Professor Stuart has examined this question at length, and decides "that the opposite opinion, which makes βαπτίζω a *frequentative* (if by this it is designed to imply that it is necessarily so by the laws of formation, or even by actual usage), is destitute of a solid foundation, I feel constrained, on the whole, to believe. The lexicographers who have assigned this meaning to it, appear to have done it on the ground of theoretical principles as to the mode of formation. They have produced no examples in point. And until these are produced, I must abide by the position that a *frequentative* sense is not necessarily attached to βαπτίζω; and that, if it ever have this sense, it is by a specialty of usage of which I have been able to find no example." The termination ιζω, is, with greater probability, supposed by others to add to the primitive word the signification of *to cause*, or *to make*, like the termination *ize* in *legalize*, to make legal; *fertilize*, to make fertile. According to this hypothesis, if βαπτω signifies *to immerse*, βαπτίζω signifies *to cause to be immersed*. This makes the two words nearly or quite synonymous. But, however nearly two words may agree with each other in their original import, it seldom happens that they continue to be used in practice as equally fitted for every place which either of them may occupy. We must, therefore, examine the usus loquendi, to ascertain the peculiar shades of meaning which they acquire. In studying the preceding table of examples, the following things may be observed:—

1. βαπτω more frequently denotes slight or temporary immersion, than βαπτίζω. Hence, the English word *dip*, which properly denotes slight or temporary immersion, is more frequently its appropriate rendering. In nearly one-half of the examples in which βαπτίζω occurs in the literal sense, it signifies the immersion which attends drowning, or the sinking of ships.

2. Βαπτω appears, in some cases, to be used in the secondary sense *to color*, without including its primary signification *to immerse*. No example occurs in which βαπτίζω has lost the primary meaning. A similar fact may be observed in the use of the English words *older* and *elder*. The words have the same primary meaning; or, rather, they are different forms of the same word: yet, while *older* has inflexibly retained its primary meaning, *elder* has

adopted a secondary signification, in which it denotes an officer without regard to age.

3. Βαπτω sometimes signifies *to dip up:* βαπτιζω never takes this sense.

DEDUCTION FROM TABLE II.

Though lexicographers frequently assign numerous significations to a word, they regard one as the primary or radical meaning from which all the rest are derived. If meanings have no relation to each other, they do not belong to the same word: hence *to lie*, signifying to be recumbent; and *to lie*, signifying to speak falsehood, though agreeing in orthography and pronunciation, are accounted different words, because their significations are independent of each other. No one imagines that there are two Greek verbs, βαπτιζω. We must, therefore, seek for one primary or radical meaning, and endeavor to account by it for all the uses to which the word is applied.

An important distinction needs to be made between the proper meaning of a word, and the accidental signification which it may obtain from the connection in which it is used. This distinction may be illustrated by the following passage:—" If I wash myself with snow water, and make my hands never so clean; yet thou shalt plunge me in the ditch, and mine own clothes shall abhor me."[1] In this sentence the word *plunge*, besides its proper meaning, obtains the signification *to defile*, from the connection in which it is used. This accidental signification is the most prominent and important idea conveyed by the word; yet it is not, strictly speaking, any part of its meaning. We may substitute *defile* for it, and the general sense of the passage will be conveyed; yet *to plunge* and *to defile* are different things. We must not conclude that we have ascertained the meaning of a word, when we have found another word which may be substituted for it in a particular sentence.

Since the lexicons give *immerse* for the primary meaning of βαπτιζω, let us try the meaning in the examples in which the word occurs, that we may ascertain whether this signification will suffice to account for all the uses to which the word is applied.

In the several examples, in which the word is applied to sinking ships, it obtains the accidental signification to *cause to sink to the*

---

[1] Job ix. 30, 31.

bottom. On this account it has been explained, in such connections, by the word βυθιζω, *to throw into the deep.* But the fact that immersed ships sink to the bottom is not affirmed by the word βαπτιζω. It is a natural consequence of their immersion. There is no necessity for supposing it to be included in the meaning of the word. The same distinction must be made in the examples which relate to drowning. The drowning is a consequence of the immersion, and is not included in the meaning of the word βαπτιζω. In several of the examples the immersion denoted by the word is clearly distinguished from the effect produced by it. So in § 3, we must distinguish between the immersion and the purification resulting from it. The immersion only is properly denoted by the word. All the other examples in Class I. perfectly agree with the sense *to immerse;* and some of them clearly require it. From Ex. 36, 37, 38, 39, it appears that substances which float on water are not baptized. This proves conclusively that *the mere application of water to a part of the surface does not satisfy the meaning of the word.* Ex. 41 proves that sinking to the bottom is not necessary to its meaning; but the other examples just referred to, prove that descent below the surface is indispensable.

The examples in Class II. require the meaning *to immerse.* The same is true of the examples in Class III. The propriety and force of the metaphorical allusions cannot be understood, if the word does not signify *to immerse.*

After thoroughly examining the collection of examples, we find that they fully establish the meaning *to immerse.* Christ, in giving the commission, must have employed the word in its usual sense. The commission is given in the language of plain command, and every other word in it is used in its ordinary signification. We are not at liberty to seek for extraordinary meanings, but are bound to take the words according to their ordinary import, where no reason to the contrary exists. What they mean, according to the ordinary rules of interpretation, is the meaning of Christ's command; and, if we do not receive and observe it in this sense, we are disobedient to his authority.

Let us now re-examine the collection of examples, trying any of the other significations which have been proposed, as, to wash, to purify, to wet, to sprinkle, to pour. The experiment will soon convince us that none of these is the proper meaning of the word.

Immersion, and nothing but immersion, will always satisfy its demands.

CONFIRMATION OF THE RESULT.

The correctness of our deduction is confirmed by the circumstances which attended some of the baptisms recorded in the Bible. The forerunner of Christ is called "the Baptist," because he administered this rite. He was sent to baptize, and it must be supposed that he understood the meaning of the word. Now, if a small quantity of water will suffice, why did John resort to the Jordan for the administration? The reason must have been that which the inspired historian has expressly assigned for his baptizing in Enon, near to Salim; namely, "because there was much water there." The people were baptized by John in the Jordan. In this river our Lord was baptized, and his own example explains the meaning of his command.

The baptism of the Ethiopian eunuch is very circumstantially described. The style in which he travelled forbids the supposition that he had no drinking vessel, in which a sufficient quantity of water might have been brought into the chariot to wet the hand of the administrator. But, if they chose not to perform the rite in the chariot, there was certainly no need for both of them to go into the water, if the mere wetting of Philip's hand was sufficient. Why did they both go into the water? and why did the sacred historian so particularly state this fact? "They both went down into the water, both Philip and the eunuch, and they both came up out of the water." These circumstantial facts are described in language which no one ought to misunderstand, and which no one ought to overlook, who desires to know his duty.

The Greek language continued to be spoken for many years after the times of the apostles. During all this period they, to whom the word $\beta\alpha\pi\tau\iota\zeta\omega$ was vernacular, understood it to signify *immerse;* and immersion has always been the practice of the Greek church to the present day. The Greeks must have understood the meaning of their own word. The Latin fathers also understood the word in the same way; and immersion prevailed in the western as well as in the eastern churches, until near the time of the reformation. Affusion was allowed instead of immersion, in case of sickness; but it was accounted an imperfect baptism. The testimony to these several facts I prefer to give in the words of Professor Stuart:—

"In the writings of the apostolic fathers, so called, *i. e.*, the writers of the first century, or, at least, those who lived in part during this century, scarcely anything of a *definite* nature occurs respecting baptism, either in a doctrinal or ritual respect. It is, indeed, frequently alluded to; but this is usually in a general way only. We can easily gather from these allusions that the rite was practised in the church; but we are not able to determine, with precision, either the manner of the rite or the stress that was laid upon it.

"In the Pastor of Hermas, however, occurs one passage (Coteler. Patr. Apostol. I., p. 119, sq.), which runs as follows: 'But this seal [of the sons of God] is water, *in quam descendunt homines* morti obligati, *into which men descend* who are bound to death, but those ascend who are destined to life. To them that seal is disclosed, and they make use of it that they may enter the kingdom of God.'

"I do not see how any doubt can well remain, that in Tertullian's time the practice of the African church, to say the least, as to the mode of baptism, must have been that of *trine immersion*.

"Subsequent ages make the general practice of the church still plainer, if, indeed, this can be done. The Greek words καταδυω and καταδυσις were employed as expressive of *baptizing* and *baptism*, and these words mean *going down into the water*, or *immerging*.

"The passages which refer to immersion are so numerous in the fathers, that it would take a little volume merely to recite them.

"But enough. 'It is,' says Augusti (Denkw. VII., p. 216), 'a thing made out,' viz., the ancient practice of immersion. So, indeed, all the writers who have thoroughly investigated this subject conclude. I know of no one usage of ancient times which seems to be more clearly made out. I cannot see how it is possible for any candid man who examines the subject to deny this.

"That there were cases of exception allowed, now and then, is, no doubt, true. Persons in extreme sickness or danger were allowed baptism by affusion, &c. But all such cases were manifestly regarded as exceptions to the common usage of the church."

BURIAL IN BAPTISM.

The significancy of baptism requires immersion. Paul explains it: "Know ye not that so many of us as were baptized into Jesus Christ, were baptized into his death? Therefore we are buried with him by baptism into death; that, like as Christ was raised up from the dead by the glory of the Father, even so we also should walk in newness of life."[1] And again: "Buried with him in baptism, wherein also ye are risen with him through the faith of the operation of God, who hath raised him from the dead."[2] Peter alludes to the same import of the rite, when he says: "The like figure whereunto even baptism doth also now save us (not the putting away of the filth of the flesh, but the answer of a good conscience toward God) by the resurrection of Jesus Christ."[3]

The faith which we profess in baptism is faith in Christ; and the ceremony significantly represents the great work of Christ, on which our faith relies for salvation. We confess with the mouth the Lord Jesus, and believe in the heart that God has raised him from the dead.[4] His burial and resurrection are exhibited in baptism, as his broken body and shed blood are exhibited in the supper. In both ordinances our faith is directed to the sacrifice of Christ. Under the name of sacraments they have been considered outward signs of inward grace; and, in this view of them, they signify the work of the Holy Spirit within us. But faith relies, for acceptance with God, on the work of Christ. It is a perverted gospel which substitutes the work of the Spirit for the work of Christ as the object of our faith; and it is a perverted baptism which represents the faith that we profess, as directed, not to the work of Christ, the proper object of faith, but to the work of the Holy Spirit in our hearts.

Objection 1.—There is an antithesis between the burial and resurrection which are here mentioned. The resurrection is moral, being to newness of life; and the same appears in the parallel passage in Colossians, where it is said to be "by the faith of the operation of God." If the resurrection is moral, the antithetic burial cannot be physical.

---

[1] Rom. vi. 3, 4.   [2] Col. ii. 12.   [3] 1 Peter iii. 21.
[4] Rom. x. 9.

If consistency of interpretation requires the burial to be moral the baptism must also be moral. The Quakers suppose that the baptism first mentioned in the passage is moral: " So many of us as were baptized into Christ." But Pedobaptists admit that physical baptism is intended in this clause. Now, in passing from physical baptism at the beginning of the passage, to moral resurrection at its close, there must be a point in the progress where we pass from what is physical to what is moral. Where is that point? some have imagined that it stands between the clause last quoted, and that which immediately follows, " were baptized into his death;" they suppose that " to be baptized into Christ," is physical; but that to be baptized into his death is moral. The passage in Galatians has been quoted as parallel : " For as many of you as have been baptized into Christ, have put on Christ." The first clause in this verse, they say refers to physical baptism; and the last to moral. But this is an erroneous interpretation. To put on Christ, is to put on his religion by outward profession, the profession which is made in baptism. The baptism and the profession are alike, in implying a moral change in the subject, only so far as he is sincere. Some are physically baptized, who do not morally put on Christ; but this, though unquestionably true, is directly contradicted by the passage, if the proposed interpretation of it is correct. So in the passage under consideration, it is affirmed that the same persons, and the same number of persons that are baptized into Christ, are baptized into his death. This could not be true, if the first baptism is physical, and the second moral. Between these two clauses, therefore, there is no place for a division between what is physical and what is moral.

We extend our examination further to find a place for the division, and we find it plainly marked by the word " should;" even so we also should walk in newness of life. Here the obligation to suitable morals is deduced from what goes before. This obligation is deduced from the physical baptism with which the passage begins, and everything in the passage, until we arrive at the word " should," is closely connected with this physical baptism, and explanatory of it. These intermediate links of explanation are necessary to connect the moral obligation at the close, with the physical baptism at the outset of the passage. If these intermediate links were moral, the proper position for the word "should," would be in the first sentence—thus, so many of us as are baptized into Christ, *should* be baptized into his death.

In the parallel passage referred to in Colossians, the expression is "Buried with him in baptism." The word baptism stands without adjuncts. It is not *baptism into death; but simply baptism.* If the word baptism, thus standing alone, can signify something wholly moral, it will be difficult to reject the Quaker interpretation of these passages, and of "baptizing" in the commission. In the preceding verse, circumcision is mentioned; but that we may know physical circumcision not to be intended, it is expressly called "the circumcision made without hands;" and "the circumcision of Christ." No such guard against misinterpretation attends the mention of baptism; and when it is recollected that Christians are not bound to receive physical circumcision, but are bound to receive physical baptism, we must conclude that physical baptism is here intended. The completeness of Christians requires the moral change denoted by circumcision, and also the obedience rendered in physical baptism. In all who are thus complete, this physical act is performed "in faith of the operation of God." This passage does not, like that in Romans, deduce moral obligation from baptism; and, therefore, the word *should* is not introduced: but it affirms the completeness of true believers in their internal moral change, and in their very significant outward profession of it.

Objection 2.—Everywhere else in Scripture, water is an emblem of purification; and it violates all analogy to suppose that in baptism it is an emblem of the grave, which is the place of putridity and loathsomeness.

That water in baptism is an emblem of purification, is clear from the words "Arise, and be baptized, and wash away thy sins." But that water is an emblem of nothing but purification, cannot be affirmed. In numerous passages it is an emblem of afflictions, of deep afflictions, without any reference to purification. When the Saviour said, "I have a baptism to be baptized with;" an immersion is intended, not into a means of purification, but into sufferings and death.

The grave is a place of putridity and loathsomeness, but not until the corruptible body is deposited in it; and when it leaves the grave, the corruptible will put on incorruption. Even the grave, therefore, is a place of regeneration and purification; and, instead of bearing no analogy to the purifying water of baptism, the analogy is striking.

Some of the Scripture allusions to baptism, are made to it as a purifying rite, but this is not true of all. An exception is found in 1 Cor. x. 2. On this Professor Stuart remarks: "Here, then, was the cloud which first stood before them, and then behind them; and here were the waters of the Red Sea, like a wall on their right hand and on their left. Yet neither the cloud nor the waters touched them. 'They went through the midst of the sea upon *dry* ground.' Yet they were *baptized in the cloud and in the sea.* The reason and ground of such an expression must be, so far as I can discern, a surrounding of the Israelites on different sides by the cloud and by the sea, although neither the cloud nor the sea touched them. It is, therefore, a kind of figurative mode of expression, derived from the idea that baptizing is surrounding with a fluid. But whether this be by immersion, affusion, suffusion, or washing, would not seem to be decided. The suggestion has sometimes been made, that the Israelites were *sprinkled* by the cloud and by the sea, and this was the baptism which Paul meant to designate. But the cloud on this occasion was not a cloud of rain; nor do we find any intimation that the waters of the Red Sea sprinkled the children of Israel at this time. So much is true, viz., that they were not *immersed.* Yet, as the language must evidently be figurative in some good degree, and not literal, I do not see how, on the whole, we can make less of it, than to suppose that it has a tacit reference to the idea of *surrounding* in some way or other." This author urges the objection which we are considering, as his "principal difficulty in respect to the usual exegesis;" yet we have here, according to his own exposition, an allusion to baptism, without any reference to purification. Another such reference is found in 1 Peter iii. 21, and again in the words of Christ before quoted, "I have a baptism to be baptized with."

Objection 3.—Very little resemblance can be found, between a man's being dipped in water, and Christ's being laid in a sepulchre hewn out of a rock. The supposed allusion requires resemblance.

Positive proof of allusion must be attended with difficulty; because, if it be mere allusion, it is always made without express affirmation. The proof of allusion must therefore be circumstantial; yet there may be circumstances which exclude all rational doubt of its existence.

If there is no resemblance between immersion and Christ's burial, the passage before us contains no allusion. If the resemblance is so slight, that but few persons are able to perceive it, the probability is, that the supposed allusion exists only in the fancy of those who imagine they see it. But if men have generally believed that allusion exists in the passage, the fact goes far to prove, that there is resemblance.

Have men generally believed in the existence of the supposed allusion? It is not necessary to examine the writings of authors attached to every different creed, and differing from each other in their views of baptism. Professor Stuart tells us their opinion in few words: "Most commentators have maintained, that συνεταφημεν has here a necessary reference to the mode of literal baptism, which they say, was by immersion; and this, they think, affords ground for the employment of the image used by the apostle, because immersion (under water) may be compared to burial (under the earth). It is difficult, perhaps, to procure a patient rehearing for this subject, so long regarded by some as being out of fair dispute." Now this general agreement of commentators, answers the objection which we are considering, far more successfully than any efforts of ours to point out the resemblance, which these commentators have perceived. The fact that it is seen is the best proof that it exists. The Scripture nowhere affirms that Paul, in this passage, alluded to a resemblance between immersion and Christ's burial; and, therefore, "the common exegesis" cannot be sustained by positive proof from Scripture; but it finds proof, the best proof that the nature of the case admits, in the fact that men generally have seen and felt the allusion.

Although positive proof of the common exegesis cannot be found in Scripture, a circumstantial proof may be drawn from the passage itself, amounting to little less than full demonstration. After making mention of baptism into Christ's death, Paul, before he refers to Christ's resurrection, goes out of the usual course to speak of Christ's burial. This was not necessary for the moral instruction which he designed to convey, if nothing but moral conformity to Christ's death was intended. It was not necessary for the purpose of finding an antithesis to the resurrection of Christ. The Scriptures usually speak of Christ's rising *from the dead, not from the grave:* and his death is the common antithesis to his resurrection. An example occurs in the present chapter, "If we have been planted together in the likeness of his death, we shall be also in the likeness of his resurrection." In Colossians, after the passage "Buried with him in baptism," the antithesis is again made, between the death (not the burial) of Christ, and his resurrection: "Wherefore if ye be dead with Christ, from the rudiments of the world, why, as though living in the world, &c."[1] "If ye then be risen with Christ, seek those things which are above," &c. "For ye are dead, and your life is hid with Christ in God."[2] Why did the apostle step out of the usual course, in two different passages to mention the burial of Christ? and to mention it in connection with baptism? It cannot be accounted for if the common exegesis be rejected.

The objection states that little resemblance can be found between immersion and Christ's burial: and the same might be said with respect to the resemblance between a loaf of bread, and the body of Christ. A well executed picture of the crucifixion, such as may be seen in Catholic chapels, has much more resemblance to the body of Christ, than is furnished by a piece of bread; yet, considering all the ends to be answered by the Eucharist, the divine wisdom has determined that we should keep Christ's death in memory, not by looking at a crucifix, but by the eating of bread. In like manner, some means might have been devised for representing the burial and resurrection of Christ, supplying a nearer resemblance than is furnished by immersion in water. But when we consider that baptism not only represents the burial and resurrection of Christ, but also our fellowship with him in both, and the consequent removal or washing away of our guilt, nothing could more conveniently, aptly, and instructively accomplish all these ends at once.

---

[1] Col. ii. 20. [2] Col. iii. 1,—3.

ARGUMENTS FOR ANOTHER MEANING.

Argument 1.—There are many reasons for supposing that βαπτιζω, being a derivative from βαπτω, has a less definite and less forcible sense than the original. And yet even βαπτω does not always signify a total immersion. This is perfectly evident from Mat. xxvi. 23: "He that dippeth his hand with me in the dish." Mark has it 'ο εμβαπτομενος, he that dippeth himself. Now, whatever liquid the dish contained, it cannot be supposed, that Judas plunged his hand all over in that liquid; much less that he dipped his entire person.

What the "many reasons" are, for supposing that βαπτιζω has a less definite and less forcible signification than βαπτω, the argument does not inform us. The mere fact that it is a derivative, furnishes not the slightest proof; for derivatives may be amplificative or intensive. To assume that they must be diminutive, would be utterly fallacious. The termination ιζω, whether it be frequentative, or causative, is not diminutive. Our examination of the preceding tables has shown, that the primitive generally denotes a slight and temporary immersion; but that the derivative, in nearly one-half of the examples in which it is used, literally signifies total and permanent immersion. This fact is decisive against the supposition, that βαπτιζω is less definite and forcible.

But if the less forcible primitive βαπτω had been used in the commission, no sufficient reason would exist, for supposing anything less than dipping to be intended. The meaning even of this word, is clearly to dip. The numerous examples of its use which have been adduced, establish this point; and even the very example brought forward in the argument, proves it. Judas dipped his hand in the dish. He did not wash, purify, wet, sprinkle, or pour his hand; but he dipped it. To dip, therefore, according to this very example, is the meaning of βαπτω; and if this word had been employed in the commission, the command would have been, "Go teach all nations, dipping them." Dipping was commanded in many of the ceremonies prescribed in the Old Testament, and the word βαπτω expresses the duty enjoined. No one imagines that it signifies, in these cases, to sprinkle or pour. Had this word been used in the commission, Christian worshippers would be less obedient than the Israelites, if they satisfied themselves with any thing less than dipping.

But it is alleged, that the word does not always denote total immersion. On re-examining the Table of Examples, we find that frequently, in the use of βαπτω, less frequently in the use of βαπτιζω, the immersion is not total; but, in no case, does this arise from any defect in the meaning of either verb. When a teacher directs his pupil to dip his pen in the ink for the purpose of writing, no one understands that an immersion of the whole pen is intended. When we read, "Send Lazarus, that he may dip the tip of his finger in water, and cool my tongue;"[1] every one understands that the whole of the part designated, *the tip of the finger*, is to be immersed. The difference in the two cases does not arise from any difference in the meaning of the verb dip. It is the same word in both cases, and has the same meaning; but the purpose for which the act is to be performed determines the extent to which the immersion is to proceed. If the pupil should stupidly mistake the teacher's design, the command would be explained, "Dip the nib of the pen in the ink;" and this is all that the first command meant. The greater definiteness of the last command, does not arise from any greater definiteness given to the verb *dip*. It is definite in the last case, and was equally definite in the first; but in the first, by a very common figure of speech, the whole pen was put for a part. The teacher relied on the nature of the case to limit the meaning of his command, and language is always sufficiently definite, so long as there is no danger of being misunderstood. We say that a pen is dipped, when in strict language the nib only is dipped; but the nib is totally immersed, and hence, in its proper meaning, to dip signifies total immersion. In all cases where the command is to dip, so far as depends on the meaning of the word, total immersion must be understood; and if we had received the commission in English, Go teach all nations, dipping them, it might safely be left to the common sense of mankind to determine whether partial or total immersion was intended.

The middle voice of Greek verbs is used, when an agent acts for his own benefit. This sufficiently explains Mark's use of εμβαπτομενος in the example cited in the argument. What Judas

---

[1] Luke xvi. 24.

dipped in the dish, is said by Matthew to have been his hand. A hand may be totally immersed in the cavity of an empty dish, or of a dish containing solids; but the probable meaning in the present case is, that something which the hand held, was dipped in a liquid which the dish contained. The hand, by a figure of speech, is put for what it held; and the dish, by a like figure, is put for what it contained: but amidst these figures, the word dip retains its literal and proper meaning; and nothing was literally and properly dipped, except what was totally immersed.

If the reader will again look through the examples in which βαπτιζω occurs, he may observe that, with very few exceptions, they are all cases of total immersion. Among the few exceptions, there are three (Ex.'s 31, 35, 49) in which the immersion is partial by expressed limitations: "up to the head;" "up to the waist;" "up to the hilt." The fact that these limitations are expressed, demonstrates that without them, the word would signify total immersion. This is the word which is used in the commission, without any limiting clause, and without anything either in the context, or the nature of the subject, to suggest that partial immersion was intended. Because an example may be found, in which, from the nature of the case, the immersion denoted is partial, we are not justified in inferring that partial immersion is here intended. The humble and teachable disciple desires to know and do what his divine Master meant that he should do; and the language of the command is as definite, as if it had been expressed in English, "Go, teach all nations, immersing them." It does not read *totally* immersing; but if any one will refuse total immersion until he finds this expressly written, we must leave him to his own conscience, and to the judgment of Him who gave the command.

Argument 2.—Βαπτιζω does indeed signify *to immerse* but it also signifies *to wash*, and under this last meaning, ceremonial purification is included. The Syrian leper was commanded to wash in Jordan; and the act of obedience to this command, is expressed by βαπτιζω. A dispute between the Jews and John's disciples about his baptism, is called "a question about purifying."[1] The Hebrew purifications were performed in various ways; chiefly by sprinkling consecrated water. Among their rites,

---

[1] John iii. 25.

"divers baptisms" are mentioned.[1] The word *divers* is the same that is applied to spiritual gifts in Rom. xii. 6, and signifies, *of different kinds*. Now, the baptisms could not be of different kinds, if they were all performed by immersion. Moreover, one of these kinds is expressly stated in the context to be "sprinkling."[2] Further, the Pharisees are said to have baptized themselves, after returning from market, when nothing more than the washing of hands is intended. They are also said to have held the baptism of pots, cups, brazen vessels, and tables; or, as the last word should have been translated, of beds, or the couches on which they reclined at meals. That all these purifications, and especially of the beds, were performed by immersion, is wholly incredible.

If *to immerse*, and *to wash* or *purify*, are two different senses of βαπτίζω, the question arises, in which of these senses did Christ use the term in the commission? We are not at liberty to take either of them at our pleasure. When a teacher commands his pupil to "dip the pen in the ink," the pupil may, by turning to Johnson's Dictionary, find that the word dip has four senses; and that one of these is *to wet, to moisten*. This sense is exemplified by a quotation from Milton:

"A cold shuddering dew dips me all o'er."

With so high authority for this interpretation of *dip*, the pupil may conclude to wet or moisten the pen, by putting the ink into it in some other way: and he may adopt this conclusion with the less hesitation, because all the purpose for which he understands the command to have been given, will be as well accomplished. But when he has filled his pen in some other mode, has he obeyed his teacher's command? Every one knows that he has not. But why? Does not the word dip signify to wet or moisten? We answer, it does not usually signify this; and the usual sense, is that in which the teacher employed the term. So Christ used the word βαπτίζω in its usual sense; and we as truly disobey his command, if we do not obey it in the sense which he intended, as if we substituted some other command in its place. What the usual sense of the word was, the examples which have been adduced fully establish.

But does βαπτίζω signify *to wash?* Lexicographers say that it

---

[1] Heb. ix. 10. [2] Ver. 13.

does, just as Johnson says that *to dip* signifies *to wet* or *moisten*. Words acquire secondary or accidental significations, from peculiar connections, or tropical usage; and these are enumerated by lexicographers as distinct meanings. Nor are they to be censured for this. Their design is, to give a view of the language, and not a mere collection of primary meanings. Our care, however, should be, when strict accuracy is required, to distinguish what is merely accidental in the signification of a word, from what is its true and proper meaning. *To immerse* and *to wash*, cannot both be the primary meaning of βαπτιζω. The last meaning cannot account for the use of the word, in the various examples in which it occurs; and the other meaning, *to immerse* could not well be derived from it. On the other hand, to immerse, accounts fully and satisfactorily for every use of the word. It must therefore be the primary sense; and so lexicographers have decided. The secondary sense, which is unknown to a large part of the examples, is, in strict criticism, merely the purpose for which the immersion happens to be performed. When the immersion is designed for the purpose of washing, or of ceremonial purification, the accidental signification to wash or purify is ascribed to the word: but its proper meaning remains unchanged, just as the proper meaning of βαπτω, in Job ix. 30, remains unchanged, by the accidental signification, *to defile*, which it acquires. In sound criticism, such accidental significations of words are not, strictly speaking, any part of their meaning, as was stated on p. 34. They are ideas, not expressed by the words, but suggested by the connection in which they are used.

A further proof that βαπτιζω does not signify to wash, to purify, to wet, to sprinkle, or to pour, may be drawn from the fact, that the copiousness of the Greek language supplies distinct words to express all these several ideas. If Jesus designed to command any one of these acts, why did he not use the proper word for denoting it? Why did he employ a word which properly denotes a different act, and which, therefore, could not convey his meaning, or must convey it very doubtfully?

The Syrian leper was commanded to wash in Jordan, and, for this purpose, he immersed himself in the river. The word βαπτιζω, denotes the immersion; and informs us, not only that he obeyed

MEANING OF BAPTIZE. 49

the command, but also how he obeyed it. He did not wash, by sprinkling a few drops on his face.

We are informed that "there arose a question between some of John's disciples and the Jews about purifying."[1] What the precise question was, we are not told; and it is impossible to determine, what its relation was to John's baptism. But the passage contains no proof, that to *baptize* and to *purify* are identical.

Paul says of the Hebrew worship: "Which stood in meats, and drinks, and divers baptisms, and carnal ordinances." It is true, as stated in the argument, that the same word "divers" is applied to the gifts mentioned in Rom. xii. 6; but these "gifts" were all *gifts*. They were gifts of various kinds; but the variety did not cause any of them to cease to be gifts. In like manner, the divers baptisms, or immersions, mentioned in this passage, are all *immersions*. Their variety does not change them into something different from *immersions*. The immersion of divers persons and things, at divers times, under divers circumstances, and for divers kinds of uncleanness, constitutes divers immersions, without the supposition that some of them were performed by sprinkling. Had the phrase been, divers sprinklings, instead of divers immersions, no one would have inferred that some of these sprinklings were performed by immersion.

But it is alleged, that Paul has informed us in the context, that some of these divers baptisms were performed by sprinkling. This is a mistake. Paul mentions in the context, "the sprinkling of the ashes of an heifer, sanctifying to the purifying of the flesh." He classifies the various rites under four heads: 1. Meats. 2. Drinks. 3. Divers immersions. 4. Carnal ordinances, or ordinances concerning the flesh. Under the last of these heads, the sprinkling which sanctified to the purifying of the flesh, was manifestly included. The assumption that it was one of the divers baptisms, is unauthorized and erroneous.

In maintaining that sprinkling and immersion are divers baptisms, the argument opposes the position usually taken by the advocates of sprinkling. Jewish baptisms were divers; but Christian baptism Paul declares to be one: "One Lord, one faith, one baptism." In explaining this passage, the advocates of sprinkling

---

[1] John iii. 25.

4

allege that sprinkling and immersion are merely different *modes* of the same rite; but different modes of one baptism do not constitute divers baptisms. If sprinkling is really a different baptism, how can the use of it be reconciled with the unity of the Christian rite?

The word βαπτιζω, in Mark vii. 4, does not signify the mere washing of the hands. This act is expressed in the preceding verse, by νιπτω, the proper word for denoting it. Instead of confounding the meaning of the two words, the sense of the passage requires that they should be carefully distinguished. The act which one of them denotes, was performed on ordinary occasions; but the act denoted by the other, was performed on extraordinary occasions: "when they came from the market." Some understand an immersion of the things brought from the market; some, an immersion of the arm up to the elbow; and some, an immersion of the whole body. I suppose the last to be the true meaning; but, for our present purpose, there is no necessity of deciding between these interpretations. According to either of them, the word retains its usual signification to immerse.

What has been said on this passage, will assist in explaining a similar one in Luke: "When the Pharisee saw it, he marvelled that he had not first washed [baptized] before dinner."[1] Jesus had been mingling with a crowd of people, who had "gathered thick"[2] around him; and the danger of ceremonial defilement was as if he had come from the market. Hence, the Pharisee expected him to use immersion before dinner, as necessary to the proper sanctity of a religious teacher.

The immersion of beds, the argument rashly pronounces incredible. Dr. Gill, in his comments on the passage, has proved that such immersions were practised, by quoting at length the regulations of the Rabbins respecting them. To pronounce the statements of the Bible incredible, unless the words be taken in an unusual sense, is not honorable to divine inspiration.

Argument 3.—The Jewish rites were of two kinds; some, atoning; others, purifying. The Christian sacraments are a summary of the Jewish rites: the eucharist corresponding to those which were atoning, and baptism to those which were purifying. If both of them took the place of the atoning rites, by referring to the

---

[1] Luke xi. 38.   [2] Ver. 29.

work of Christ, the Christian system would be defective, in having no ceremony to represent the purifying work of the Holy Spirit. But if baptism represents this, it is sufficient to perform it in any mode that will represent purifying; and especially by sprinkling, which is the mode that was commonly employed for this purpose.

It is better to learn the design of the Christian rites, from the Holy Scriptures, than from our own reasonings, as to what is necessary to render the Christian system complete. The supper represents the atoning work of Christ, and it, at the same time, represents our feeding on Christ by faith, which is produced by the influence of the Holy Spirit. Because the supper represents the atoning work of Christ, we have no right to confine it to this single purpose, and refuse to eat and to drink, because these acts do not represent a part of Christ's work. Baptism represents our purification from sin; but it, at the same time, represents our fellowship with Christ in his burial and resurrection; and if we so perform it as to make it serve one of these purposes only, we do what no one claims the right to do with respect to the other Christian ceremony. We mutilate an ordinance of Christ, and render it unfit to fulfil all the purposes which his wisdom had in view.

Argument 4.—The language of the New Testament, although written in Greek letters, is not the Greek of classic authors; but modified by peculiarities of Hebrew origin. On this account, it avails but little, in ascertaining the sense of βαπτιζω in the New Testament, to collect examples of its use by profane authors. The examples in which the word has reference to purification, Cl. I. § 3, are numerous in the Greek Scriptures. As the primitive βαπτω loses the original sense *to dip*, when it takes the secondary sense *to color;* so βαπτιζω was used by the Hebrews in the sense *to purify*, without regard to the primary sense *to immerse*. By profane writers, the word was usually construed with the preposition εις; but, in the Scriptures, it is usually construed with the preposition εν, and sometimes with the dative without a preposition. This peculiarity of construction may be regarded as proof, that the sense of the word is not identical with that in which it is employed by Greek classic authors.

We cheerfully admit that the Greek of the New Testament contains many Hebrew idioms. It is also true, that some of the words are used to denote things which were unknown to writers unacquainted with the religion of the Hebrews; and these words must therefore be used in a peculiar sense. But notwithstanding all this, the language of the New Testament is Greek. This language, because of its general prevalence, was wisely selected to be the vehicle of the New Testament revelation. The Holy Spirit made the revelation for the benefit of mankind, and not for the Jews exclusively. The selection of a language which was generally understood among the nations, was in accordance with this design; provided the words were generally employed in their known signification. But if the words were used in senses to which men were unaccustomed, the prevalence of the language was a strong objection to its use. Men would unavoidably be misled, by taking words which were familiar in the customary sense.

Βαπτιζω did not denote something peculiar to the Hebrew religion or customs, but an act which had no necessary connection with religion, and which was as well known in every heathen land as it was in the land of Judea. If a peculiar use of it could be proved to have prevailed in Judea, it might still be questioned, whether, in a revelation designed for all nations, the Holy Spirit would have conformed to this peculiar usage. But no such proof exists. Not a single passage can be found, either in the Septuagint, or the New Testament, in which the word departs from its ordinary signification. When it denoted immersion, performed for the purpose of ceremonial purification, the meaning of the word was precisely the same, as if the immersion had been performed for any other purpose. Βαπτω frequently occurs in the Old Testament in commands which enjoin religious observances. Yet no one concludes that this word had a Hebrew sense different from that which it obtained among the Gentiles; and the supposition that βαπτιζω had a peculiar Hebrew sense, is destitute of foundation.

The language of Christ, "I have a baptism to be baptized with," cannot be explained, on the supposition that the Hebrew mind attached the sense *purify* to the word *baptize*. To render the phrase intelligible and expressive, we must admit the classical sense *immerse*.

Josephus was a Jew, and wrote soon after the time of Christ. From his use of the word, we may learn what it signified to the mind of a Jew. Table II. contains several examples from this author, in not one of which does the supposed Hebrew meaning *to purify* appear; but the meaning in all is precisely the same as in the Greek of gentile authors.

That the Hebrews attached the ordinary meaning to the word, may be learned from Jewish proselyte baptism. All admit that this was immersion. Many have maintained that this baptism was practised as early as the time of Christ. If it was, the fact decides what the word meant in that age and country. But if, as is more probable, the practice did not originate till the second century, the proof is still decisive, that the Jews had not been accustomed to a different sense of the word.

The use of immersion for the purpose of purifying, was not confined to the Hebrew nation. One design of bathing, a process which classic Greek sometimes expresses by βαπτίζω, is the cleansing of the body. The dipping denoted by βαπτω, in Ex. 36 and 38, is clearly for the purpose of cleansing. The peculiarity in the Hebrew use of these words is, that the immersion which they signify, was performed for the purpose of *religious* purification. This resulted from the religious character of the nation, and not from a peculiar sense of the terms. Immersion, when performed for religious purification, does not cease to be immersion.

We admit that βαπτω has a secondary sense *to color*, as well as the primary sense to dip; but both these senses are found in classic, as well as sacred literature. The case, therefore, furnishes no analogy which can give countenance to the supposition, that *to purify* is a secondary sense, in which the primary sense of βαπτίζω is lost. No one pretends that this secondary sense is found in classic Greek.

The alleged peculiarity of construction in the New Testament, does not prove that the word has a different meaning in Scripture, from that which prevailed in uninspired writings. As, in English, we say *to dip into*, or *to dip in*; so, in Greek, βαπτίζω is construed with either εις or εν. Both these prepositions agree perfectly with the sense *to immerse*. Were one of them invariably used in the Scriptures in construction with the verb, the circumstance would furnish no valid argument for a peculiar meaning in the sacred writing. Though εν is commonly used, εις is also found;[1] and the

---

[1] In classic Greek also, both constructions are found. Ex. 45 has εις; Ex. 17 has εν.

example in which it occurs, Mark i. 9, so connects the sacred use of the word with the classical, as to deprive the argument for a peculiar meaning, of the plausibility which an invariable use of one construction might be supposed to give it. The fact that both constructions appear in the inspired writings, supplies additional assurance that the meaning of the verb is not peculiar. We feel that the Greek language is the same, whether we read it on the sacred or the classic page. Dr. Campbell, in his notes on Matt. iii. 11, says:—
" *In water—in the Holy Spirit* . . . . . . Vulgate *in aqua* . . . . *in Spiritu Sancto.* Thus also the Syr., and other ancient versions. . . . . I am sorry to observe that the Popish translations from the Vul. have shown greater veneration for the style of that version than the generality of Protestant translations have shown for that of the original. For in this the Latin is not more explicit than the Greek. Yet so inconsistent are the interpreters last mentioned, that none of them have scrupled to render εν τω Ιορδανη in the sixth verse, *in Jordan*, though nothing can be plainer, than that if there be any incongruity in the expression *in water*, this *in Jordan* must be equally incongruous. But they have seen that the preposition *in* could not be avoided there without adopting a circumlocution, and saying, *with the water of Jordan*, which would have made their deviation from the text too glaring. The word βαπτιζειν, both in sacred authors, and in classical, signifies, *to dip, to plunge, to immerse,* and was rendered by Tertullian, the oldest of the Latin fathers, *tingere*, the term used for dyeing cloth, which was by immersion. It is always construed suitably to this meaning."

Argument 5.—If it were the case that βαπτιζω clearly signifies *to dip*, or *immerse all over* in water, when applied to other subjects, it would by no means certainly follow, that it has this signification, when applied to the Christian rite of *baptism*. The word supper in English, and δειπνον in Greek, have a very different sense, when applied to the eucharist, from what they have in ordinary cases. Eating a morsel of bread does not constitute a supper, in the ordinary sense; but it is called a supper, in this religious rite. Now, if the word which denotes one Christian rite, has a sense so very different from its usual sense; why may it not be so, with the word which denotes the other Christian rite? Why may it not signify, instead of a complete dipping or washing, the application of water in a small degree?

This argument claims, that words may have a peculiar sense in religious rites. It does not claim this for Greek words only; for it does not object to *supper* as a proper rendering of δειπνον. It claims that these words, both the Greek and the English, have a sense unknown elsewhere, when they are applied to the eucharist. There is, therefore, no necessity in controverting the argument, to transport ourselves to the foreign territory of the Greek language; but we are at liberty to meet it, and try its validity, on English ground. It does not object that *immerse* is an improper rendering of βαπτιζω; but it claims that these words, when applied to a religious rite, may have a meaning which they possess in no other case. We are consequently at liberty, in trying the validity of the argument, to use the word *immerse* as a correct translation of the Greek verb.

The whole argument rests on what is supposed to be a peculiar use of a single word, δειπνον; and it deserves special consideration, that there is but a single instance of this peculiar signification, even with respect to this word. The instances are exceedingly numerous, in which other words are used with reference to religious rites; and even δειπνον is frequently used with reference to the paschal supper. In all these instances it is invariably true, that words when applied to religious rites, have the same signification as in other cases, and are subject to the same rules of interpretation. If δειπνον in 1 Cor. xi. 20, is an exception, it is a solitary exception. It is certainly the part of true criticism, in determining the meaning of βαπτιζω, to follow the general rule rather than the single exception. Besides, we have frequent use of βαπτω with reference to religious rites. The Jewish priests seem never to have thought, that, when Moses enjoined dipping in religious rites, he meant a diminutive dipping, or one that might be performed by sprinkling; and no one has suggested, that these priests mistook the meaning of their lawgiver. Is it not infinitely more probable, that βαπτιζω follows its kindred word βαπτω, in obeying the general rule, than that it follows a very different word in a solitary deviation from all rule and analogy?

If on a single instance we may establish a rule, that words, when applied to a religious rite, may have a meaning which they obtain nowhere else; who will limit the application of this rule, and tell us, how many of the words which apply to religious rites, obtain an extraordinary meaning, or how far their meaning differs from that which they obtain elsewhere? Perhaps the words, which, in the institution of the supper, are rendered *eat* and *drink*, although they have this meaning everywhere else, signify, when applied to a religious rite, nothing more than *to handle* and *to look upon.* Who will determine for us? Has the legislator of the Church committed to any one a lexicon of ritual terms, by which his simple-hearted disciples may find out what he meant? Or has he given to any persons on earth authority to decree what ceremonies they may think proper, by assigning to all the ritual terms of Scripture what sense they please?

That the terms used in reference to religious rites, may sometimes have a figurative rather than the literal meaning, a secondary sense rather than the primary, may be admitted. But this is what happens in all other speaking or writing, and the same rules of criticism are to be applied in this as in other cases. We must prefer the literal and primary signification, if nothing forbids it. We understand the word *is*, in the phrase "This is my body," to signify *represents;* because the literal primary signification would make the sense absurd and false. But this word has the same signification, when not applied to a religious rite, in the phrase, "The field *is* the world." For the same reason, the phrase "As often as ye drink this cup," is to be interpreted according to a common figure of speech, as often as ye drink the liquor contained in this cup. The same literal sense of the terms, and the same rules of figurative interpretation, are found here, as in all other cases.

The premises stated in the argument, cannot, in any view of them, justify the conclusion that baptism may be administered by using a small quantity of water. The proper conclusion would rather be, that we ought to change our mode of administering the eucharist. If we do not literally and fully obey the divine command when we restrict ourselves in this ordinance to a morsel of bread and a few drops of wine, we do wrong so to restrict ourselves; and we ought rather to correct the error than establish it as a precedent.

It deserves to be noticed, further, that $\beta\alpha\pi\tau\iota\zeta\omega$ and $\delta\epsilon\iota\pi\nu o\nu$ are not applied to the two religious rites in the same manner. One of them is found in the words of Christ's command; the other is not, but is, at most, merely a name which the rite has received.

Our conduct, in obeying the commands of Christ, must be regulated, not by the names which His institutions may receive, but by the words of his commands. Believers are said, in Scripture, to be *buried* with Christ in baptism, at least twice as often as the Eucharist is called a supper. Baptism may, therefore, be called a burial; but no one would infer hence that the body should be left for a long time under the water, as in a real interment. Baptism represents a real burial, in which the body of Christ continued three days in the grave. The eucharist represents the free and abundant communion in which the Lord sups with His people,[1] in which a great supper is spread,[2] and which will be perfected at the marriage supper of the Lamb.[3] Yet Christ did not say, "Go, teach all nations, *burying* them;" nor, "Take a *supper* in remembrance of me." His command in the latter case is, "*Eat* this bread and *drink* this cup;" and he did not institute this ordinance as a supper, but "after supper." Now, if the command is *eat, drink*, could this command be obeyed any otherwise than by eating and drinking? Would it suffice merely to apply the bread and cup to the lips? In like manner, when Christ said, "Go, teach all nations, immersing them," can the command be obeyed in any other way than by performing a real immersion? In the eucharist, he commanded to eat bread and drink wine, but not to take a full meal; and we know, from the circumstance that this ordinance was instituted immediately after the disciples had taken a full meal, that a full meal was not intended. The Corinthians, when they converted this ordinance into a full meal, did truly eat and drink, yet they did not fulfil the command more strictly and literally than we do; while, on the other hand, they departed from the example, and manifest intention of Christ, and were censured for so doing by the Apostle Paul.

We have suggested that the eucharist may possibly be called a supper, because of the spiritual feast which it represents. So one of the Jewish feasts was called the Passover, because of what it commemorated. But, after all, it is not certain that the eucharist is, in Scripture, called a supper. The eucharist is several times mentioned in the New Testament, but is never called the Lord's Supper, unless in this instance; and many learned men are of

---

[1] Rev. iii. 20.   [2] Luke xiv. 16.   [3] Rev. xix. 9.

opinion that, what is here called by this name, is not the eucharist itself, but the Love Feast which was anciently celebrated in connection with it. Perhaps it denotes the perversion which the Corinthians made of the eucharist. The phrase is without the definite article in the original text, and might be rendered "a supper of the Lord." Paul does not deny that the Corinthians had made a supper of it, but he denies that it was a supper *of the Lord*—a supper which the Lord had instituted, or which he approved. What proof, then, is there, that the Holy Spirit has ever called the eucharist by the name Lord's Supper? We have no objection to the name in itself considered; but, when so much is made to depend on it, the authority for it needs to be examined. If a universal law of Biblical interpretation, respecting ritual words, is to be established on a single fact, the fact should be well ascertained.

Everywhere throughout the New Testament, the words *baptize* and *baptism* are applied to one of the Christian rites; if the word *supper* is ever applied to the other, it is but in a single instance, and it may be that it is there applied to it as converted by abuse into a full meal. The word *baptize* was used in Christ's command, and directly expresses the act commanded. The word *supper* was not used in the command; and, if it be used as a name of the institution, is not directly descriptive of it. The two cases have no analogy between them to sustain the argument.

Argument 6.—The circumstances attending the baptisms of the New Testament, do not, in any case, prove that they were administered by immersion.

They who urge this argument have alleged that, in the account of Christ's baptism, the phrase " went up straightway out of the water," ought to have been translated, " went up straightway *from* the water."[1] The emendation of the translation leaves us without proof, they say, that he went *into* the water to be baptized. We admit, in this case, the correction of the translation. This clause, we concede, does not prove that Christ was in the water. But we have proof of this, in another verse of the same chapter: "And were baptized of him *in* Jordan."[2] The testimony of Mark to the same point, is very decisive. His record of the transaction

---

[1] Matt. iii. 16.   [2] Matt. iii. 6.

may be properly translated thus: "And was immersed by John into the Jordan."[1]

In the account of the eunuch's baptism, the phrases, "they went down into the water," and "they came up out of the water," have been subjected to a similar criticism. It has been alleged that these may be translated with equal propriety, "they went down *to* the water," and "they came up *from* the water." This we deny. The preposition απο used in the former case, is not found here, and our translators have, in the present case, rendered the prepositions εις and εκ according to their usual import. The opponents of immersion do not deny this, or maintain that they *must* be translated otherwise; but a departure from their ordinary signification ought not to be supposed without necessity. That these prepositions signify *into* and *out of*, in the common use of them by Greek authors, might be proved by innumerable citations; but, instead of these, the following extracts from Robinson's Lexicon ought to suffice:—

"Απο is used of such objects as before were *on*, *by*, or *with* another, but are now separated from it (not *in* it, for to this εκ corresponds)." "Εκ [is] spoken of such objects as before were *in* another, but are now separated from it."

This decides that our common version gives the true sense of the passage, in the rendering, "they went up *out of* the water." It follows that they must have been *in* the water when the baptism was performed; and that they must have gone down *into* the water for its performance.

It has been argued that, if going down into the water proves immersion, Philip was immersed as well as the eunuch; for they both went down into the water. If we maintained that *going down into the water* signifies going beneath its surface, this argument would be applicable; and it might also be argued against us that the clause which the inspired historian has added, "he baptized him," is superfluous. But we understand the immersion to be denoted by this last phrase; and which of the two persons was immersed, the context clearly shows. But while the phrase, *they went down into the water*, does not express the immersion, it proves it. No other satisfactory reason, for going into the water, can be

---

[1] Mark i. 9.

assigned. But in truth this circumstantial proof is not needed. The phrase, "he baptized him," states expressly what was done.

In the passage, "John was baptizing in Enon, near to Salim, because there was much water there,"[1] it has been alleged that the proper translation is *many waters;* and it is argued that the waters were many small springs or rivulets, not adapted to the purpose of immersion, but needed for the subsistence and comfort of the crowds that attended John's ministry.

The word rendered *water* properly denotes the element, and not a spring or rivulet. It was used in the plural, as we use the word *ashes* to denote the element, and not separate collections of it. In the phrase "ofttimes it hath cast him into the fire and into the water,"[2] fire is singular, and water is plural in the original text. If the latter word was put in the plural form, to denote the different collections of the element into which the afflicted youth fell at different times, the word fire would, for the same reason, need to be plural. Hence the phrase *many waters* does not signify *many small springs* or *streams.* When Isaiah said, "The nations shall rush like the rushing of many waters;"[3] when David said, "The Lord on high is mightier than the noise of many waters, yea, than the mighty waves of the sea;"[4] and again: "He drew me out of many waters;"[5]— when John said, "His voice was as the sound of many waters;"[6] the supposition that many little springs or rivulets are intended, is inadmissible. The same phrase, *many waters*, is used for the river Euphrates.[7] It follows, therefore, that the proposed change of translation, can be of no avail to lessen the evidence of the passage in favor of immersion. As to the allegation, that the water was needed for the subsistence and comfort of the people; we answer, that this, whether true or not, is not what the historian has stated. "John was baptizing, because there was much water." Water was needed for baptizing; and the connection of the clauses shows that the place was selected with reference to the administration of the rite.

Argument 7.—In several cases the circumstances which attended baptism forbid the belief that it was administered by immersion.

This is a dangerous argument. If the Holy Spirit affirms that

---

[1] John iii. 23.   [2] Mark ix. 22.   [3] Isaiah xvii. 13.
[4] Ps. xciii. 4.   [5] Ps. xviii. 16.   [6] Rev. i. 15.
[7] Jer. li. 13.

persons were baptized, and if *to baptize* signifies *to immerse*, it becomes us to receive his testimony; and, if any difficulty respecting the probability of the fact presents itself to our imagination, we should ascribe it to our ignorance. If an ordinary historian relates what cannot be believed, when understood according to the established laws of language, we do not invent new laws to relieve his veracity; but we pronounce his statement incredible. They who urge this argument, should beware lest they impugn the veracity of the Holy Spirit.

It has been imagined that there was not sufficient water to be obtained in Jerusalem for the immersion of three thousand on the day of Pentecost. Jerusalem was the religious capital of a religious nation, whose forms of worship required frequent ceremonial purifications. These purifications were not performed exclusively by the sprinkling of consecrated water; but in various cases, the defiled person was required to wash his clothes, and bathe himself in water.[1] Provision for such bathing was needed throughout the land. At Cana, an obscure town of Galilee, a poor family unable to supply a sufficient quantity of wine for a wedding feast, had six water pots of stone containing two or three firkins apiece, for the purpose of purifying.[2] Such provision was specially needed at Jerusalem, the centre of their worship. Here their sacrifices were to be offered, and here the whole nation were required to assemble for their appointed feasts; and these they were forbidden to celebrate, if in a state of defilement. In preparation for these feasts, we know from the express testimony of John, that the people went up to Jerusalem "to purify themselves."[3] Some provision, therefore, must have existed, accessible to the people, and sufficient for their use, at these great gatherings. The privilege which was open to the whole multitude out of every nation under heaven at this pentecostal feast, belonged equally to the apostles, and to the three thousand who were baptized; for all these were Jews, fully entitled to enter the temple, and unite in all the public services of the nation. If any of the rulers were inclined to hinder them, they as yet feared the people; for when these baptisms were performed, the administrators and subjects had "favor with all the people."

---

[1] Lev. xiv. 8, 9; xv. 5, 8, 11, 22; xvi. 26, 28.   [2] John ii. 6.
[3] John xi. 55.

If, therefore, any one persist in asking where water was found to immerse so many, we ask in turn where was water found sufficient for the purifying of the assembled nation?

In Jerusalem, as it now is, there are large cisterns of water on the grounds attached to private dwellings; and we may suppose that, when the city was in its ancient prosperity, such reservoirs were far more numerous. It is probable that access to these, as to rooms for keeping the Passover, was often obtained by the assembled worshippers. Of the converts who were baptized on the day of Pentecost, it is likely that many resided in the city; and if the use of private tanks was needed for baptism, their tanks were doubtless at the service of the apostles. There were also public pools, of which Chateaubriand, who visited Palestine about the beginning of the present century, gives the following account:—

"Having descended Mount Zion on the east side, we came, at its foot, to the fountain and pool of Siloe, where Christ restored sight to the blind man. The spring issues from a rock, and runs in a silent stream. The pool, or rather the two pools of the same name, are quite close to the spring. Here you also find a village called Siloan. At the foot of this village is another fountain, denominated in Scripture Rogel. Opposite to this fountain is a third, which receives its name from the blessed Virgin. The Virgin's fountain mingles its stream with that of the fountain of Siloe.

"We have now nothing left of the primitive architecture of the Jews at Jerusalem, except the Pool of Bethesda. This is still to be seen near St. Stephen's Gate, and it bounded the temple on the north. It is a reservoir, one hundred and fifty feet long, and forty wide; the pool is now dry, and half filled up. On the west side may also be seen two arches, which probably led to an aqueduct that carried the water into the interior of the temple."

The dimensions of the Pool of Bethesda, as given by Maundrell, are one hundred and twenty paces long, forty broad, and eight deep. Even the smaller dimensions given by Chateaubriand, indicate a sufficient supply of water in this single pool for the whole pentecostal baptism. A doubt has been recently raised, whether the excavation measured by these travellers, is identical with the ancient Bethesda: and attention has been directed to a neighboring intermittent fountain, the water of which, instead of flowing equably, sometimes rises by a sudden movement, and, after a time, subsides to its former level. This has been thought to agree with John's account of the ancient pool: "For an angel went down at a certain season into the pool, and troubled the water."[1] The hypothesis is liable to strong objections, which our purpose does not require us to present. Nor is it necessary for us to defend the correctness of the tradition, which points to this excavation as the ancient Bethesda. Much water was needed in the city; and, when so many tanks were dug at great labor and expense, it is altogether probable that a cavity, which could hold a large supply of the needed element, was not permitted to remain useless. If it contained water, the pool, by whatever name called, may have been the baptizing place on that memorable day.

But the Pool of Bethesda was not the only reservoir sufficiently capacious for the immersion of three thousand. The facilities for travelling which the present times afford have rendered visits to the old world frequent; and men now living, have greatly increased our knowledge of its geography and antiquities by their investigations. The learned Dr. Robinson has twice explored Palestine, with a special view to biblical illustration; and the result of his researches has been given to the world in a large work abounding with valuable information. The Rev. George W. Samson has also visited the same country within a few years, and has directed particular attention to the question now before us, in a short but excellent work entitled, "The Sufficiency of Water for Baptizing at Jerusalem, and elsewhere in Palestine, as recorded in the New Testament." In this work, the present condition of the pools at Jerusalem, six in number, is described; and the dimensions of five, according to the measurement of Dr. Robinson, are given in feet as follows:—

	Length.	Breadth.	Depth.
Pool of Bethesda	360	130	75
Pool of Siloam	53	18	19
Old or Upper Pool in the Highway of the Fuller's Field	316	{200 / 218}	18
Pool of Hezekiah	240	140	
Lower Pool of Gihon	595	{245 / 275}	{35 / 42}

[1] John v. 4.

The depth of the Pool of Hezekiah varies, its bottom being an inclined plane, and the sides of the Lower Pool of Gihon, which covers more than four acres of ground, are sloping. In these any convenient depth of water for baptizing might be readily obtained. When facilities for immersion were so abundant we can have no plea for inventing a new meaning for the word which the sacred historian has employed in recording the baptisms at Jerusalem. If we were unable to offer any probable conjecture with respect to the supply of water, we ought still to receive the testimony of the Holy Spirit according to the proper import of his words, and to believe his statement to be true; but the investigations which have been made remove all difficulty.

It has been further imagined, that there was not time for the immersion of so many; but this difficulty is not one which ought to impair the credibility of the narrative. Many, if not all of the seventy whom Christ had commissioned, were probably present on the occasion; and the apostles had undoubted authority to command their services in the administration of the rite. With so many agents, the work required but little time. In modern revivals, the number of persons immersed on profession of faith is sometimes large; and, from observing the time required, some have maintained that the apostles themselves could have baptized all the converts on the day of Pentecost. Sprinkling, if performed with the solemnity due to a religious rite, would require not much less time than immersion. We may therefore believe the sacred narrative, without inventing a new meaning for the word baptize.

It has been supposed that the baptism of the Philippian jailer and his household could not have been by immersion; because it took place at night, and in the prison. As to the time; the persecution which had been raised against Paul and Silas, and the relation which the jailer sustained to the government of the city, rendered it more convenient to administer the immersion at night than to postpone it till the next day. As to the place; there is no proof that it was administered in the jail. Paul and Silas had been brought out, and had preached the Word to the jailer, and "to all that were in his house." After the preaching, they must have left the house for the administration of baptism; for it is expressly stated that the jailer afterwards " brought them into his house and set meat before them."[1] Where the rite was performed we are not told. There may have been, as is common in the East, a tank of water in the prison enclosure; and we know, because the inspired historian has so informed us, that there was a river[2] near at hand. There was, therefore, no want of water.

Argument 8.—Jesus said to his disciples, "John truly baptized with water; but ye shall be baptized with the Holy Ghost not many days hence."[3] This promise was fulfilled on the day of Pentecost. The Spirit was then poured out upon them; and since Christ called this baptism, we have proof that pouring is baptism.

The Holy Spirit is not a material agent; and all representations of his operation, drawn from material things, are necessarily imperfect. To immerse in the Spirit, and to pour out the Spirit, are figurative expressions, and the things which they signify are conceived to bear some resemblance to immersion in water, and to the pouring out of water. But the resemblance is in our conception, and not in the things themselves; for between what is spiritual and what is material, there cannot, strictly speaking, be any likeness. Different figures may be employed to represent the same thing, and if the figurative expressions *pour out the Spirit*, and *baptize with the Spirit*, referred to precisely the same thing, it would not follow that the figures by which they represent it are identical. But if the figures are not identical, they can furnish no proof that *to pour* is *to baptize*.

God had promised by the prophet Joel, "I will pour out of my Spirit;"[4] and Christ had promised his disciples, "Ye shall be immersed in the Holy Spirit."[5] Both the promises were fulfilled on the day of Pentecost; but the two promises exhibit the influence of the Spirit then communicated, in different aspects. In one it is viewed as proceeding from God, and is likened to water poured out; in the other it is viewed as affecting all the powers of the apostles, surrounding and filling them, as water surrounds and imbues substances which are immersed in it. The figures, therefore, not only differ from each other, but are employed to represent different things. Hence, they can furnish no proof that *to pour* is *to baptize*.

---

[1] Acts xvi. 34. [2] Acts xvi. 13. [3] Acts i. 5.
[4] Acts ii. 17. [5] Acts i. 5.

ARGUMENTS AGAINST LITERAL OBLIGATION.

Argument 1.—Baptism is a mere ceremony, and, in the sight of God, is of far less importance than moral duties. In instituting it, Christ did not design to bind his followers to the very letter of his command; but intended that they should be at liberty to accommodate the mode of their obedience to circumstances which might arise, provided they accomplished the end which he had in view. He commanded his disciples to wash the feet of one another. This command was given at a time when the washing of feet was a usual act of hospitality; and we now rightly judge, that since this usage has passed away, we ought to fulfil the command in some other way. So he commanded to immerse, when immersion for the purpose of purification was in almost daily use; but to us, whose ordinary ablutions are partial, another mode of representing purification is better adapted. This has been the judgment of the pious; and God's abundant blessing on them, shows that they have his approbation.

Baptism is indeed a ceremony; but it is a ceremony of God's appointing. In moral duties arising from the relations which we bear, and founded on reasons which we are able to comprehend, the duty must vary according to the varying relations, and there is scope for the exercise of enlightened reason; but positive institutes are founded on the mere will of the lawgiver, and with respect to them, to obey or disobey is the only question, and the only variety. A ceremony of positive institution may possibly be in itself of little moment; but obedience in performing it, is of great value in God's sight; and disobedience to mere ceremonial requirements, he has in some cases punished in an exemplary manner. If he abundantly blesses many who neglect the baptismal command, the fact proves his great goodness, and not their innocence.

They who, acknowledging a departure from the letter of Christ's command, satisfy themselves with the belief that they attain all the ends of baptism, though they be not immersed, assume that they fully comprehend the subject, and all the ends which the lawgiver had in view. Is not this arrogating too much? It is certainly safer to believe that Christ is wiser than we are, and to render implicit obedience to his precepts. If baptism represents the burial and resurrection of Christ, as well as the washing away of sin, they do not attain all the ends of baptism who neglect immersion. We have reason to believe that positive institutes were in part given, to test and to promote the spirit of obedience. They who fail to comply strictly with the divine precepts, not only fail to accomplish these ends which infinite wisdom had in view, but counterwork the designs of the lawgiver.

The command to wash one another's feet, is not parallel to that which enjoins baptism. The latter, the advocates of sprinkling acknowledge to be of perpetual obligation, a Christian ceremony of positive institution; but the former they do not so regard. This is not the proper place to enter on the inquiry, whether the washing of feet was designed to be a ceremony of perpetual obligation. In our judgment it was not. If it can be made to appear that we have judged wrong, it will be our duty, not to make our error an argument for disobedience, but to amend our practice, and conform strictly to every divine requirement.

Argument 2.—When Christ instituted the eucharist, he commanded, "this do."[1] Yet no one imagines that we are bound to do all that he did on that occasion. He met in an upper room, and at night; and he reclined while eating. We do not suppose ourselves under obligation to imitate him in these particulars; but only to do so much as is necessary to the moral ends of the institution. By the same rule of interpretation, we are not bound to a literal compliance with the command of baptism.

No reason exists for supposing that the pronoun "this," in the command "this do," refers to the place, the time, or the manner, in which Christ ate the last supper. It evidently refers to the acts of eating bread and drinking wine; and precisely what it does signify, is what we are bound to do; and precisely what the word *baptize* signifies, is what we are bound to do in obeying the command which enjoins baptism. To relieve ourselves from the obligation of strict obedience, on the plea that the moral ends of Christ's institutions may be attained without it, is to legislate for Christ.

Argument 3.—Christ designed his religion to be universal, and adapted to every climate of earth, and every condition and rank among men. Immersion is not suited to cold climates—is frequently impossible to the infirm and sick—is repulsive to the delicate and refined; and the invariable observance of it cannot have

---

[1] Luke xxii. 19.

been required by him who said, "My yoke is easy, and my burden is light."

Our simple reply to this argument is, that it is Christ's command. We dare not, by our fallible reasonings from general principles, attempt to determine the will of our divine lawgiver, when we have in our possession his express command on the very subject. Christ knew all the climates of the earth, and all the conditions and ranks among men, and he has adapted his religion to these as far as appeared best to his infinite wisdom. If the infirm and sick cannot obey, there is an end of responsibility in their case. If the delicate and refined will not, they must leave the pleasure of obedience to those, who think it no humiliation to tread where they find the footsteps of their Lord and Master. Though Christ's yoke is easy, it is still a yoke; and pride and false delicacy may refuse to wear it; but love can make it welcome and delightful.

Section III.—SUBJECTS OF BAPTISM.

THOSE ONLY ARE PROPER SUBJECTS OF BAPTISM WHO REPENT OF SIN AND BELIEVE IN CHRIST.

Repentance and faith are associated graces in the hearts of the regenerate, each of them implying the existence of the other. Sometimes one of them is particularly mentioned as a qualification for baptism, and sometimes the other. They manifest themselves by confession of sin; by profession of dependence on Christ, and subjection to his authority; and by holy obedience.

John the Baptist required repentance, with its appropriate fruits, in those whom he admitted to baptism. It has been denied that the rite which he administered was identical with Christian baptism; but, for our present purpose, nothing more is necessary than to satisfy ourselves, that John did not require more spiritual qualifications for his baptism, than were required by Christ and his apostles. If he proclaimed repentance to be necessary because the kingdom of heaven was at hand, it could not be less necessary after the kingdom was established. That John did require repentance, as a qualification for baptism, the following Scriptures testify: "Repent ye, for the kingdom of heaven is at hand . . . . . .

and were baptized of him in Jordan, confessing their sins."[1] "Bring forth, therefore, fruits meet for repentance; and think not to say within yourselves, We have Abraham to our father."[2]

During the personal ministry of Christ, he made and baptized disciples. "There he tarried and baptized."[3] "The Lord knew how the Pharisees had heard that Jesus made and baptized more disciples than John."[4] Those only were baptized by Christ, who were made disciples; and discipleship implies repentance and faith.

The commission which Christ gave to his apostles, connects faith and discipleship with baptism as qualifications for it: "Go, preach the gospel to every creature. He that believeth, and is baptized, shall be saved."[5] "Go, make disciples of all nations, baptizing them."[6]

In executing the commission of Christ, the apostles and their fellow-laborers required repentance and faith as qualifications for baptism. Several passages in the Acts of the Apostles clearly indicate this: "Repent and be baptized, every one of you, in the name of Jesus Christ. . . . . Then they that gladly received the word were baptized."[7] "When they believed Philip preaching the things concerning the kingdom of God, and the name of Jesus Christ, they were baptized, both men and women."[8] "And the eunuch said, See, here is water; what doth hinder me to be baptized? And Philip said, If thou believest with all thine heart, thou mayest."[9] "Can any man forbid water, that these should not be baptized which have received the Holy Ghost as well as we."[10] "Whose heart the Lord opened, that she attended unto the things which were spoken of Paul. And when she was baptized."[11] "He was baptized, he and all his straightway . . . . and rejoiced, believing in God with all his house."[12] . . . "Many of the Corinthians hearing, believed and were baptized."[13]

In the Epistles of the New Testament, baptism is mentioned in such connections as prove that all the baptized were believers in Christ: "Know ye not, that so many of us as were baptized into

---

[1] Matt. iii. 2, 6. [2] Matt. iii. 8, 9. [3] John iii. 22.
[4] John iv. 1. [5] Mark xvi. 15, 16. [6] Matt. xxviii. 19.
[7] Acts ii. 38, 41. [8] Acts viii. 12. [9] Acts viii. 36, 37.
[10] Acts x. 47. [11] Acts xvi. 14, 15. [12] Acts xvi. 33, 34.
[13] Acts xviii. 8.

Jesus Christ were baptized into his death."[1] "Buried with him in baptism, wherein also ye are risen with him through faith."[2] "Ye are all the children of God by faith; for as many of you as have been baptized into Christ have put on Christ."[3] "Baptism doth now save us, ... the answer of a good conscience toward God."[4]

All these quotations from Scripture harmonize perfectly with each other, and incontrovertibly establish the truth, that repentance and faith are necessary qualifications for baptism. This is universally admitted with respect to adult persons; but a special claim is urged in behalf of infants, and the practice of administering the rite to them has prevailed very extensively. The arguments in its defence will be examined in the Chapter on Infant Membership.

Section IV.—DESIGN OF BAPTISM.

BAPTISM WAS DESIGNED TO BE THE CEREMONY OF CHRISTIAN PROFESSION.

The religion of Christ was intended for the whole world, and it is made the duty of his followers to propagate it. Men are required not only to receive, but also to hold forth the word of life. The lepers who found abundance of food in the Syrian camp, could not feast on it by themselves while their brethren in the city were famishing; and, if any one thinks that he can enjoy the blessings of religion, and shut up the secret in his own breast, he mistakes the nature of true Christianity. The light kindled within must shine, and the Spirit of love in the heart must put forth efforts to do good.

Profession is, in general, necessary to salvation. With the heart, man believeth unto righteousness; and with the mouth, confession is made unto salvation.[5] Divine goodness may pardon the weakness of some, who, like Joseph of Arimathea, are disciples secretly through fear; but it nevertheless remains a general truth, that profession is necessary. Christ has made the solemn declaration, "Whosoever shall be ashamed of me, and of my words, in this adulterous and sinful generation; of him also shall the Son

---

[1] Rom. vi. 3.   [2] Col. ii. 12.   [3] Gal. iii. 26, 27.
[4] 1 Peter iii. 21.   [5] Rom. x. 10.

of man be ashamed, when he cometh in the glory of his Father with the holy angels."[1]

Profession is the appointed public outset in the way of salvation The apostles exhorted, " Save yourselves from this untoward generation."[2] The world lies in wickedness, and under the curse of God. They who would be saved, should escape from it, as Lot escaped from Sodom. God calls: " Come out from among them, and be ye separate."[3] This call is obeyed, when converted persons separate themselves from the ungodly, and publicly devote themselves to the service of Christ. They then set out in earnest to flee from the wrath to come. The resolution to flee must first be formed in the heart; but the public profession may be regarded, in an important sense, as the first manifest step in the way of escape.

The profession of renouncing the world, and devoting ourselves to Christ, might have been required to be made in mere words addressed to the ears of those who hear; but infinite wisdom has judged it better that it should be made in a formal and significant act, appointed for the specific purpose. That act is baptism. The immersion of the body, as Paul has explained, signifies our burial with Christ; and in emerging from the water, we enter, according to the import of the figure, on a new life. We put off the old man, and put on the new man: "As many of you as have been baptized into Christ, have put on Christ."[4]

The place which baptism holds in the commission, indicates its use. The apostles were sent to make disciples, and to teach them to observe all the Saviour's commands; but an intermediate act is enjoined, the act of baptizing them. In order to make disciples, they were commanded, " Go, preach the gospel to every creature." When the proclamation of the good news attracted the attention of men, and by the divine blessing so affected their hearts, that they became desirous to follow Christ, they were taught to observe his commandments, and first to be baptized. This ceremony was manifestly designed to be the initiation into the prescribed service; and every disciple of Christ who wishes to walk in the ways of the Lord, meets this duty at the entrance of his course.

The design of baptism is further indicated by the clause " bap-

---

[1] Mark viii. 38.   [2] Acts ii. 40.   [3] 2 Cor. vi. 17.
[4] Gal. iii. 27.

tizing them into the name of the Father, and of the Son, and of the Holy Ghost." The rendering of our version, "*in* the name of," makes the clause signify that the administrator acts by the authority of the Trinity; but the more literal rendering "*into* the name of," makes it signify the new relation into which the act brings the subject of the rite. He is baptized into a state of professed subjection to the Trinity. It is the public act of initiation into the new service.

The design of baptism proves its importance. The whole tenor of the gospel forbids the supposition that there is any saving efficacy in the mere rite: but it is the appointed ceremony of profession; and profession, we have seen, is, in general, necessary to salvation. As the divine goodness may pardon disciples who fear to make public profession, so it may, and we rejoice to believe that it does pardon those, who do not understand the obligation to make ceremonial profession, or mistake the manner of doing it. But God ought to be obeyed; and his way is the right way, and the best way. Paul argues from the baptism of believers, their obligation to walk in newness of life. The ceremony implies a vow of obedience, a public and solemn consecration to the service of God. The believing subject can feel the force of the obligation acknowledged in the act, and Paul appeals to this sense of obligation: "Know ye not, that so many of us as were baptized into Jesus Christ were baptized into his death?"[1] Though it is an outward ceremony, it is important, not only as an act of obedience, but as expressing a believer's separation from the world, and consecration to God, in a manner intelligible and significant, and well adapted to impress his own mind and the minds of beholders.

The faith which is professed in baptism, is faith in Christ. We confess with our mouths the Lord Jesus Christ, and believe in our hearts that God has raised him from the dead.[2] If the doctrine of the resurrection be taken from the Gospel, preaching is vain, and faith is vain. So, if the symbol of the resurrection be taken from baptism, its chief significancy is gone, and its adaptedness for the profession of faith in Christ, is lost. Hence appears the importance of adhering closely to the Saviour's command, "immersing them."

---

[1] Rom. vi. 3.   [2] Rom. x. 9.

The obligation to make a baptismal profession of faith, binds every disciple of Christ. Some have converted the Eucharist into a ceremony of profession; but this is not the law of Christ. Baptism was designed, and ought to be used, for this purpose. If infant baptism be obligatory, the duty is parental; and if it be a ceremony in which children are dedicated by their parents to the Lord, it is a different institution from that in which faith is professed. He who has been baptized in infancy, is not thereby released from the obligation to make a baptismal profession of faith in Christ. If it be granted, that his parents did their duty in dedicating him to God, he has, nevertheless, a personal duty to perform. The parental act of which he has no consciousness, cannot be to him the answer of a good conscience toward God. Had it left an abiding mark in the flesh, an argument of some plausibility might be urged against the repetition of the ceremony. But the supposed seal of God's covenant is neither in his flesh, nor in his memory, and his conscience has no Scriptural release from the personal obligation of a baptismal profession.

Section V.—CONNECTION OF BAPTISM WITH CHURCH ORDER.

It will be shown hereafter, that in a Church, organized like the primitive churches, none but baptized persons can be admitted to membership. On this account, the present chapter on baptism has been introduced, as a necessary preliminary to the subsequent discussions on church order.

CHAPTER II.

LOCAL CHURCHES.

SECTION I.—MORAL CHARACTERISTICS.

A CHRISTIAN CHURCH IS AN ASSEMBLY OF BELIEVERS IN CHRIST, ORGANIZED INTO A BODY, ACCORDING TO THE HOLY SCRIPTURES, FOR THE WORSHIP AND SERVICE OF GOD.

ASSEMBLY.

The word *church*, when it occurs in the English New Testament, is, with one exception, the rendering of the Greek word εχχλησια. The Greek word, however, sometimes appears in the original text, when it could not, with propriety, be translated *church*. No one would render Acts xix. 32, "For the *church* was confused;" or verse 39, "It shall be determined in a lawful *church*;" or verse 41, "He dismissed the *church*." It is hence manifest, that the two words do not precisely correspond to each other in signification.

The meaning of an English word, is ascertained by the usage of the best English authors. By such writers, the word CHURCH is often employed to denote religious societies, consisting of persons who, because of the wide extent of territory which they occupy, never assemble in one place for divine worship. The principles on which these societies are formed, are various; their modes of government differ from each other; and they do not agree in the doctrines which they profess. If we should refuse to call any one of these societies *a church*, the usage of the best English writers might be cited against us; and the usage of such men is the law of the language.

But the disciples of Christ have another law, to which they appeal when they seek direction in forming and organizing churches. This law is contained in the Holy Scriptures. The question then is not, what does the English word *church* mean, or to what religious societies may the name be applied; but what is *a church*, according to the teaching of the inspired word.

The Greek word εκκλησια denotes *an assembly;* and is not restricted in its application to a religious assembly. But every reader of the New Testament discovers, that the first Christians were formed into religious assemblies, to which epistles were directed; and which acted, and were required to act, as organized bodies. The word is ordinarily used, in the New Testament, to denote these assemblies; and it is only with this use of the term, that we are at present concerned.

The Greek word denotes *an assembly;* and, in this particular, differs from the English word *church*, which is often used to signify *the house* in which men assemble for religious worship. The word "churches," in Acts xix. 37, denotes the temples in which the heathen gods were worshipped; but this is the exception before referred to, in which the Greek word εκκλησια does not appear in the original text. This word never denotes *the house* in which the worshippers assemble. The word συναγωγη was used, not only for the assembly, but also for the house in which the assembly met; and hence, we read "He hath built us a synagogue."[1] But the word εκκλησια differs from it in this particular. The passage of Scripture which most favors the opinion, that the word was applied to a material edifice, is, "Have ye not houses to eat and to drink in? or despise ye the Church of God, and shame them that have not?"[2] Here an antithesis has been supposed, between the private dwellings of the Corinthian Christians, and their house of public worship. But this interpretation weakens the force of the passage. The word "despise," like the word "shame" which follows, has persons for its object; and the injurious treatment which it implies, would be far less criminal, if it affected merely the material edifice in which the church assembled.

The word εκκλησια, as used by classic Greek authors, signified *an assembly*. It was used to denote the assembly of the citizens in the democratic towns of Greece, met to decide on matters appertaining to the State. With this use of it, precisely agrees that which is found in Acts xix. 39: "It shall be determined in a lawful assembly." The multitude there convened, were not a lawful

---

[1] Luke vii. 5.   [2] 1 Cor. xi. 22.

ecclesia. But we learn from the last verse of the chapter, that the word was not restricted in its use to a lawful ecclesia, for it is applied to the very company congregated on this occasion. "He dismissed the assembly." In the Septuagint, it is the word usually employed to denote the assembly of Hebrew worshippers, called the Congregation of the Lord; but it is also applied to assemblies not organized for religious purposes or business of state.[1] On the whole, therefore, when we meet with the word, we are sure of an assembly, and of nothing else, so far as depends on the word itself.

When we turn to the New Testament, and examine the use of this word in its application to the followers of Christ, we find it for the most part so employed that an assembly is manifestly denoted. "If he shall neglect to hear them, tell it unto the church," "but if he neglect to hear the church," &c.[2] The church in this passage, is an assembly, addressed by the party complaining, and addressing the party offending. Frequently the churches have their place of meeting specified, and are hence called the church at Jerusalem;[3] the church at Antioch;[4] the church at Corinth;[5] the church at Ephesus, &c.,[6] and when mention is made of the Christians in a district of country, so large as to render their habitual and frequent meeting for the worship of God impracticable, the term church is not applied to them in the singular number. Hence, we read, "the churches throughout all Judea, Galilee, and Samaria;"[7] the churches of Galatia;[8] the churches of Macedonia;[9] the churches of Asia.[10] It is clear, from these passages, that the term in the singular number, denoted the separate local assemblies in those districts or countries, and not the whole number of Christians inhabiting a kingdom or province. This is further confirmed by the fact, that the meeting of the Christians in the city of Corinth, is called the meeting of *the whole Church*, if the whole church be come together into one place.[11] If they had been called the church at Corinth, merely as belonging to a class of persons widely scattered through Achaia or the whole world, to

---

[1] Ps. xxvi. 5; Judith vi. 16; xiv. 6.   [2] Matt. xviii. 17.
[3] Acts viii. 1.   [4] Acts xiii. 1.   [5] 1 Cor. i. 2.
[6] Rev. ii. 1.   [7] Acts ix. 31.   [8] Gal. i. 2; 1 Cor. xvi. 1.
[9] 2 Cor. viii. 1.   [10] 1 Cor. xvi. 19.   [11] 1 Cor. xiv. 23.

whom, contemplated in the aggregate, the name church was given; the phrase "the whole church" would necessarily denote the entire aggregate; and it could not be said with truth that the whole church was assembled, when only the Christians in the city of Corinth formed the assembly.

Further proof that the word denoted a particular or local assembly, appears in this, that the churches are mentioned as distinct from one another. "They ordained elders in every church."[1] Also in this, that the churches were compared with each other: "For what is it wherein ye were inferior to other churches?"[2] "No church communicated with me as concerning giving and receiving, but ye only."[3] "As distinct bodies, they sent and received salutations,"[4] and held intercourse by messengers.[5]

By the proof which has been adduced, it is fully established that the word *church*, in such names as The Church of England, The Church of Scotland, The Presbyterian Church, The Episcopal Church, The Methodist Church, does not correspond in signification with the Greek word εκκλησια. These churches never assemble in one place, because their members are dispersed over too large an extent of territory. They are, therefore, not churches in the New Testament sense of the word. It is true that some of these churches have supreme judicatories in which the power of the whole body is supposed to be concentrated; and in these the whole church is conceived to be assembled: thus, the Presbyterian Church has its General Assembly. But whenever the General Assembly of the Presbyterian Church is mentioned, the very title indicates that the Assembly is one thing, and the Church another. The Assembly may be seen in some spacious room, transacting the business of the Church; but no one will affirm that the Church itself is literally there; and no one calls the Church itself an assembly. The people of the United States are conceived to be assembled in Congress; and the people of the several states in their several legislative assemblies; but no one understands this to be literally true, and no one calls the people of the United States or of any single state an assembly. But whenever the word εκκλησια is used, we are sure of an assembly; and the term is not applicable to bodies or societies of men that do not literally assemble.

---

[1] Acts xiv. 23.   [2] 2 Cor. xii 13.   [3] Phi. iv. 15.
[4] Rom. xvi. 16; 1 Cor. xvi. 19.   [5] 2 Cor. viii. 23.

In defending the Presbyterian form of church government, it has been argued that the term ecclesia is applied in the New Testament to denote all the Christians in a large city, when their number was so great that they could not all assemble for worship in one place. In a large city of the present day, a single denomination of Christians may have many churches assembling at their several places of worship at the same hour. The same division of the worshipping assemblies, is supposed to have existed in ancient times; and yet, it is remarked, we never read in the New Testament of several churches in one city; and it is inferred that the word εκκλησια in the singular number, included in these cases all the separate worshipping assemblies.

Dr. Dick[1] urges the argument just stated, and refers particularly to the church at Jerusalem, and the church at Antioch, as bodies too large for all the members to assemble in one place. It is unfortunate, however, for the argument, that these very churches are expressly declared in the Holy Scriptures to have assembled. Although the disciples in Jerusalem were numbered by thousands, yet, when their number "had multiplied,"[2] the apostles gathered the whole multitude together, and directed them to choose out from among themselves seven men to have charge of the distribution to the poor. And when Paul and Barnabas returned to Antioch, after having performed a tour of missionary labor, it is left on record that they gathered the church together, and rehearsed what the Lord had done by them.[3] Against these express declarations of the sacred historian, the conjecture that the number of disciples in these cities was too great to permit them to assemble in one place, is entitled to no consideration.

It is further argued by Dr. Dick, that all the disciples in Jerusalem could not have assembled in one place, because of the persecution to which they were exposed. But an important fact is here overlooked. For a considerable time after the day of Pentecost, the Christians had "favor with all the people."[4] The rulers were opposed to them; but the favor which they had among the people stayed the hand of persecution. While this state of things lasted, they remained one church, one assembly. But when persecution

---

[1] Theology, § 96, 98. [2] Acts vi. 1, 2. [3] Acts xiv. 27.
[4] Acts ii. 47.

scattered them, they were compelled to hold their assemblies in several places, and they are no longer regarded as constituting one church; but the historian, with strict regard to accuracy of language, calls them "churches."[1]

If the word εκκλησια in the singular number, could denote several distinct assemblies in a large city, no good reason can be assigned why it might not also denote the assemblies of Christians throughout a province or kingdom. But it is admitted that when applied to these, the word is always used in the plural form. All this exactly accords with what was before stated—that the word always assures us of an assembly.

MEMBERS.

Whether the assembly denoted by the word εκκλησια was religious or political, lawful or unlawful, the word itself does not determine. We must look beyond the word itself, to learn the character of the members who composed the churches of the New Testament; and the purpose for which they were associated.

The character of the persons who composed the New Testament churches, may be readily learned from the epistles addressed to them. They are called "The elect of God;"[2] "Children of God by faith;"[3] "Sanctified in Christ Jesus, called to be saints;"[4] "Saints in Christ Jesus;"[5] "Followers of the Lord;"[6] "Beloved of the Lord."[7] No doubt can exist that these churches were, in the view of the inspired writers who addressed them, composed of persons truly converted to God.

We may learn the same from the Acts of the Apostles. The first church admitted to membership those who repented and gladly received the word;[8] and the Lord added to the church daily such as should be saved.[9] Some have preferred to translate the passage last cited, "The Lord added to the church such as were saved." The former rendering does not so fully determine that the persons added had already undergone a saving change. Neither rendering, however, gives the precise sense of the original, which,

---

[1] Acts ix. 31. [2] Col. iii. 12. [3] Gal. iii. 26.
[4] 1 Cor. i. 2. [5] Phil. i. 1.   [6] 1 Thes. i. 6.
[7] 2 Thes. ii. 13. [8] Acts ii. 39, 41. [9] Acts ii. 47.

by the use of the present participle, describes the salvation as neither future nor past, but in present progress. Men who had entered the way of salvation, and were making progress therein, were added to the church in Jerusalem, and all the members of the church were persons of like character, for the multitude were " of one heart."[1] When persecution scattered this first church, its dispersed members formed other churches precisely like the parent church in the character of the members. None were admitted but as believers in Christ.

What has been said must not be understood to imply that none but true believers ever entered the primitive churches. We know from the Acts of the apostles, that Ananias, Sapphira,[2] and Simon the Sorcerer,[3] had a place for a time among the true disciples of Jesus; and we know from the apostolic epistles, that false brethren were brought in unawares into the churches.[4] But we are clearly taught that they were considered intruders, occupying a place that did not properly belong to them, and were ejected when their true character became apparent. Although, even in apostolic times, such men obtained admittance into the churches, they crept in unawares,[5] and, therefore, if we would tread in the footsteps of the apostles, we cannot plead their authority for admitting into the churches any who are not true disciples of Christ.

In our definition of a church, we have called it an assembly of believers in Christ. This definition tells what a church is according to the revealed will of God, and not what it becomes by the criminal negligence of its ministers and members, or the wicked craft of hypocritical men who gain admittance into it. When we study the word of God to ascertain what a church is, we must receive the perfect pattern as presented in the uncorrupted precepts of that word, and not as marred by human error and crime.

ORGANIZATION.

A church is an *organized* assembly. The organization cannot be certainly inferred from the mere name. This is supposed to signify, properly, an assembly legally called together or summoned;

---

[1] Acts iv. 32.   [2] Acts v. 1.   [3] Acts viii. 13.
[4] Gal. ii. 4.   [5] Jude 4.

and the derivation of the word from εχχαλεω, *to call out*, accords with this meaning. A legal summons implies obligation to obey it; and the persons who were under this obligation must be supposed to have been bound, not only to assemble, but also to co-operate with one another in the business for which the assembly was convoked. Although the term was sometimes applied to an assembly not legally convened, or a loose and disorderly assembly, yet it commonly signified an assembly of persons bound to act together as a body for some specified object. This is true of the New Testament churches.

The church at Jerusalem is clearly distinguished, in the sacred narrative, from the loose multitude that heard Peter's sermon on the day of Pentecost. Many of these became "added to the church;" but the church, it is manifest from the record, was a distinct and separate body, and their union and co-operation are plainly exhibited in the sacred history.

A passage in the first epistle to the Corinthians shows that the church at Corinth was a distinct assembly, not including others who might chance to be present in their meeting: "If the whole church be come together into one place, and all speak with tongues, and there come in those that are unlearned or unbelievers."[1] Had the church been a loose or unorganized assembly, these visitors who came in would have formed a part of it. But the distinction between them and the church is marked and clear. Moreover, the phrase, "If the whole church be come together," manifestly implies that there was a definite number of persons who were expected to convene, and who, when convened, constituted the entire body. This would not be true of an unorganized assembly. Let it be further noted, that the word εχχλησια is here used to denote the body, not as actually assembled, but as a body of which it was possible for some of the members to be absent when others were present. Sometimes the word was used to denote an actual assembly, as in the passage, "When ye come together in the church"[2]— that is, in the assembly or public meeting: but in the phrase, "If the whole church be come together," the term manifestly applied to the church, not as a body actually assembled, but as organized. Their organization had doubtless a reference to their assembling

---

[1] 1 Cor. xiv. 23.   [2] 1 Cor. xi. 18.

for the purpose of carrying the design of their organization into effect; and the name εκκλησια was given to the body because of its actual assembling, or because the members were obliged to assemble by the terms of their organization.

This distinction in the use of the term, as sometimes denoting an organized body, and sometimes an actual assembly, appears also in the Septuagint. The Congregation of the Lord was an ecclesia, whether actually assembled or not; but, in the phrase, "in the day of the assembly," the term εκκλησια is used to denote the actual assembly that stood before Mount Sinai. This is the meaning of the word in 1 Cor. xiv. 34, "Let your women keep silence in the churches"—that is, in the assemblies, or public meetings. It is added: "For it is a shame for a woman to speak in the church." This shame does not attach to her as a member of an organized body, but as being in a public assembly.

The English word *church* always refers to an organized body; but it does not necessarily imply an actual assembly, being very frequently applied to bodies that never actually assemble. On this account, it is not an accurate rendering of εκκλησια, when this term denotes an actual assembly without reference to organization. Dr. Doddridge has very properly rendered Acts vii. 38: "This is he that was in the assembly in the wilderness." If this principle of translation were applied throughout the New Testament, and the word church were admitted only when an organized body is intended, something would be gained in respect of perspicuity.

We have not argued the organization of the primitive churches from the mere use of the Greek name ecclesia. The name was appropriately used to denote an organized assembly; but this was not its exclusive signification. Other considerations which have been adduced, prove that the local churches of the New Testament were, in general, organized bodies; but a doubt exists with respect to the churches or assemblies in private houses, of which four cases are mentioned.[1] In those times, houses had not been erected for the special accommodation of Christian assemblies; and meetings for religious worship were doubtless often held in private houses. That in some cases a regularly organized church may have held its stated meetings in a private house, is by no means

---

[1] Rom. xvi. 5; 1 Cor. xvi. 19; Col. iv. 15; Philem. 2.

improbable. But we cannot affirm that every Christian assembly to which the word ecclesia was applied, was a regularly organized church. We may admit that the word *assembly* would be a more suitable rendering in these cases of meeting in private houses; and yet the proof is abundant that the churches commonly spoken of in the New Testament were organized assemblies.

INDEPENDENCE.

Each church, as a distinct organization, was independent of every other church. No intimation is anywhere given that the acts of one church were supervised by another church, or by any ecclesiastical judicatory established by a combination of churches. In the direction given by Christ, for settling a difficulty between two members, the aggrieved brother is commanded to report the case to the church, and the action of the church is represented as final. The church at Corinth excommunicated the incestuous person, by its own act and without reference to a higher judicatory. As if to settle the question of church independence, Paul, though possessing apostolic authority, and though he commanded the act to be done, yet required it to be done by the assembled church, as the proper agent for performing the work. Again, when the same individual was to be restored, the action of the church became necessary, and this action completed the deed. In the book of Revelation, distinct messages were sent to the seven churches of Asia. The character and works of each church are distinctly and separately referred to; and the duties prescribed are assigned to each church separately, and that church alone is required to perform them.

The only case in which there is an appearance of appeal to a higher judicatory, is that which is recorded in Acts xv. This was not a case of appeal to a higher judicatory established by a combination of churches, but to the single church at Jerusalem, with the Apostles and Elders; and the decree, when issued, went forth with the authority of the Holy Ghost.

DIVINE RULE.

After we have proved that the primitive churches were organized societies, an important question arises, Whether we are under obligation to regulate the church order of the present time in conformity to ancient usage. Was that usage established by divine authority, and designed to be of perpetual obligation; or was the whole matter of order and government left to human prudence? If the primitive churches consisted wholly of baptized believers, are we now at liberty to receive unbelievers and unbaptized persons? If the primitive churches were independent organizations, are we now at liberty to combine many churches in one organization? If the ancient pastors were all equal in authority, are we now at liberty to establish gradations in the pastoral office, and give one minister authority over others?

It must be admitted, that the Scriptures contain very little in the form of direct precept relating to the order and government of churches. But we have no right to require that everything designed for our instruction in duty, should be made known to us only in the way of direct command. Judicious parents give much instruction to their children by example; and this mode of instruction is often more intelligible and more useful than precept. It was made the duty of the apostles to teach their converts whatsoever Christ had commanded, and to set the churches in order. If, instead of leaving dry precepts to serve for our guidance, they have taught us, by example, how to organize and govern churches, we have no right to reject their instruction, and captiously insist that nothing but positive command shall bind us. Instead of choosing to walk in a way of our own devising, we should take pleasure to walk in the footsteps of those holy men from whom we have received the word of life. The actions of a wise father deserve to be imitated by his children, even when there is no evidence that he intended to instruct them by his example. We revere the apostles, as men inspired with the wisdom which is from above; and respect for the Spirit by which they were led, should induce us to prefer their modes of organization and government to such as our inferior wisdom might suggest.

But the Apostles designed that their modes of procedure should be adopted and continued. Paul commended the church at Corinth, because they had kept the ordinances as he had delivered them. Some things which needed further regulation, he promised to set in order when he came; evidently implying that there was an order which ought to be established. Titus, whom he had instructed, he left in Crete,[1] to ordain elders in every city, and to set in order the things that were wanting. To Timothy, he said: "The things which thou hast heard of me, the same commit thou to faithful men who shall be able to teach others also."[2] As matters of church order formed a part of his own care and action, and a part of what he had committed to Titus, so we must believe that they formed a part of that instruction which he had given to Timothy, to be transmitted by him to other faithful men, and by them to their successors.

The commission which the Lord gave to his apostles, required them to teach the observance of all that he had commanded. Many discourses which he delivered, previous to his crucifixion, are mentioned in the four gospels, without being recorded at length; and he doubtless delivered many others of which no mention is made. In the interviews which he had with the apostles after his resurrection, we are informed that he discoursed with them on the things pertaining to the kingdom of God;[3] and that this subject was so prominently before them, as to induce the inquiry, "Lord, wilt thou at this time again restore the kingdom to Israel?"[4] They were the chosen and commissioned agents for establishing his kingdom, having been appointed by him to "sit upon twelve thrones, judging the twelve tribes of Israel."[5] They were to proceed on the work assigned them, and were now waiting in Jerusalem, until they should be endued with power from on high for its successful prosecution. But what directions he gave them, in the interesting conversations that have not been committed to record, we have no other means of knowing than the precepts and examples which they have left. His parting command and promise were, "Teach them to observe all things whatsoever I have commanded you; and lo! I am with you alway, even unto the end of the world."[6] This plainly implies that commands had been given to them, which were to be observed to the end of time; and that these

---

[1] Titus i. 5.   [2] 2 Tim. ii. 2.   [3] Acts i. 3.
[4] Acts i. 6.   [5] Matt. xix. 28.   [6] Matt. xxviii. 20.

were to be learned from their instructions. The organization and government of the churches, which were to hold forth the word of life, and be the golden candlesticks, among which the glorified Jesus was to walk,[1] were matters intimately pertaining to his kingdom; and it cannot be supposed that he gave no instruction respecting them. Whatever he had commanded on these points, the commission required that they should teach men to observe; and the accompanying promise of his presence till the end of the world, clearly demonstrates that the observance was to be perpetual. We arrive, therefore, at the conclusion that, whatever the apostles taught, whether by precept or example, had the authority, not only of the Holy Spirit by which they were guided into all truth, but also of their Lord who had commissioned them.

It may be objected, that the example of the apostles is clearly not always to be followed; as, for instance, the conduct of Paul in shaving his head at Cenchrea,[2] in purifying himself at Jerusalem,[3] and in having Timothy circumcised.[4] But how do we know that these acts of Paul are not to be imitated? We learn it from the instruction and example of the same great apostle. He has taught us to distinguish between acts of personal obligation and acts performed from regard to the weakness and prejudice of others. He became all things to all men. To the Jews he became a Jew, that he might gain the Jews. He had Timothy circumcised, because of the Jews which dwelt in that quarter: and the other acts which have been cited were performed in the same accommodation to Jewish prejudice. But when it became necessary to defend the rights and privileges of Gentile converts, he boldly asserted their rights, and strenuously opposed the circumcision of Titus.[5] If, with an humble and teachable spirit, we study the instructions as well as the example of the apostles, we shall find it scarcely possible to err in deciding which of their acts were accommodated to particular circumstances, and which of them are proper examples for our imitation. If any doubt should remain in any particular case, it would be highly rash and criminal, on account of it, to throw away the benefit of apostolic example entirely.

When we have made our deductions from the instruction and

---

[1] Rev. i. 20. [2] Acts xviii. 18. [3] Acts xxi. 26.
[4] Acts xvi. 3. [5] Gal. ii. 3.

example of the apostles, we may use them with great profit to interpret the brief directions which the divine Master himself gave. Twice only, so far as the record states, did he use the word church, during all his personal ministry. In one case, he gave a promise of stability and perpetuity: "Upon this rock I will build my church; and the gates of hell shall not prevail against it."[1] From this promise we might infer, even if we had not apostolic instruction on the subject, that the church was to be built of durable materials, of living stones, of real saints. In the other case, the Master gave a precept to his disciples, with reference to personal difficulties that might arise among them: "If thy brother shall trespass against thee, go and tell him his fault between thee and him alone; if he shall hear thee, thou hast gained thy brother. But if he will not hear thee, then take with thee one or two more, that in the mouth of two or three witnesses every word may be established. And if he shall neglect to hear them, tell it to the church; but if he neglect to hear the church, let him be unto thee as an heathen man and a publican."[2] What kind of persons are concerned in the supposed difficulty? They are brethren. The direction was given to the disciples, and the very offender is called "thy brother." The direction was not designed for a case of injury from persecuting Scribes and Pharisees, but for a case of difficulty between Christian brethren. The second step in the process is thus described: "Take with thee one or two more." Who are the persons to be taken? Not persecuting Scribes and Pharisees; not strangers who will have no interest in adjusting the difficulty; but beyond all doubt, they were to be other *brethren*. In the third step it is directed, "Tell it to the ecclesia," the assembly. What assembly? The assembly of Israel, the Congregation of the Lord, collected from all places to keep their feasts at Jerusalem? The assembly of Jewish worshippers met in a synagogue? Jesus did not direct his disciples to refer their matters of grievances to such arbitrators. Evidently the ecclesia consists of the same kind of persons as those concerned in the preceding steps of the process. It is the assembly of the brethren. The constituents are Christian disciples, and none other. It is *the* assembly, and not *an* assembly that might be accidentally convened. The distinctness of the assembly,

---

[1] Matt. xvi. 18.   [2] Matt. xviii. 15, 16, 17.

and to some extent its organization, are here implied. Tell it to the assembly; an assembly actually convened, and capable of being addressed; and not a society scattered through a province or kingdom. "If he will not hear the church." The ecclesia not only hears, but decides; not only decides, but announces its decision. Here organization is clearly implied, and also right of jurisdiction: "Let him be to thee as an heathen man and a publican." This proves the decision to be final, and without appeal to a higher judicatory; otherwise the offended brother would be bound to await the issue of such an appeal. Thus we discover, that this admirable passage contains, in its brief dimensions, an epitome of the doctrine concerning church order and discipline, which was more fully developed afterwards in the instruction and example of the apostles. If the divine authority of their instructions were doubtful, these words of Jesus give them his sanction.

While we find proof that the church order established by the apostles, was designed to be perpetuated to the end of time, we do not find either precept or example for the regulation of every minute particular in the doings of a church. Marriage is a divine institution; and the rules given respecting it are obligatory, though much is left to the judgment and pleasure of the parties. So the regulations prescribed in the word of God for the organization and discipline of churches, are all obligatory, though some things are still left for human prudence to determine.

Objection 1.—A community of goods existed in the church at Jerusalem. This was the first church, and was established under the supervision of all the apostles. If primitive usage were obligatory on all succeeding time, a community of goods would be an indispensable part of church order.

We are informed, concerning the members of the first church, "Neither said any of them that aught of the things which he possessed was his own, but they had all things common."[1] But in this no intimation is given, that any church regulation was established obliging all to give up their private property. The surrender was spontaneous on the part of those who made it. It is not said that the church or the apostles called the possession of each member public property; but the accounting of it public property is

---

[1] Acts iv. 32.

attributed entirely to the owner himself. That each member had a full right to retain his property, is evident from the words of the apostle Peter to Ananias, "While it remained, was it not thine own?"[1] The crime of Ananias and Sapphira, was not that they kept back a part of their possessions, but that they lied about it. The clear recognition of their right to retain possession of the whole, is an explicit declaration from the apostle Peter, that a community of goods had not been established by apostolic authority.

If it could be proved that the apostles established a community of goods in the church at Jerusalem, we should be compelled to class the act with those acts of Paul before noticed, which were the result of peculiar circumstances. In the churches which were afterwards organized, we know that the distinction of rich and poor existed, and that the members were expected to contribute according to what they had. The possession of private property is unquestionably implied; and the apostles, who had the care of all the churches, if they had designed to make a community of goods a permanent arrangement in the churches, would not have permitted a necessary part of church order on a matter of great importance to be wholly neglected.

The circumstances of the church at Jerusalem were peculiar. From that church the gospel was sounded forth through all the world. It was regarded by Paul as having a claim on the carnal things of churches subsequently formed, in return for the spiritual things communicated. The liberality of that church in its contributions to sustain the cause of Christ was extraordinary, because the circumstances were extraordinary; and an extraordinary claim to remuneration for having impoverished themselves in support of the cause was founded on it. Paul commended the liberality of the churches of Macedonia, because "to their power, and beyond their power" they had contributed to the Lord's cause.[2] Jesus commended the liberality of the poor widow who threw all her living into the Lord's treasury. So the liberality of the church at Jerusalem was pleasing to the apostles, and also to the Lord; and the more pleasing, because it was a free-will offering, and not extorted by any church order which the apostles had established.

---

[1] Acts v. 4.   [2] 2 Cor. viii. 1, 3.

Objection 2.—The church order which you profess to deduce from the Scriptures, does not agree with that which, according to ecclesiastical history, prevailed in the times that followed the age of the apostles. There is reason, therefore, to suspect that your deductions are erroneous.

In attempting to learn from ecclesiastical history what usages prevailed in the apostolic churches, there is danger of error from two causes: the writers of ecclesiastical history were uninspired men, and therefore fallible; and the churches of the times after the apostles, may have departed from the order first instituted. Neither of these causes of error can mislead us in the course of investigation which we have pursued. The writers on whom we rely were inspired; and the churches concerning which we have inquired, were the first and purest, organized by the apostles under the infallible guidance of the Holy Ghost. Moreover, we have the assurance of inspired authority, that the Scriptures are sufficient to render the man of God perfect, thoroughly furnished unto every good work. If every duty appertaining to church order cannot be learned from the Scriptures, they have not the sufficiency and perfection which Paul ascribed to them. If ecclesiastical history can make any suggestion that will assist us in fairly interpreting the Scriptures, we may thankfully accept its aid. But if it goes beyond the Scriptures, it leaves divine authority behind it; and if it opposes the Scriptures, we must reject it, lest we make void the law of God through our traditions.

But ecclesiastical history says nothing that can lead us to suspect the accuracy of our deductions from Scripture. On the contrary, the nearer we ascend with it to the time of the apostles, the more exact is the agreement which it exhibits between the order of the churches, and that which we have ascertained from the Scriptures to have been established by Christ and his apostles.

The following quotations from Gieseler's Ecclesiastical History, will suffice to show the gradual progress of infringement on the original church order, with respect to the independence of the churches, the equality of the pastors, and the right of the people to elect their church officers. The historian considers it a progress of improvement, rendering the churches "better organized and united;" but we think it a progress towards popery:—

"The influence of the bishops increased naturally with the increasing frequency of synods, at which they represented their churches. Country churches which had grown up around some city, seem with their bishops to have been usually in a certain degree under the authority of the mother-church. With this exception, all the churches were alike independent, though some were especially held in honor on such grounds as their apostolic origin, or the importance of the city in which they were situated."—A. D. 117, 193.[1]

"We have seen that the sphere of individual influence amongst the bishops was gradually enlarging, many churches in the city and its vicinity being united under one bishop, a presbyter or a country bishop presiding over them. But we have now to speak of a new institution, at first found chiefly in the east, which had the effect of uniting the bishops more intimately amongst themselves. This was the Provincial Synod, which had been growing more frequent ever since the end of the second century, and in some provinces was held once or twice a year. * * * By these associations of large ecclesiastical bodies, the whole church became better organized and united."—A. D. 193, 324.[2]

"When once the idea of the Mosaic priesthood had been adopted in the Christian church, the clergy soon began to assume a superiority over the laity. * * * * The old customs, however, were not yet entirely done away. Although the provincial bishops exercised a very decided influence in electing a metropolitan, the church was not excluded from all share in the choice."—A. D. 193, 324.[3]

Objection 3.—God has in other cases unfolded his plans of operation gradually; and it is at least probable, that, in planting the church, the principles of church order were incorporated in the organization seminally, to be developed afterwards in the progress of Christianity. It is, therefore, improper to take for our model, the first embryo of the church.

God has been pleased to unfold the plan of his grace gradually. The first revelation of it in the garden of Eden, was exceedingly obscure; but, like the dawn of day, the light continued to increase, until at length the Sun of righteousness arose, and the full revelation of the gospel was given to mankind. This progress was made by new light from heaven. From time to time were

---

[1] P. 102. [2] P. 152. [3] P. 156.

added new revelations from God, through inspired men, whom he commissioned to make known his will. Now, if the principles of church order, inculcated by Christ and his apostles, were left too imperfect for our guidance, the analogy suggests that the additional disclosure which is needed, ought to come down from above. But the objection does not claim, and no one will pretend, who does not claim infallibility for the church, that the progressive change made in church order, was directed by inspired men. What Christ and the apostles planted, could not possibly receive any further improvement, unless God gave the increase; and since we have no proof that the increase was from God, we may fear that men marred the Lord's work, instead of mending it.

In the developments which God makes of his plans of operation, the progress is ever towards perfection: but in the change of church order, to which the objection refers, the progress terminated in the revelation of the Man of Sin. All the steps in the progress tended to this full disclosure. If the wisdom which directed it was from above, we ought to follow its entire guidance. The doctrine of church infallibility must be admitted, and we must take it in all its consequences. The doctrines and practices of the Roman church, however contrary to the word of God, must be taken as developments of the seminal truth which the Bible contains. If we are not willing to go all this length, where shall we stop? Is there a point in the progress of the church, at which it attained its highest perfection, and from which it sunk into the depths of the papal apostasy? If so, how can we ascertain which this point was? If the word of God does not tell us, and if we have no infallible church to tell us, we are left in the dark on this important subject. The only escape from this darkness, is, by flight to the sure word of prophecy, to which we do well to take heed as unto a light that shineth in a dark place.

But were the changes of church order which took place, a development of principles inculcated by Christ and his apostles? If Christ forbade his disciples to call any man master, and constituted them all brethren—is prelacy, or the Roman hierarchy, a development of the principle which he inculcated? If he made final the decision of an ecclesia of the brethren, to which an injured brother might tell his grievance—is the establishment of appellate tribunals a development of his principle? If he established a converted church-membership—is not the admission of unconverted members, a corruption rather than a development of his principle? The progress of the divine development is towards that ultimate state, in which the wicked will be completely and for ever separated from the righteous. His destruction of the old world by a flood, from which righteous Noah was preserved, was a step in this development. After corruption and idolatry had again prevailed, another step was taken, in the call of Abram from his kindred, and the removal of him to a different land in which his descendants were to be a separate nation, maintaining a purer religion. Another separation was made, when John the Baptist preached, "Think not to say within yourselves, we have Abraham to our father;" "The axe is laid unto the root of the trees;" "Whose fan is in his hand," &c. From that time, a converted church-membership was established, which was to be separate from the world, though not removed out of the world. The next step will be, its complete and final separation. Now, after Christ, with his forerunner and apostles, has established a converted church-membership, the admission of unconverted members is a step, not in the direction of God's progressive development, but in a direction backward. Instead of leading to a more perfect state, it leads back to that state which it was a grand aim of John's ministry to alter.

Objection 4.—The mode of church organization and government, which you profess to have deduced from the Scriptures, is not wise, and, therefore, cannot be from God.

The consideration of this objection will be reserved for Chapter X., Section I.

DESIGN.

Every man, as an accountable creature, is bound to worship and serve God; but to render this worship and service apart from all his fellow-creatures, would not accord with his social nature. Many acts of devotion and obedience may be performed more advantageously and more acceptably, by companies of men, than by each man separately. Prayer is acceptable to God, though poured forth from a solitary heart excluded from all the world, and unknown to all the world: but a special promise is recorded in the word of God, for the encouragement of united prayer. Union tends to strengthen our faith, and warm our devotions; and the united petition rises with more acceptance to the ear of him who hears and answers prayer. Churches are companies of men who assemble for united prayer. The first church prayed fervently and effectually, when the number of their names was one hundred and twenty;[1] and they continued in prayer when their number was increased to thousands.[2] When Peter was in prison, prayer was made for him by the church.[3] Praise also is acceptable to God, though offered in secret; but when Paul and Silas sang praises unto God in the prison,[4] their companionship strengthened their hearts, and gave increased sweetness and power to their music. United praise entered largely into the worship of the ancient temple; and the members of Christian churches are enjoined to speak to one another in psalms, and hymns, and spiritual songs, singing and making melody in their hearts to the Lord.[5] The duty and acceptableness of church praise, may be inferred from the words, "In the midst of the church will I sing praise unto Thee."[6] The commemoration of Christ's death in the breaking of bread, is an ordinance committed to the churches. The disciples at Troas, and at Corinth, assembled for this purpose. By the union of Christians, greater efficiency is given to efforts for the spread of the gospel. Hence from the churches sounded out the word of the Lord. Association in public assemblies, gives opportunity for the spiritual instruction, which Christ commanded in the commission given to his ministers; and for the members of the church to promote each other's spiritual interests by mutual exhortation. Accordingly Paul enjoins: "Forsake not the assembling of yourselves together, but exhort one another; and so much the more, as ye see the day approaching."[7] These are among the important purposes, for which it is the will of God that believers in Christ should form themselves into churches.

---

[1] Acts i. 14, 24.   [2] Acts ii. 42; iv. 24.   [3] Acts xii. 5.
[4] Acts xvi. 25.   [5] Eph. v. 19.   [6] Heb. ii. 12.
[7] Heb. x. 25.

Section II.—CEREMONIAL QUALIFICATION FOR MEMBERSHIP.

BAPTISM IS A PREREQUISITE TO MEMBERSHIP IN A LOCAL CHURCH.

The considerations presented in chapter 1, section 4, determine the proper position of baptism in the course of Christian obedience. It stands at the head of the way. In this act, the believer gives himself to God, before he gives himself to the people of God, to walk with them in church relation. The duties connected with church-membership are included among the commands which are referred to in the commission, and which are to be taught after baptism. The members of every Christian church must profess subjection to Christ. They cannot walk together in obedience to his commands, unless they are agreed on this point. As profession is necessary to church-membership, so is baptism, which is the appointed ceremony of profession. Profession is the substance, and baptism is the form; but Christ's command requires the form as well as the substance. In reading the Scriptures, it never enters the mind that any of the church-members in the times of the apostles were unbaptized. So uniformly was this rite administered at the beginning of the Christian profession, that no room is left to doubt its universal observance. The expression, "As many of you as have been baptized into Christ, have put on Christ,"[1] might in some other connection suggest that *all* had not been baptized. But it follows the declaration, "Ye are all the children of God by faith in Jesus Christ," and is added to prove the proposition; but it could not prove that *all* were in the relation specified, if the phrase, "as many as," signified only *some*. The same phrase is used by Gamaliel, where all are intended: "And all, as many as obeyed him, were scattered."[2] The same phrase, with the same meaning, is used in Rom. vi. 3: "So many of us as were baptized into Christ, were baptized into his death." Paul argues from this, the obligation of all to walk in newness of life. It follows, therefore, that all the members of the Galatian churches, and of the church at Rome, were baptized persons; and the same must be true concerning all the primitive churches. We conclude, therefore, that the authority of Christ in the commission, and the usage

---

[1] Gal. iii. 27.   [2] Acts v. 36.

established by the apostles, give baptism a place prior to church-membership.

Many unbaptized persons give proof that they love God, and are therefore born of God, and are children in his spiritual family. If they belong to Christ, it may be asked, why may they not be admitted into his churches? That there are such persons among the unbaptized, we most readily grant; for such persons, and such only, are entitled to baptism. To every such person, an apostle of Christ would say, "And now why tarriest thou? arise, and be baptized." We have not the authority of apostles, but we have the words of Christ and the apostles in our hands; and we owe it to our unbaptized Christian brother, to tell him, by their authority, his proper course of duty.

Objection 1.—Many good men do not understand the words of Christ and the apostles as we do, and consequently do not obey in this particular; yet they give satisfactory evidence, in other ways, that they love God, and conscientiously obey him. Paul says: "Him that is weak in the faith, receive ye;" and he urges, as a reason for receiving him, that "God has received him." Now, if we have satisfactory proof that God has received an unbaptized Christian brother, we are bound to receive him.

We admit the obligation to receive such a brother, but not in any sense that requires an abandonment or neglect of our own duty. We ought not to despise the weak brother. We ought not, by our knowledge, to cause the weak brother to perish. We ought to receive him into our affections, and endeavor to promote his best interests; but if he, through his weakness, disobeys God in any particular, our love for him degenerates into weakness, if it induces us to disobey also. We owe nothing to a weak brother which can render it necessary for us to disobey God. If a weak brother feels himself reproved when we yield our personal obedience to the Lord's command, we are not at liberty to neglect the command, for the sake of keeping the unity of the Spirit in the bond of peace. As I am bound to exercise my affection for a weak brother in such a manner as not to neglect my duty, so is a church. Every church owes its first obligation to Christ, and is bound to regulate its organization and discipline in obedience to Christ's command. If, by strict adherence to the divine rule, we cannot secure the co-operation of a weak brother, we must do our duty, and leave the result to God. Nothing in the law of church organization forbids the receiving of a brother into membership, who is weak in the matter of eating herbs, the case to which Paul refers. But if a church be required, for the accommodation of a weak brother, to give up the principles of organization learned from Christ, and adopt others, she owes it to Christ, and to the weak brother himself, firmly to refuse.

Objection 2.—If baptism is a prerequisite to church-membership, societies of unbaptized persons cannot be called churches; and the doctrine, therefore, unchurches all Pedobaptist denominations.

Church is an English word; and the meaning of it, as such, must be determined by the usage of standard English writers. Our inquiry has been, not what this English word means, or how it may be used. We have sought to know how Christ designed his churches to be organized. This is a question very different from a strife about words to no profit. In philological inquiries, we are willing to make usage the law of language; and we claim no right, in speaking or writing English, to annul this law. But our inquiry has not been philological. We have not been searching English standard writers, to know how to speak; but the Holy Bible, to know how to act. Even the Greek word ecclesia was applied to assemblies of various kinds; and we are bound to admit the application of it to an assembly of unbaptized persons, solemnly united in the worship of God. But we have desired to know how an ecclesia, such as those to which Paul's epistles were addressed, was organized; and we have investigated the subject as a question of duty, and not of philology. The result of our investigation is, that every such ecclesia was composed of baptized persons exclusively.

Section III.—FALSE PROFESSORS.

The disciples of Christ, in obeying their Master's command to love one another, are liable to mistake the proper objects of the love enjoined. Men who have not the Christian spirit, frequently assume the Christian name; and, since none but God can search the heart, such men frequently obtain admittance among the followers of Christ, and are for a time reckoned true disciples. For wise reasons, some of which we are able to comprehend, Christ did not pray that his people should be taken out of the world. Though the relation which they sustain to the men of the world is often an occasion of painful trial, it gives an opportunity for duties that are profitable to themselves and to mankind, and honorable to God. In like manner, their relation to false professors, gives occasion for the exercise of patience and forbearance, and of careful self-examination.

Local churches possess external organization; and in this organization, human agency is employed. Men unite in it, on the principle of mutual recognition of each other as disciples of Christ. Since God has not endowed the members of a church with the power to search the heart, it is possible for persons, whose hearts have not been sanctified by the Holy Spirit, to obtain admission into a local church. It is not Christ's law that such persons should be received; but they obtain admittance through the fallibility of those to whom the execution of the law has been intrusted.

Since every church on earth has probably one or more false professors in it, and since Christ has not authorized the admission of false professors, it may be questioned whether, strictly speaking, there is a Christian church on earth. But it may be questioned, with equal propriety, whether any individual man should be called a Christian, since no man is fully conformed to the law of Christ. Some, on the other hand, have thought that because no church on earth is perfectly free from false professors, it is folly to aim at a perfect church. But we may, with equal propriety, charge any individual man with folly who is striving after personal perfection. The duty of every individual is, to press toward the mark, for the prize of the high calling of God in Christ Jesus; and the duty of every church, and of every church-member, is, to strive in every lawful way for church perfection. Though full perfection may not be attained, yet approach to it sufficiently rewards our continual effort; and, apart from all respect to reward, we are obliged to this course, by the command of Christ.

It may be objected, that if the Lord had designed the churches to be free from false professors, he would not have committed the management of them to fallible men. We may grant that it was not God's purpose to preserve the churches free from false professors by the exertion of his omnipotence. Had this been his purpose, it would not have failed to be accomplished. But, as in other parts of God's moral government, responsible agents are employed who have laws prescribed, which as free agents they may or may not obey. The fact that the law is not obeyed, disproves neither its perfection nor its obligation.

But the objection may be presented in another form. The failure of a church to keep out false professors, does not necessarily arise from moral delinquency in its members; it may be wholly owing to the unavoidable fallibility of human judgment. Since their failure is not criminal, it is not a violation of divine law; and, therefore, the divine law does not provide for a perfectly pure church.

The objection in this form would be embarrassing, if the church which admits a false professor, were the only party concerned in the transaction. But the false professor himself is a party, and the most responsible party. He does not love Christ; and this want of love not only unfits him for a place in the church, but is criminal. He is certainly in fault; and it too often happens that the members of the church are also in fault. Were they less conformed to the world, the distinction between Christians and men of the world would be more apparent, and fewer cases of mistake in the reception of members would occur. Churches are often criminally careless, both in the reception of members, and in the discipline of them when received. If the piety of churches were very fervent, men of cold hearts could not remain happy among them, and could not continue to have their true character concealed.

The possession of love to Christ is required of every one who seeks admission into a Christian church. The members who admit him are required to demand a credible profession made in obedience to Christ's command. Beyond this they cannot go, and here their responsibility ceases. But in every case in which a false professor is admitted, the law of Christ is violated by one or both of the parties.

CHAPTER III.

THE CHURCH UNIVERSAL.

Section I.—MEMBERSHIP.

THE CHURCH UNIVERSAL IS THE WHOLE COMPANY OF THOSE WHO ARE SAVED BY CHRIST.

Whether the term church is used in the Scriptures to denote the whole body of Christ's disciples, is simply a question of fact. Were we to regard it as an etymological question, we might doubt whether a word, which always assures us of an assembly, could be used to denote a body that has never assembled on earth since the time of the first persecution, which scattered the disciples from Jerusalem. But some reason for such an application of the term may exist; and, if we ascertain the fact that it is so applied, the reason for this peculiar use will afterward become a proper subject of inquiry.

The following are examples in which the word is used with this wide signification: "Gave him to be the head over all things to the church."[1] "Unto him be glory in the church by Christ Jesus throughout all ages, world without end."[2] Let any one attempt to interpret these and similar passages, on the supposition that the term church always denotes a body of Christians assembling at one place—as the church at Rome, at Corinth, or at Ephesus— and he will become fully convinced, that the interpretation is inadmissible. In some of the passages the extension of the term to the whole body of believers, is perfectly apparent. In others, though it is not so apparent that the entire body is intended, yet

---

[1] Eph. i. 22. [2] Eph. iii. 21.

this signification perfectly harmonizes with the use of the term, the context, and scope of the passage.

We shall hereafter investigate the question, whether the term church, in this wide signification, includes those who profess faith in Christ, but are not true Christians. Such false profession has become very common in modern times; but we are inquiring into the use of the term in apostolic times, when fewer motives to false profession operated. Even in those ancient times, some intruded themselves into the brotherhood, who were false brethren, brought in unawares. But the intrusion of such persons was not authorized by the head of the church; and in our effort to ascertain what the church is, we should seek to know what it is as Christ instituted it, rather than what it is as man has misconceived or corrupted it.

After having ascertained the fact that the word is used in the extended sense, the next inquiry which presents itself respects the reason or propriety of this use.

Some have thought that this use of the word is not properly collective, but generic. When we say, gold is heavier than sand, the terms gold and sand are used generically. Were they used collectively to denote all the gold and all the sand in the world, the proposition would not be true; for there is a far greater weight of sand in the world, than of gold. But the comparison is made between the two kinds of matter, without regard to the quantities of them that exist. In the generic use of names to denote the various kinds of unorganized matter, the noun is not preceded by an article: thus—fire, air, earth, and water, as names of elements, are used without an article. So *man* is used generically without an article; and we do not say, *the man*, unless some particular man is meant. When the names of other organized bodies are used generically, the definite article *the* generally precedes them: thus we say, the horse is more tractable than the mule; the cedar is more durable than the oak. So the phrase, the church, is supposed by some to be used generically to denote the kind of organization existing in local churches.

It is an argument in favor of this opinion, that the idea of an assembly is thus fully retained in the signification of the word. Each local church is an assembly.

This generic theory is advocated by Mr. Courtney, a fictitious character in "Theodosia Ernest," a popular work recently published, which maintains, in general, the true doctrine of Scripture on baptism and church organization. The arguments of Mr. Courtney, on the question now before us, are the best that I have met with; we shall, therefore, proceed to examine them.

The question is not, whether the phrase, *the church*, may be grammatically used in a generic sense; but whether the Scriptures do so employ it. This also is simply a question of fact. We must examine the passages in which the word extends its signification beyond a single local church, and endeavor to determine, whether in these cases it is generic or not.

"Upon this Rock I will build my church; and the gates of hell shall not prevail against it."[1]

This is the first text which Mr. Courtney examines in relation to this question. He regards the church which was to be built, as a visible organization; and maintains that no visible organization more extensive than a local church, was instituted by Christ. He hence infers that a local church is the thing here intended; and that the term obtains an extended signification, by being used generically. To this argument, we oppose two objections: 1. There is no proof that the church referred to in the passage, is a visible organization in the sense of Mr. Courtney. The opposing force denoted by the phrase "the gates of hell," is not such an organization; and the text contains no proof that the church differs from it in this particular. 2. The passage does not admit a consistent interpretation, on the supposition that the word "church" is to be taken generically.

It is agreed by all, that this text does not refer to any particular local church—as the church at Jerusalem, at Corinth, or at Rome. The promise of perpetuity was not designed to apply to any one of these churches. One of them may be totally scattered by persecution; another may waste away by gradual decay; and a third may be so overrun by corruption as to become a synagogue of Satan, and no longer a church of Christ. By the universal consent of interpreters, the proper application of this text extends beyond any one local church, and somehow embraces the followers of Christ throughout the world; but how the word church obtains the extended signification, is the question. Most interpreters have

---

[1] Matt. xvi. 18.

supposed that it is used as a collective name for the whole body of Christ's people; but some, with Mr. Courtney, suppose it to be merely a generic use of the term—and our present inquiry is confined to this point: Is the word church, in this passage, a collective or a generic term?

When collective terms are used to denote the subject of any affirmation, what is affirmed may respect the entire body signified by the term, or it may respect the individuals composing that body. On this distinction, a well known rule of grammar is founded: "A noun of multitude, or signifying many, may have a verb or pronoun agreeing with it, either in the singular or plural number, yet not without regard to the import of the word, as conveying unity or plurality of idea." When we say the crowd is large, because the verb is in the singular number, the largeness is predicated of the crowd as a whole; and the meaning is, that there are many persons in it: but when we say the crowd are large, the largeness is predicated of the individuals who compose the crowd; and the meaning is, that it consists of large men. On the same principle the pronouns which refer to collective nouns, may be either singular or plural according to the sense. We may say the crowd is large, but we fear not to meet it; or the crowd are large, but we fear not to meet them. The pronoun *it* refers to the crowd as a whole; and the pronoun *them* to the individuals who compose it.

With regard to generic nouns, our grammars do not give, and the usage of language does not authorize any such rule. In every well constructed sentence in which they are found, the verbs and pronouns which agree with them are always singular; and the things affirmed respecting them always relate to the individuals, and not to the genus or species as a whole. We say "the oak is large," but never "the oak are large;" and the largeness which this sentence predicates of the oak, relates to the dimensions of each single tree, and not to the number of individuals contained in the species.

To illustrate the use of generic terms, appropriate reference is made in Theodosia to the passages in the book of Job, which speak of behemoth, leviathan, and the war horse. All these passages may serve also to exemplify the rule laid down in the preceding paragraph. The verbs and pronouns are all singular; and the things affirmed all relate to the individual animals, and not to their several species considered collectively.

Let us now apply this rule to the interpretation of the text under consideration. On the supposition that church is here a generic term, the rule determines the sense to be, that each individual church is built on the rock, and each individual church has the promise that the gates of hell shall never prevail against it. But this, as Mr. Courtney himself has admitted, cannot be the meaning of the passage.

But is the rule universal? May there not be exceptions, in which the affirmations that refer to generic terms, relate to the species as a whole, and not to the individuals? That there are exceptions, is admitted. A sentence may be so constructed that, if interpreted according to the rule, it makes no sense, or a sense known not to have been intended by the writer: we are, therefore, compelled to account it an exception. Such a sentence Mr. Courtney has given us: "The jury is '*built*' upon the '*rock*' of the constitution, and the councils of tyrants can never 'prevail against' or overthrow it." This sentence does not conform to the rule. It was constructed for the purpose of furnishing a parallel to the words of Christ: but we may well doubt whether Mr. Courtney himself would ever write such a sentence in the ordinary course of composition. Besides, it does not appear that the sentence expresses what is required by its supposed parallelism to the words of Christ. The promise of perpetuity to the church had not failed, when corruption overspread all the earth, except in the valleys of Piedmont, or the mountains of Wales. But if tyranny had banished the mode of trial by jury from all the earth except in a single obscure court, would any writer say, The jury is built, &c., and the councils of tyrants have not prevailed against it? Any one who should speak or write thus, would depart from all the usual forms of language.

Another difficulty still remains, arising from the use of the pronoun my: "I will build my church." Although the phrase, *the horse*, may be used generically, the phrase, *my horse*, is never so used; and the presence of the pronoun is very unfavorable to the interpreting of "*my* church" as generic. Mr. C. thinks that the juries in the dominions of Queen Victoria, acting by her authority, may be generically called her jury: but if her Majesty, in an address to Parliament, should say, "My jury is built on the rock of the constitution, and the councils of tyrants can never prevail against it," we may well doubt whether her language would be understood.

In the interpretation of Scripture, unusual forms of expression are never to be supposed without necessity; and the most natural interpretation, that interpretation which most nearly conforms to the usus loquendi, is always to be preferred. The difficulties which attend the interpretation of the text under consideration, when the phrase, my church, is taken generically, vanish when it is understood to be a collective term, including the whole body of Christ's people in every age and country.

The rule which has been given respecting generic nouns might be illustrated by innumerable examples. It is said of leviathan: "The arrow cannot make him flee."[1] The intrepidity here attributed to him, is attributed to each individual animal of the species. It belongs to the whole species, yet not to the whole as an aggregate body, but to every individual. We may say, "The hyena is ferocious; and no human skill has ever tamed him." The ferocity here attributed to the hyena belongs to each individual of the species; and the taming of any one hyena would falsify the assertion. On the same principle, the declaration of Christ, The gates of hell shall never prevail against it, cannot be true, if the pronoun "it" refer to church as a generic noun; for not only one, but many, very many, individuals of the genus have been prevailed against.

Scarcely any rule of language is without exception. Men consult convenience in speaking or writing; and, when they have no fear of being misunderstood, they allow themselves much liberty in the use of words and forms of speech. If any one choose to try his skill in inventing sentences which will not conform to the rule that we have stated, he may succeed; but he will find, on careful examination, that there is some peculiarity which allows the departure from rule. Mr. C. has very properly regarded the generic noun as "representative." One individual is contemplated and spoken of, as representing every individual of the genus. If a noun, generic in its form, is so used as not to retain the "representative" character, but to denote the entire genus directly, and without

---

[1] Job xli. 28.

representation, it becomes in fact a collective noun. It is possible to construct sentences of this kind, which will be apparent exceptions to the rule; and if the text under consideration be an exception of this kind, the word church, instead of being generic or representative, is collective. If the term "church" signifies a local church, considered as a representative of all local churches, the promise that the gates of hell shall never prevail against it, must belong to every local church. But this is not true; and, therefore, the generic interpretation of the passage is inadmissible.

"Because I persecuted the church of God."[1] "Beyond measure I persecuted the church of God, and wasted it."[2] "Concerning zeal persecuting the church."[3]

These passages cannot be relied on for proof, that the signification of the word church ever extends beyond the limits of a local assembly. During the time of Saul's persecution, the only church in existence, so far as we have information in the sacred history, was the church of Jerusalem. Of this church he made havoc, and to this church the three texts above quoted may be understood to refer. But when it has been ascertained from other Scriptures, that, in some manner, the word obtains a more extended signification, the possibility is suggested that it may have a wider signification in these texts. Paul does not say that he persecuted the church which was at Jerusalem. Although this was the only church in existence at the time of his persecution, many others had been planted before he wrote these words. Had his mind, in speaking of his persecutions, been fixed on the church at Jerusalem as a local assembly, it would have been natural to distinguish it from the numerous other local churches that had afterwards originated. When Paul wrote, the church at Jerusalem was no longer *the* church, but only one of the churches. It is, therefore, probable that he used the phrase, the church, in its wide signification; and the question again comes up, How does it obtain this extended signification? Is it as a collective or as a generic term?

When Christ met Saul on his way to Damascus, he said to him, "Why persecutest thou me? I am Jesus whom thou persecutest." The meaning of this language may be learned from the words

---

[1] 1 Cor. xv. 9.   [2] Gal. i. 13.   [3] Phil. iii. 6.

which, we are informed, he will use on the last day, "Inasmuch as ye have done it unto one of the least of these my brethren, ye have done it unto me."[1] His charge was brought against Saul, because he persecuted his followers, the members of his mystical body. This persecution is explained elsewhere: "Many of the saints did I shut up in prison. And when they were put to death, I gave my voice against them. And I punished them oft in every synagogue, and compelled them to blaspheme; and being exceedingly mad against them, I persecuted them even to strange cities."[2] The saints were the objects of Saul's persecution, and not an institution of Christ called the church. It was not the institution that he put into prison, condemned to death, and compelled to blaspheme, but "men and women;" were the objects of his hatred and fury. He did not persecute the institution, either as the individual institution in Jerusalem, or as a genus, of which this individual institution served as a specimen and representative. But he persecuted the saints; and the term church denotes the saints in no other way than as a collective noun. As a generic term, the word church could not denote the object of the persecution.

As in the former case, so in this, Mr. C. constructs a sentence which he considers parallel to the words of Paul. "I am a cotton planter, and yet I am not worthy to be called a cotton planter, because, some twenty years ago, I was bitterly opposed to Whitney and the cotton-gin." Here the name cotton-gin is clearly generic. The object of dislike is the machine or organ, and not the wood and iron which composed it. Just so, if the persecution of Saul was directed against the church generically understood, it was against the church as an organization, and not against the men and women who were members of it. But the exceeding madness of Saul was against the persons, not against their ecclesiastical organization.

In the sentence, "I persecuted the church and wasted it," there is a peculiarity which deserves to be noticed. As the object of persecution, the term church conveys plurality of idea; for the persecution fell on the individual members, and not on the body as a unit: but as the object of the wasting, unity of idea is presented; for it was the body, and not each individual member, that was laid waste. This two-fold use precisely accords with what is

---

[1] Matt. xxv. 40. [2] Acts xxvi. 10, 11.

known concerning collective nouns, and recognised in the rule of grammar before cited; but it ill accords with the usage respecting generic nouns. A cotton planter might hate and oppose the cotton-gin as a genus; but how he could lay it waste generically or representatively is not clear. No good writer would say, *he destroyed the snake and the tree in the island*, using the terms snake and tree generically; but, to express the meaning in language which usage approves, he would say, "he destroyed the snakes and the trees in the island." Other sentences may be constructed in which the uncouthness of such generic use of nouns may be less apparent, but it is never in accordance with prevalent usage. Common sense, which Mr. Courtney very highly and very justly commends, seeks to interpret language according to common usage; and it will naturally and readily understand Paul to mean that he wasted the church by persecuting its members; and, therefore, conceived of the church as a collection of men, and used the name by which he designated it as a collective, and not as a generic noun.

The distinction between an organization, and the individuals composing it, is very strongly drawn by Mr. C. when he inveighs against various ecclesiastical organizations of the present day, and charges them with being rebels against Christ; but, at the same time, explains, that he does not make this charge against the individual members. If common sense will keep this distinction steadily in view, when interpreting the texts under consideration, it will clearly perceive, that the object of Paul's hatred and persecution was not the organization, but the men and women, whom he regarded as worthy of death; not because of the organization, but because of their being Christians.

"To the intent that now unto the principalities and powers in heavenly places, might be known by the church the manifold wisdom of God."[1]

"Unto him be glory in the church by Christ Jesus throughout all ages, world without end. Amen."[2]

Mr. Courtney thinks the term church used generically in both these passages. According to his custom, he constructs sentences which he regards as parallel. The first is: "In order that unto kings and princes, in their palaces and on their thrones, might be

---

[1] Eph. iii. 10.   [2] Eph. iii. 21.

made known through the engine [steam-engine] the manifold skill of the inventor." As the skill of the mechanic is exhibited in the construction of the steam-engine, so the wisdom of God is exhibited to the admiration of angels in the institution of the church; that is, of local churches as a genus. This he understands to be the import of the first passage.

Paul's mind, when he penned this chapter, was filled with grand subjects—the unsearchable riches of Christ, the love of Christ which passeth knowledge, and the manifold wisdom of God. In the beginning of the epistle, he had spoken of the great scheme of salvation, in which God "has abounded toward us in all wisdom and prudence." This wonderful scheme, in which Christ is exhibited as the wisdom of God, and into which the angels, those bright intelligences that have long contemplated the wisdom of God in creation and providence, desire to look, that they may learn the higher wisdom displayed in redemption; this wonderful scheme, in all its glorious provisions, was still before the mind of Paul when he wrote the third chapter of the epistle. The whole context proves this. It was the wisdom of God in the redemption and salvation of the universal church, that, in his view, engaged the attention of angels. How does the sublimity of the thought vanish, in Mr. Courtney's interpretation of the passage! It represents the angels as learning the manifold wisdom of God, from the institution of local churches, and their adaptedness to the purposes for which they were designed. These bright spirits leave their celestial abodes, and come down to contemplate a local church of the right order, and admire the manifold wisdom of God in the contrivance of such a machinery; and its superiority to the ecclesiastical organizations of human contrivance. Lest my reader may suspect that I misrepresent Mr. Courtney's interpretation of the text, I will quote his words:—

"The idea in the first of these two passages is, that the angels of God, who are elsewhere called principalities and powers, might look at this wonderful contrivance of Jesus Christ for the execution of his laws, and the promotion of the comfort and piety of his people, and see in it evidences of the wisdom of God. It was a divine contrivance, and characterized by infinite wisdom. *Nothing else could possibly have done so well.* Men have not believed this. *Men* have all the time been tinkering at God's plan and trying to mend it. *Men* have set it aside, and substituted others in its place; but to the angels it appears the very perfection of wisdom. And it was one object of God in having the church established, that his wisdom might, through it, be known to those heavenly powers and principalities. But now, what was this plan? What was this church? It was, as we have seen, a local assembly, in which each member was the equal of every other, and by whom, in the name of Christ, and by authority from him, his ordinances were to be administered, and his laws enforced."

The sentence constructed as a parallel to the other text, is as follows: " Let the poetry of Shakspeare be honored in the theatre by managers and actors, even to the end of time." We make no objection to this sentence, but its parallelism to the text fails in an important particular. Paul did not say, " Be glory in the church to the end of time." Local churches, like theatres, exist only in the present world; and when the end of time arrives, they will cease to exist. It is therefore impossible that this text should refer to local churches, either as a genus, or as individuals; for it speaks of glory in the church, world without end.

Several passages in the New Testament speak of the church as identical with THE BODY OF CHRIST. It, therefore, becomes important in our present inquiry, to investigate the meaning of this last phrase. Mr. Courtney commences this investigation, by citing Romans xii. 4, 5: "As we have many members in one body, and all members have not the same office, so we being many, are one body in Christ, and every one members one of another."

From this passage, we learn that the body of Christ is not a conglomeration of all the local churches. They who hold this opinion, may defend it from the arguments of Mr. Courtney, as best they can. The members of Christ's body are individual Christians, and not churches: but the question remains, whether it includes all Christians, or only some of them. Mr. C. thinks it perfectly clear that, in this passage, it signifies only the saints who were members of the church at Rome, to whom this epistle was addressed; and he quotes, as decisive on this point, the words, " I say to every man that is among you,"[1] putting the pronoun " you" in small capitals. But this is not the only pronoun which might be

---

[1] V. 3.

so distinguished in the passage. Paul says, "We, being many, are one body in Christ,"[1] including himself among the members of Christ's body, to which the saints at Rome belonged. But Paul was not a member of the local church at Rome. When he wrote this epistle, he had never seen that church; but expected to see them for the first time, when he should make his contemplated journey into Spain.[2] It is hence clear, that the body of Christ included more than the members of that local church. The same may be inferred from ver. 13, "distributing to the necessities of saints." The kind affections, which Paul enjoined on them to exercise, were not to be confined to the saints at Rome, as if they only were members of this body; but all saints were to be accounted co-members with them, and entitled to their sympathies. This appears also in the words, "given to hospitality." Rome was the centre of the Roman empire, the great city of the world, to which men flocked from all nations; and the hospitality here enjoined, must be understood to have for its objects, not the members of that local church only, but all the disciples of Christ who might visit the metropolis.

Mr. Courtney's exposition of the phrase "the body of Christ," is liable to a serious and fatal objection. It converts the beautiful figure which the Holy Spirit employs to represent the union between Christ and his people, into a monster, having one head and many bodies. Every local church is considered a body of Christ; and he is therefore the head of as many bodies, as there are local churches in the world. In Paul's view, Christ's body is one, and not many, though consisting of many members. "We, being many, are one body." His doctrine contemplates one God, one Lord, one Spirit, one faith, one hope, one baptism, and also one body;[3] but the doctrine of Mr. C. destroys the last of these seven unities, and makes it, not one, but thousands.

The doctrine of Mr. C. cannot be relieved from this objection, by the consideration that the churches, though many, are generically one. The members of the church at Rome, were members of a particular, and not of a generic church. A generic church cannot have actual existence, any more than a generic horse, which is neither black, white, bay, nor speckled; but exists only as a mental conception. Mr. C. objects strongly to the opinion, that

---

[1] V. 5.   [2] Rom. xv. 24.   [3] Eph. iv. 4—6.

the term church denotes the church universal, because, he alleges, that this universal body exists only in the imagination; but this misapplied objection falls with crushing weight on his own ideal church generic.

"Now ye are the body of Christ, and members in particular."[1] As the other body of Christ means, according to Mr. C., the church at Rome, this body of Christ means the church at Corinth. The same difficulty as before, recurs here. Paul considered himself a member of the church here intended: "By one Spirit are WE all baptized into one body."[2] And it appears,[3] that he was not the only apostle whose membership was in this church: "God hath set some in the church; first, apostles." Peter had a party in this church, who said, "We are of Cephas;"[4] but no one has hence inferred, that Peter's church-membership was at Corinth—and there is as little proof that Paul and Apollos, though made heads of factions there, had membership in that particular locality. Paul does indeed say to the Corinthians, "Ye are the body of Christ;" but he says also, "By one Spirit are WE all baptized into one body." Paul contemplated the saints at Corinth, as members with himself and all the apostles, of that one body in which the one Spirit operated; and by whose operation, all, whether Jews or Gentiles, are brought into one body. So it is said in another place, "He hath broken down the middle wall of partition between us [Jews and Gentiles], to make in himself of twain one new man, and that he might reconcile both unto God in one body."[5] This one body, this one new man, was not the local church at Corinth, or any other local church, or the church generic; but the universal church, the body of which Christ is the head, and all his people are members.

"And gave him to be head over all things to the church, which is his body, the fulness of him that filleth all in all."[6] This passage declares the church, and the body of Christ, to be identical; and what is affirmed, by no means agrees with the supposition that the body intended, is a local church, the church at Ephesus. Christ was not made head over all things, for the special benefit of this church; and this church was not the fulness of him

---

[1] 1 Cor. xii. 27. [2] V. 13. [3] V. 28.
[4] 1 Cor. l. 12. [5] Eph. ii. 14, 16. [6] Eph. i. 22, 23.

that filleth all in all. Nor can this passage refer to the church generic. The nouns in apposition, "body and fulness," forbid this interpretation. The word body is generic in the phrase "the body without the Spirit is dead," and the generic use of it in this case, is apparent to common sense; but common sense cannot comprehend how the body of Christ can be generic. His literal body was not a genus; and to suppose his mystic body to be a genus, perplexes common sense, and obscures plain Scripture. The word "fulness" is abstract; and to take it generically, requires a generalization of abstractions which confounds common sense. Besides, if "the church" signifies the church at Ephesus, or any other local church, as a representative of the genus, it follows that each particular church, however small, is the fulness of him that filleth all in all. This notion, therefore, multiplies not only the body of Christ, but also the divine fulnesses, to an extent equal to the number of local churches; but the context leads to the true interpretation of the passage — an interpretation simple, clear, and free from all obscurity. The grand scheme of redemption and salvation by Christ, filled the expanded mind of Paul. The gathering together of all things in Christ, the riches of the glory of his inheritance in the saints, and the admission of the Gentiles to be follow-citizens with the saints, and of the household of God, are subjects which engaged his thoughts, and burst forth from his full soul, in the sublime language in which he here writes. And who are the saints that constitute Christ's inheritance, among whom the Ephesians had been admitted as fellow-citizens? Unquestionably not the church at Ephesus. They can be no other than the whole redeemed people of Christ, the whole household of faith. Jews and Gentiles were united under the gospel; constituted one fold, under Christ, the one shepherd; one body, of which he is the head; one family, gathered together in him; one house, over which he, the Son, presides. This body was not a local church. The epistle to the Hebrews was not addressed to a local church; and Paul says of all the Hebrew Christians, "Whose house are we, if we hold fast the confidence, and the rejoicing of the hope firm unto the end."[1] Amongst these Hebrew Christians, believing Gentiles had been received into the same family as members of the

---

[1] Heb. iii. 6.

same household. To this united family, the entire household, the whole context alludes; and any interpretation which turns the thought from this great body, to a local church, is wholly unsuited to the subject of the apostle's discourse.

In commenting on the last verse of the third chapter, we argued that the church there referred to cannot be local, either particular or generic, because it is to endure world without end. The same argument applies to the interpretation of the phrase, the body of Christ. If it signifies a local church, or the genus of local churches, it is not immortal and indivisible. If the church at Rome was the body of Christ referred to in Rom. xii., that body saw corruption. Every local church, and the genus of local churches, will cease to exist; and the mystical body of Christ, according to this interpretation, will cease to exist, having yielded to dissolution. The promise that the Lord would not suffer his Holy One to see corruption, was fulfilled in respect of his flesh; much more may we expect it to be fulfilled, in respect of his spiritual body.

In the context, Paul refers to the church under other figures: "a building;" "the whole building;" "a holy temple." These figures do not present to our view an edifice, or genus of edifices, temporary as local churches; but a structure that, with the foundation on which it is built, will endure for ever. It is no objection to this view, that the indefinite article is used in the phrases, "a holy temple," "a habitation of God." Mr. C. notices this last phrase, and seems to infer from it that God has many such habitations. But the inference is unauthorized. He who says that God is *an* infinite being, does not authorize the inference that there are many infinite beings.

The fourth chapter of the epistle abounds with the same subject, and exhibits it clearly and impressively. Paul exhorts the Ephesians to keep the unity of the Spirit. This one Spirit was not confined to the local church at Ephesus; but actuated the saints everywhere. He adds: "For there is one body, and one Spirit; even as ye are called in one hope of your calling."[1] The oneness of the body, like that of the Spirit which vitalized and actuated it, was not confined to this local church, but included all who were called with "the one calling." The church at Ephesus does not

[1] V. 4.

appear to have included any of the apostles among its members; but the one body of which Paul speaks had apostles in it, with other ministers, who were designed by the head of the church for the perfecting of the saints, the edifying *of the body* of Christ. All the saints are included in this body; and the design was, that "all should come in the unity of the faith, unto a perfect man, unto the measure of the stature of the fulness of Christ." Christ's body is to be perfect and complete; and all the ministry, appointed and given by the ascended Saviour, was designed to effect this: but all the labor of these is not expended on any one local church. The conception of one head with many bodies never entered Paul's mind; but, in his view, as the head is one, so the whole body is one.

In the fifth chapter, we meet again with the same subject: "The husband is the head of the wife, even as Christ is the head of the church; and he is the Saviour of the body."[1] Here the church is again presented to view as the one body, of which Christ is the one head and Saviour; and there is no intimation that the church is more than one. Everything which follows in the chapter respecting the church, agrees with its unity: "Husbands, love your wives, even as Christ also loved the church, and gave himself for it; that he might sanctify and cleanse it with the washing of water by the word; that he might present it to himself a glorious church, not having spot, or wrinkle, or any such thing. * * * * * No man ever yet hated his own flesh; but nourisheth and cherisheth it, even as the Lord the church: for we are members of his body, of his flesh, and of his bones. For this cause shall a man leave his father and mother, and shall be joined unto his wife, and they two shall be one flesh. This is a great mystery: but I speak concerning Christ and the church."[2]

Mr. Courtney thinks he finds a key to the interpretation of all this in the words first quoted: "the husband is the head of the wife."[3] As the wife here referred to is not any one wife in particular, but is to be understood generically, so, he thinks, the church is to be understood generically throughout the passage. But at verse 28, the generic form of speech is dropped, with respect to the wife, and the plural substituted: "so ought men to love their

---

[1] V. 23.   [2] Eph. v. 25—32.   [3] V. 23.

wives as their own bodies." Yet the plural *churches* is nowhere found in the passage. When the husband is singular, the wife is singular; and when husbands are spoken of in the plural, wives also are mentioned in the plural. This accords with what is said elsewhere: "Let every man have his own wife, and let every woman have her own husband."[1] When one of these correlative terms is used generically, the other is also used generically. When Christ and the church are named together, Christ is not generic, and yet the church is supposed to be. Christ, as the husband of the church, is one; but the church, as the wife of Christ, is, according to the interpretation, not one, but a genus—a whole family of wives! This polygamy, introduced into the interpretation of Paul's words, is wholly discountenanced by the scope of the discourse, and particularly by the clause, "and present it to himself a glorious church"—one glorious church, and not a family of churches.

But Mr. C.'s interpretation represents the object of Christ's conjugal love as the institution. Though the churches are many, the institution is but one; and in this view, the notion of polygamy is excluded. But the institution, apart from the churches instituted, is a mere abstraction: and is the bride of Christ a mere abstraction? Is it an abstraction that Christ loved and gave himself for, that he might sanctify and cleanse it with the washing of water by the word? It was not an abstraction that he designed to perfect and present to himself. He did not expend his love and sufferings to perfect the ecclesiastical institution. Nor was it his design to perfect the instituted churches, and present them to himself as a glorious family of churches. The object to be presented is *a* church. The bride, the Lamb's wife, is but one. Another consideration effectually excludes Mr. C.'s interpretation of this passage. The presentation of Christ's bride to him is reserved for the future world, when the marriage supper of the Lamb will be celebrated. But then, according to Mr. C.'s interpretation, Christ will have no bride; for local churches, as individuals and as a genus, will not then exist.

"And fill up that which is behind of the afflictions of Christ in my flesh for his body's sake, which is the church."[2]

This passage agrees with Eph. i. 22, 23, in declaring that the

---

[1] 1 Cor. vii. 2.   [2] Col. i. 24.

church and the body of Christ are identical. What was said on the other text, is applicable to this.

"I will declare thy name unto my brethren, in the midst of the church will I sing praise unto thee."[1]

"But ye are come unto mount Sion, and unto the city of the living God, the heavenly Jerusalem, and to an innumerable company of angels, to the general assembly and church of the first-born, which are written in heaven, and to God the Judge of all, and to the spirits of just men made perfect, and to Jesus the mediator of the new covenant."[2]

These two passages present much difficulty to the advocates of the generic theory. The first of them contains two parallel clauses, in which "my brethren" and "the church" are corresponding phrases, and signify the same persons. The brethren of Christ are the "many sons" whom he, as the captain of their salvation, is conducting to glory.[3] He declares God's name to the brethren, and in the midst of the church, the assembly of these brethren, he celebrates the praise of God. This is the church universal; for he says, concerning them, in presenting them to the Father, "Behold, I and the children which God hath given me."[4] This cannot be consistently interpreted of a local church, either single or generic.

The other text describes the same company, not on their way to glory, but already arrived in the heavenly city. To them all, as the brethren of Christ, and sharers of the glory which the Father had given him, and joint heirs with him of the inheritance, belong all the dignity and rights of first-born sons. Their names are enrolled as citizens of the New Jerusalem. Believers on earth are citizens of the same city: "The Jerusalem which is above is free, which is the mother of us all."[5] Our citizenship is above. We are made "fellow-citizens with the saints, and of the household of God."[6] Paul says, concerning the saints yet on earth: "Ye are come to the church of the first-born." All make one household, one church. Some having already arrived, and others on the way. The river Jordan separated two and a half tribes of ancient Israel, on the one side, from the remaining tribes who were on the other

---

[1] Heb. ii. 12. [2] Heb. xii. 22—24. [3] V. 10.
[4] V. 13. [5] Gal. iv. 26. [6] Eph. ii. 19.

side; but they constituted one nation, and they united as one, in their festal assemblies, in the earthly Jerusalem. So death separates the saints below from the saints above; but they are one—one company, one church; and the heavenly Jerusalem is the place of their joyful meeting in one glorious and happy assembly. This is the church in which there will be glory to God by Jesus Christ, throughout all ages, world without end.[1]

The text last considered shows clearly the propriety of applying the term ecclesia to the entire body of the saints. Though they do not meet in one assembly on earth, they belong to the assembly above, and are on their way to join it. They have been called out of the world, with the heavenly calling which is the summons to meet in the assembly. In obedience to this summons, they quit the world, count themselves no more of it, and are on their march to the city of which they claim to be citizens, and to the company with which they are to be eternally united. As the church at Corinth were an ecclesia, considered as bound to assemble in one place, though not actually assembled; so believers in Christ, considered as bound for heaven and on their way thither, are one ecclesia with the saints who have already arrived at the place of final meeting.

Some have thought that the extended sense of the word is metaphorical; like body, flock, fold, house, temple, applied to the same subject. They suppose it to mean the whole body of Christ's disciples, not literally assembled, but bearing a relation to each other, similar to that which the members of a local church bear to each other. But, on the general principle of interpretation, the literal meaning is to be preferred whenever the subject admits it. The other terms cannot be taken literally; but a literal assembly of Christ's disciples is not only possible, but is expected by all of them, and is in part the hope of their calling. Besides, if we have not mistaken the sense of the passage last considered, this literal assembly is presented to view in it, and the relation which the saints on earth bear to the church above. To this may be added, that the term church is used as explanatory of the metaphorical phrase the body of Christ, a use to which it would be less adapted if the terms are alike figurative. But the question concerning the reason

---

[1] Eph. iii. 21.

of applying the term to denote the universal church, is wholly distinct from the question whether a universal church exists. The first question may remain undecided, without affecting in the least the doctrine concerning the existence and nature of the universal church.

In the first use of the term ecclesia that occurs in the New Testament,[1] it denotes the church universal. No local church at that time existed; and it is, therefore, improbable that the application of the term to the universal church, should be a metaphor derived from its local signification. When the first church at Jerusalem was formed, it included, for a considerable time, all the disciples of Christ, and was the universal church, as far as it was practicable for that body to be assembled on earth. The distinction of local churches never existed until the church at Jerusalem was scattered: it is, therefore, improbable that the name of the universal body was derived from that of the particular associations subsequently formed. Even the term, as contained in Christ's directions,[2] was first applicable to the one church at Jerusalem, and was not applicable to the separate local churches until the first church had become dispersed.

The most remarkable use of ecclesia as a classical word, is its application to the democratic assemblies of the Grecian cities. It is not to be supposed that the name given to those assemblies, implied in itself the powers of the assemblies or the qualifications to membership in them. It would be useless, therefore, to look to the mere word for information respecting the qualifications of church members, or the nature and design of ecclesiastical organizations. It denoted, in the political use of it, the assembly of all those who had the full rights of citizenship; and the place of assembling was in the city to which they belonged. These particulars agree well with the application of the term to the church universal, which includes all the citizens of the heavenly Jerusalem, whose place of meeting is in the glorious city.

In the Septuagint, the word is applied to the body called in the Hebrew Scriptures the Congregation of the Lord. This use of it corresponds better with the Christian use in application to the universal church, than to local churches. The Hebrew ecclesia

---

[1] Matt xvi. 18.   [2] Matt. xviii. 17.

was the assembly of all in the whole nation, who could lawfully unite in the worship of Jehovah according to the forms prescribed in the ceremonial law. The place of this general meeting was in the city Jerusalem. In this city the first Christian ecclesia assembled. It consisted of Jews, who were attached to their holy city, their temple, and the forms of worship to which they had been accustomed. At first they had no conception that gentiles were to be admitted to equal privileges in the Christian dispensation; and they probably expected that Jerusalem was to be the great centre of Christian worship, as it had been for the people of Israel; but persecution soon taught them their mistake. Driven from the city of their affections, and scattered abroad through the earth, they learned to look to another city in which they were to unite in the worship of God, beyond the reach of persecution. They regarded themselves as strangers and pilgrims in the earth, travelling to the city prepared for them by God. As the Israelites, members of the Congregation of the Lord, had been accustomed to travel from all parts of the land which they inhabited, to appear before the Lord in Jerusalem, and to keep their sacred feasts in his presence; so the spiritual Israel are on their pilgrimage to the heavenly Jerusalem, to unite in the great congregation, and enjoy the bliss which God has prepared for them. The pious Hebrews, when journeying to their holy city, longed to appear before God in the great congregation; and often directed their prayers towards his holy temple. In this distant worship, little companies of them would naturally unite in the exercise of like affections, and for mutual encouragement and benefit. So the Christian pilgrims to the heavenly Jerusalem unite in temporary associations, for the worship of God and their spiritual good. Such are the local churches in which they unite on earth.

Although the term church occurs much more frequently in the New Testament in its application to local churches, than to the church universal; yet it is apparent on the face of the sacred pages, that membership in this was far more important than in those. Little is anywhere said of membership in a local church; but the common recognition of Christians is as members of the church universal, the great brotherhood: "Of this way,"[1] "the

---

[1] Acts xi. 2.

sect everywhere spoken against,"[1] "having their names in the book of life."[2] Phebe is mentioned as "a servant of the church at Cenchrea," but she is also recognised as "our sister,"[3] and this relation to the great fraternity, the universal family, has everywhere the chief prominence.

Thus far we have had no occasion for the distinction which theologians have made between the church visible and the church invisible. We have supposed all who profess Christ to be true believers. In apostolic times, the exceptions were comparatively few; and, moreover, in those days, true believers did not delay to receive baptism, the appointed ordinance of profession. In this state of things, there was no practical necessity for the distinction referred to; and the apostle addressed the professors of religion who composed the churches, as true saints, members of the universal ecclesia, citizens of the heavenly Jerusalem, heirs of the incorruptible inheritance.

In this state of things which we have contemplated, the church universal includes all the local churches; but yet it does not include them as organizations. We have before noticed, that the members of the universal church are individual Christians, and not local churches. Moreover, all the local churches taken together do not make up the church universal; for it includes the saints in heaven as well as those on earth. Besides, there may be saints on earth, as the Ethiopian eunuch, who belong to the family of saints, and have not yet been received into any local church.

Section II.—VISIBILITY.

THE MEMBERS OF THE UNIVERSAL CHURCH ARE KNOWN BY THEIR PROFESSION OF CHRIST AND THEIR OBEDIENCE TO HIS COMMANDS.

The religion of Christ was not designed for concealment. From its very nature, it cannot be hid. It inclines every one who possesses it, to do good to all mankind, and to make known the gospel by which all mankind are to be blessed. At every point of contact with human society, Christian benevolence will exhibit itself.

---

[1] Acts xxviii. 22. [2] Phil. iv. 3. [3] Rom. xvi 1.

Christ's followers are described as lights in the world.[1] They are a candle which is lighted, not to be put under a bushel, but that it may give light to all who are in the house.[2] They are a city on a hill, which cannot be hid.[3] They are commanded, "Let your light so shine before men, that they may see your good works, and glorify your Father which is in heaven."[4] Their obedience to this command has distinguished them in all ages, and made them visible to the world.

The disciples of Christ are bound to profess their attachment to him before the world. This obligation is taught in such passages as the following: "If thou shalt confess with thy mouth the Lord Jesus, and shalt believe in thine heart that God hath raised him from the dead, thou shalt be saved."[5] "Whosoever shall confess me before men, him will I confess also before my Father which is in heaven."[6]

But something more than mere profession is necessary to distinguish the true followers of Christ. Many say Lord, Lord, who do not the things which he has commanded. To such persons, however loudly they may profess his name, he will say, "Depart from me, ye that work iniquity."[7] He recognises those only as his followers who are obedient to his precepts; and he has taught us to recognise them in the same manner: "By their fruits ye shall know them."[8] "Ye are my friends, if ye do whatsoever I command you."[9] A life of holy obedience to Christ is readily distinguishable from the common course of this world; and where it is exhibited, men cannot fail to see it.

The visibility of the church consists in the visibility of its members. Our Divine Master came, "a light into the world;" and all his followers are lights; some of them burning and shining lights, and others stars of less magnitude. But, as the constellations of heaven have no other light to render them visible than that which the several stars emit, so it is with the church. All its light is the light of its members, and all its visibility depends on their lustre.

Writers on theology have distinguished between the church visible, and the church invisible; but a church in this world to be

---

[1] Phil. ii. 15.   [2] Matt. v. 15.   [3] Matt. v. 14.
[4] Matt. v. 16.   [5] Rom. x. 9.   [6] Matt. x. 32.
[7] Matt. vii. 21, 23.   [8] Matt. vii. 20.   [9] John xv. 14.

invisible must consist, not of children of light, but of those whose light is darkness. Were we to use these designations according to their proper import, we might call the saints in heaven the invisible church, because they are removed beyond the reach of human sight; and the saints on earth, the visible church, because they still remain on earth to enlighten this dark world. But the saints above and the saints below, make only one communion, one church; and theologians, when they mean to distinguish these two parts of the one whole from each other, are accustomed to call them the church militant and the church triumphant. By the church invisible, they mean all true Christians; and by the church visible, all those who profess the true religion. The invisible consists wholly of those who are sons of light; and the visible includes sons of light and sons of darkness in one community. We have seen that Christ does not recognise mere professors as his disciples, and that he has taught us not so to recognise them. A universal church, therefore, which consists of all who profess the true religion, is a body which Christ does not own. To be visible saints, a holy life must be superadded to a profession of the true religion; and they who do not exhibit the light of a holy life, whatever their professions may be, have no scriptural claim to be considered members of Christ's church.

Membership in a local church, is not always coincident with membership in the church universal. This appears on the one hand, in the fact that the pure light of a holy life may sometimes be so successfully counterfeited, as to deceive mankind. Paul has taught us, that Satan may transform himself into an angel of light; and that it is no marvel, if his ministers do the same.[1] John says, "They went out, that they might be made manifest that they were not all of us;"[2] and we hence infer, that they were not manifest before. But this passage teaches us, that their profession of religion, and their successful imitation of the Christian life, were not enough. It was still true, "they were not of us." Simon, the sorcerer, was thought for a time to be a convert; but when his true character was disclosed, Peter decided, "Thou hast neither part nor lot in this matter, for thy heart is not right in the sight of God."[3] If mere profession rendered him a member of the uni-

---

[1] 2 Cor. xi. 14, 15.   [2] 1 John ii. 19.   [3] Acts viii 21.

versal church, his membership in it was not affected by the discovery that his heart was not right, so long as his profession was not renounced. If membership in the local church at Samaria rendered him a member of the universal church, the local church had not disowned him. When Paul would have the incestuous person at Corinth excommunicated from that local church, he did not pronounce the sentence of excommunication by his apostolic authority; but left it with the church to perform the act.[1] So Peter did not use his apostolic authority, to exclude the sorcerer from the church at Samaria; but pronounced on his relation to the whole community of the saints. It is hence apparent that membership in a local church may be superadded to profession in those who have no part in the matter. They of whom John says, "They were not of us," were for a time members of some local church; and so are many to whom the Saviour will say in the last day, "I never knew you."

On the other hand, men sometimes judge too unfavorably. The church at Jerusalem was unwilling, for a time, to receive the converted Saul as a true disciple; but the Lord Jesus had received him, and given him the place of an apostle in his universal church.

Notwithstanding the errors which human judgment may commit in individual cases, it still remains true, that the light of piety is visible. Time often corrects these errors. The sorcerer, and John's false professors, were made manifest; and the conversion of Saul to the faith which he once destroyed, became universally admitted. Doubtless there are cases which will not be understood till the last judgment; but it nevertheless remains a general truth: "By their fruits ye shall know them." Because some cases are doubtful, and some may be mistaken, it does not follow that sin and holiness are undistinguishable, or that the world and the church are undistinguishable.

The epithet "*invisible*," applied to the true church of Christ, is not only incorrect, but it has led into mistake. Men have spoken of this church as a mere mental conception; and they have asked, whether Saul persecuted an invisible church. They seek a church possessing more visibility than proceeds from Christian profession and a life of piety; and they find it, as they think, in some form

---

[1] 1 Cor. v. 4, 5.

of organization, which they deem necessary to constitute the church. Such an organized body, they call the visible church. But Saul did not inquire, whether those whom he persecuted, as professed followers of Christ, and devotedly attached to his cause and doctrine, were also members of some external organization. He persecuted them as Christian men and women. But the existence of such men and women, like the persecutions which they suffered, was something more than a mere mental conception. Organization is not necessary to visibility; much less is any particular species of it. Rocks and mountains are as visible as plants and animals.

Section III.—UNITY.

The Unity of the universal church is spiritual.

Material bodies are formed by an aggregation of particles which have an attraction for each other. In like manner, living beings are brought together into bodies, or societies, by various attractions which subsist among them. Bees, birds, and various species of animals, exhibit the social propensity; and it operates in man, as a part of his natural constitution. Together with this innate tendency to seek society, the interests and necessities of men bind them together in various forms of association. In these cases, the principles of association are natural; and a new nature, or a new heart, is not indispensably requisite. But the church is a society, in which this qualification is indispensable. Its members are bound to one another by an attraction which is unfelt by men of the world: "If ye were of the world, the world would love his own; but because ye are not of the world, but I have chosen you out of the world, therefore the world hateth you."[1]

The distinctive principle which separates Christians from the world, and binds them together, is produced in them by the regenerating influence of the Holy Spirit. "The fruit of the Spirit is love." "Beloved, let us love one another; for love is of God."[2] "Every one that loveth is born of God."[3] "We know that we have passed from death unto life, because we love the

---

[1] John xv. 19.   [2] Gal. v. 22.   [3] 1 John iv. 7.

brethren."[1] The same spiritual influence that sheds abroad the love of God in the heart, produces love to all who bear the image of God: "He who loveth God, loveth his brother also."[2] Brotherly love was especially enjoined on the followers of Christ, by their divine Master: "A new commandment I give unto you, that ye love one another."[3] All who feel the love of Christ constraining them, are drawn by its influence to love those whom he loved, and gave himself for. Not only is brotherly love enjoined, but it flows spontaneously from the new heart: "But as touching brotherly love, ye need not that I write unto you; for ye yourselves are taught of God to love one another."[4]

Love, which is sometimes called charity in our translation of the Bible, is declared to be "the bond of perfectness."[5] It binds all the people of God together, and makes them one. It is the essential principle of that sympathy, so beautifully described in 1 Cor. xii., as subsisting between the various members of Christ's body. It is this that cements the living stones of the spiritual temple, which as it groweth together, maketh increase of the body unto the edifying of itself in love. This was the principle of union in the first church at Jerusalem, of which it is recorded: "The multitude of them that believed, were of one heart, and one soul."[6] Persecution drove the members of this church from one another; but it could not sever the tie that bound them together, and made them one. The love of the brethren was never confined to a local church. After Paul had said to the church of the Thessalonians, "Concerning brotherly love, ye have no need that I write unto you," he adds, "and indeed ye do it towards all the brethren which are in all Macedonia."[7] Their love extended beyond the boundaries of their church, into all the region round about. Wherever a child of God, a disciple of Jesus, was found, this love embraced him as one of the spiritual brotherhood. "Every one that loveth him that begat, loveth him also that is begotten of him."[8]

The bond of perfectness which unites the people of God on earth, makes them one with the church in heaven, who are made perfect

---

[1] 1 John iii. 14.   [2] 1 John iv. 21   [3] John xiii. 34.
[4] 1 Thes. iv. 9.   [5] Col. iii. 14.   [6] Acts iv. 32.
[7] 1 Thes. iv. 10. [8] 1 John v. 1.

in love. This grace is not destroyed by death, nor does death deprive it of its cementing power. Faith and hope may cease, and the unity of faith and the unity of hope belong more properly to the church on earth; but love never faileth, and the unity of love binds and will for ever bind all the redeemed together, as it binds them all to Christ.

The attraction of love, which draws all the people of God to heaven, causes them, while on their way thither, to unite with each other, as they have opportunity, in the worship and service of God. Even without a divine command not to forsake the assembling of themselves together, grace within would incline them to form such societies. It is said of the first Christians, on the memorable day of Pentecost, "They were all with one accord in one place."[1] And when their number was greatly increased by the ministry of the word, it is said, "All that believed were together."[2] The word "together" is a translation of the same Greek phrase that is rendered in the first verse "in one place." The new converts were of one heart and one soul with the original one hundred and twenty; and formed with these one society accustomed to meet for the worship of God. The unity of this assembly was disturbed by persecution; but the tendency to assemble was not destroyed. The disciples were scattered from Jerusalem; and we immediately after read of the churches in Judea, Galilee, and Samaria. The same principle of unity pervaded the whole body; and by it, from the necessity of the case, local churches were multiplied.

The brotherly love which characterizes and unites the followers of Christ, has not for its object all who profess the true religion. Christ did not enjoin such exercise of it; but instructed his disciples to beware of wolves in sheep's clothing. These dangerous intruders into the fold were to appear as professors of the true religion; otherwise, it could not be said that they wore the clothing of sheep. Paul, in his last interview with the elders of the Ephesian church, gave a similar warning: "I know this, that after my departing shall grievous wolves enter in among you, not sparing the flock. Also of your own selves shall men arise, speaking perverse things, to draw away disciples after them."[3] He elsewhere speaks of false brethren, brought in unawares. If these false brethren had not

---

[1] Acts ii. 1.   [2] Acts ii. 44.   [3] Acts xx. 29, 30.

professed the true religion, they could not have found entrance, even for a short time. Such agents of mischief are not the proper objects of brotherly love. Even the beloved disciple, whose heart was so full of love, and who urged the duty of brotherly love with the utmost earnestness, commanded to try the spirits;[1] and directed, concerning such mischievous professors, not to receive them, nor bid them God speed.[2]

Again, all who profess the true religion do not exercise the brotherly love of true Christians. The wolves in sheep's clothing were enemies of the flock. Among others who had not their deadly designs, it was still true, even in the apostolic times, that iniquity abounded, and the love of many waxed cold.[3] In later times, the pages of what is called church history give accounts that contrast painfully with the beautiful exhibitions of brotherly love found in the Holy Scripture. Those who, according to their profession, ought to have laid down their lives for the brethren, have, in multitudes of instances, persecuted them unto death; and, while professing the true religion, have shed the blood of the saints.

From what has been said, it follows clearly that the church, the body of Christ, does not consist of all who profess the true religion. To constitute membership therein, the profession must proceed from love in the heart; in which case it will be manifested externally by obedience to his commandments. Only so far as this evidence of true discipleship appears, are we required, or even authorized, to exercise brotherly love.

Section IV.—Organization.

The church universal has no external organization.

Organization has respect to action, and is an arrangement and adaptation of parts fitting them to act together to a common end. A society is said to be organized when its members are brought into such connection and relation, that they can act together as one body. A family is a society in which persons are connected with each other in the relations of husband and wife, parent and child. They act towards each other in these relations for the common

---

[1] 1 John iv. 1.   [2] 2 John 10.   [3] Matt. xxiv. 12.

good of the family, and each family stands as a distinct whole in the community. The tie of affection which unites the members of the family, is an internal bond of union; but superadded to this, there is an external organization which makes them one family, even though the internal tie of affection were severed. A nation is a society organized for the purpose of civil government, and the common good of the whole. The members may all love their laws, institutions, and governors; and patriotism, an internal bond of union, may make them one. But an external organization is superadded which would constitute them one nation, even if patriotism failed. A local church is an assembly of believers organized for the worship and service of God. Internal piety is a bond of union; but while piety and brotherly love would bind them equally to saints of other churches, they have an external organization which brings them into special relation to each other, and constitutes them one church.

Believers in Christ may be regarded as composing one family. God is their Father, and all they brethren; but the relationship is spiritual. Believers in Christ compose a nation, a holy nation, over which Christ is the king. They obey his laws, and strive to gain conquests in his cause, but they fight not with carnal weapons; and the bond of their union to each other and to their king is spiritual. The members of a local church may be known by the record of their names in the church book; but the church of the first born are written in heaven, and no record on earth determines their membership. It may be known by their fruits of righteousness, but these are the fruit of the Spirit which dwells and operates in each member, and by immersion in which they are formed into one body.

In the preceding section, the unity of the church universal was proved to be spiritual. Unity may exist in material bodies without organization. A pebble is one, though its parts are not organically united; but in living bodies the parts are organically united, and the organism is necessary to their vitality. The church is called the body of Christ: and the members operate on each other and co-operate with each other like the members of the human body; but the organism is spiritual. The qualification of every member to occupy his proper place and perform his proper duties, is ascribed to the Holy Spirit, who divides to every man severally as he will; and who operates in and through all. Christ is the head of this body, and every member is organically united to the head: but "he that is joined to the Lord is one spirit;" and, therefore, the organization is spiritual.

Theological writers have maintained the existence of what they call the Visible Church Catholic, consisting of all who profess the true religion. They regard this as distinct from the body of true saints, which they designate the Invisible Church. The propriety of this designation we have denied, on the ground that true religion is visible in its effects. But the question as to the propriety of the names used to designate these bodies, is altogether different from the question whether these bodies actually exist. We have maintained the existence of what theological writers have called the Invisible Church, consisting of all who are spiritually united to Christ. Is there another body consisting of all who profess the true religion?

The possibility of uniting all who profess the true religion in one mental conception, and of designating them by a collective name, cannot be disputed. In this way we conceive and speak of the vegetable kingdom, the animal kingdom, &c. If it were impossible to unite all who profess the true religion in one mental conception, the doctrine that a visible church Catholic exists would be an absurdity; but this no one will assert. The existence of such a body in our mental conception is one thing, and the existence of it in fact is another. All who profess the true religion do not form one body by mere juxtaposition, as a number of men gathered together form one assembly; but they are scattered abroad everywhere over the face of the earth. The simple fact that they are alike in professing the same religion is sufficient for the purpose of mental classification; but to constitute them really one body, some species of organization is necessary. Do they compose an organized body?

The Holy Scriptures contain no proof that the followers of Christ, after the dispersion of the church at Jerusalem, ever acted together as one externally organized society. Previous to their dispersion, they were of one heart and one soul, and they were one by juxtaposition as a congregated assembly, and they united as one body in the outward services of public worship, and in such church action as the election of deacons. After their dispersion, they continued to be of one heart and one soul; and they continued to act under the influence of one Spirit to one common end. Their spiritual union and their spiritual organization continued; but their external union and external organization ceased. They no longer constituted one assembly, and they never acted together as one society. They constituted separate local churches which acted independently in their distinct organizations, but never formally united in counsel or in action as one body.

The only fact in sacred history which at all favors the opinion that the churches acted in general council, is recorded in the 15th chapter of Acts. The church at Antioch sent messengers to the church at Jerusalem to consult on a point of duty. After consultation, the church at Jerusalem, with the apostles and elders, sent forth a decree which the disciples of Christ everywhere were required to observe. There is not the slightest intimation that delegates went from the other churches, which were now numerous, and scattered through different countries. The whole church met in the council: not the entire body of those in every place who professed the true religion, but the church at Jerusalem. To this church the messengers from Antioch were sent, and before this church they laid the question. When the decision was made, it was announced, not as the decision of the universal church assembled in general council by its delegates, but as the decision of the church at Jerusalem with the apostles and elders. The decision of this church would have been entitled to respect, as the oldest and best informed of all the churches, and especially in the present case, in which the disturbers of the church at Antioch had claimed the authority of established usage in this, the mother church. But the decree of the assembled body was sent forth with an authority above that of any single church or council of churches: "It seemed good to the HOLY GHOST, and to us."[1] The inspired apostles were present in this consultation, and their decision went forth with divine authority: "Whatsoever ye shall bind on earth shall be bound in heaven."[2] No ecclesiastical council can justly claim this synod at Jerusalem as a precedent for its action, unless it can also claim to act by inspiration, and send forth its decrees with the authority of the Holy Ghost.

---

[1] Acts xv. 28.   [2] Matt. xviii. 18.

No ecclesiastical organization of modern times can, with any show of propriety, claim to be the Visible Church Catholic. No one of them includes all who profess the true religion. Some of them may claim to be THE CHURCH; but most of them have more modest pretensions, and claim to be only branches of the church. Each branch, however, has its own organization, and all the branches do not unite in one organized whole. Were there a combination of all the separate ecclesiastical organizations into one body, and were this body to act as an organized whole, it would possess no authority from the Holy Scriptures; but no such combination does in fact exist. The state of the Christian world falsifies the doctrine.

The bishop of Rome and his adherents, claim to be the Catholic or universal church. They are united by external organization, for the organization itself points out the head, the subordinate officers, and the members of the body. These hold their several positions, whatever may be their moral or spiritual qualifications. The organization is a strong one, as the history of its acts demonstrates; and this history, stained with blood, equally demonstrates that the body is not energized by the spirit of peace and love. This external organization needed an external head, and the bishop of the imperial city became the acknowledged vicar of Jesus Christ. Sitting in the temple of God, and showing himself that he is God, he claims a headship which belongs exclusively to the Lord Jesus Christ. This assumption of power is founded on the doctrine of the visible church Catholic. Destroy the foundation, and nothing remains for the superstructure to stand on. We have, therefore, good reason to regard the doctrine with suspicion, and to examine carefully its claims on our faith.

It will be instructive to notice how naturally the papal usurpation arose out of this doctrine. On the supposition that Christ instituted a universal church of external organization, the declarations and promises which have respect to his spiritual church, would naturally be applied to this external body. It would appear incredible that he should leave this body to degeneracy and corruption, after having promised to be with it always to the end of the world, and that the gates of hell should never prevail against it; and after having constituted and declared it the pillar and ground of the truth. If external organization connects the universal church with the church of apostolic times, it will be difficult, if not impossible, to set aside the pretensions of the Romanists. We may argue that they have lost the doctrine and the spirit of the apostles; but if the church is a body of external organization, the continuity of the organization must determine the true church. If its failure to preserve the truth and spirit of the primitive times has unchurched it; then these last attributes are the distinguishing characteristics of the true church, rather than external organization. Here, then, is the grand controversy between Christ and Antichrist. Jesus Christ has not two universal churches. He is not the head of two bodies, the husband of two wives. His true church is a spiritually organized body, and spiritually joined to him its only head. The body claiming to be the church on the ground of external organization is a substitute, and its head is a substitute for Christ. They first take the place of the true church and its true head, and afterwards oppose and persecute. They who see and deplore the mischief which the papal usurpation has wrought, should learn the secret of its power. The substitution of ecclesiastical organization for spiritual religion has wrought all the evil. Let the pernicious effects teach us to guard against the cause which produced them.

The doctrine of the visible church catholic, is much favored by the use of the epithet *visible*. Things are predicated of the true church which cannot be true of an invisible body. Saul persecuted the church, and this he could not have done if the church had been invisible. We fully admit the visibility of the church, but we distinguish between visibility and organization. Herod persecuted the infants of Bethlehem; but it does not follow that those babes composed an organized society. The rage of the persecuting Saul was directed against the saints, and not against their ecclesiastical organization. To have disbanded their external organization, would not have disarmed his rage. This they might have retained, if they had blasphemed the name of Jesus and renounced his doctrine. The truth and spirit of Christianity are hateful to the world; and without external organization, have been sufficiently visible to awaken the opposition and rage of persecutors.

An argument for an externally organized universal church, is derived from 1 Cor. xii. 28: "God hath set some in the church; first, apostles; secondarily, prophets; thirdly, teachers; after that miracles; then gifts of healings, helps, governments, diversities of tongues." The universal church is here meant, and the offices enumerated imply that the body to which they belong is organized; but the organization is not external. The church which includes all who profess the true religion, contains bad members, and bad officers, as well as good ones. Even in the primitive times, there were, among those who professed the true religion, false apostles and false prophets; pastors who devoured the flock; teachers who brought in damnable heresies; and governments that lorded it over God's heritage, and loved to have the pre-eminence. Considering the church as an externally organized society, these men were as truly officers in it as the most self-denying of its ministers. In the Roman church, the pontiff holds the supreme place, whatever may be his moral character. The priests hold the sacraments, and dispense their mysterious benefits, however unclean may be their hands. If a similar organization existed in apostolic times, the false apostles and other ungodly officers were truly members of the church. Now, did God "set" such men in the church? Did he set them there "for the perfecting of the saints, for the work of the ministry, for the edifying of the body of Christ?" Such men were not the ministers of God, but ministers of Satan, transforming themselves into ministers of righteousness; and the church which excludes them from its boundaries must have those boundaries determined, not by external organization, but by genuine piety. With this view, the whole context of the passage agrees. The qualifications for the officers enumerated are mentioned in the first verses of the chapter, and attributed to the Holy Spirit, dividing, not according to the vote of the church, but according to his own will. The members are brought into the body by immersion in the Spirit; and the sympathy which pervades the body is spiritual. It is no objection to this view, that some of the offices enumerated have respect to local churches, which are confessedly bodies of external organization. The man who labors in the pastorship or government of a local church, if called of God to his office, is a member of the true universal church, and qualified for his office by the Spirit that pervades and animates that body, and is required to labor with reference to the good of the whole. The local church to which he belongs, if organized according to the mind of Christ, consists of real saints; and he labors to introduce no others into their fellowship. He officiates to them as members of Christ's body, and does not bound his aims by the local organization. So Paul taught the elders of Ephesus to consider themselves laboring for the whole redeemed church: "Take heed therefore unto yourselves, and to all the flock, over the which the Holy Ghost hath made you overseers, to feed the church of God, which he hath purchased with his own blood."[1] So Peter taught the elders whom he addressed: "Feed the flock of God which is among you. * * * * Neither as being lords over God's heritage."[2] Every faithful pastor shares in the universal pastoral commission given to Peter: "Feed my sheep—feed my lambs." Though laboring for a part of the flock, he labors for the good of the whole. He who, in his official labors, limits his view to the local organization with which he is connected, and which is temporary in its duration, degrades his office; and so far yields to the antichristian spirit which substitutes external organization for spiritual religion, and a visible for an invisible head.

The opinion has been held, almost as a theological axiom, that baptism is the door into the church. It is not the door into the spiritual universal church; for men enter this by regeneration, and are, therefore, members of it before they are fit subjects for baptism. It is not the door into a local church; for, though it is a prerequisite to membership, men may be baptized, and remain unconnected with any local church. But those who hold that there is a visible church catholic, commonly maintain that it receives and includes all the baptized. They differ among themselves respecting the extent and boundaries of the church, because they differ as to what constitutes valid baptism. Since Baptists admit nothing to be valid baptism but immersion on profession of faith, those of them who hold the doctrine of a visible church catholic, make this church substantially identical with the Baptist denomination. This Baptist modification of the doctrine was its earliest form. While immersion was the universal practice of the churches, and infant baptism had not yet prevailed; before sprinkling was substituted for baptism, and babes for believers; the notion obtained, that the kingdom is the visible church catholic, and that men are

---

[1] Acts xx. 28.   [2] 1 Peter v. 1, 3.

born into it by water. In this notion, Pedobaptism and Popery originated.

Much mischief to the cause of truth has resulted from a misinterpretation of the words of Christ just referred to: "Except a man be born of water and of the Spirit, he cannot enter into the kingdom of God."[1] Not a word is said in this text about baptism and not a word in the whole discourse, of which this verse is a part, leads to the supposition that baptism was intended. But it is not necessary for our present purpose to enter into a discussion of this question. If we admit that the phrase "born of water" intends baptism, it is clear that this alone does not introduce into the kingdom; for it is also an indispensable condition, that a man be born of the Spirit. We have, therefore, the boundaries of the church so narrowed, that it includes none but those who have been both regenerated and baptized.

Persons who have been both regenerated and baptized, are the baptized part of the true universal church; but they do not of themselves constitute a church. They are not the generic church of Mr. Courtney. Each local church is liable to contain false professors; and, therefore, the genus of local churches does not consist of regenerated persons exclusively. They are not the visible church catholic of theologians. This body consists of all who profess the true religion; and, therefore, includes false professors as well as true Christians. Besides, these regenerated and baptized persons do not, in the sense of theological writers, compose a *visible* church. Their regeneration is a spiritual qualification, and is not determined by outward ceremony or external organization. This baptized part of the true spiritual church is as invisible, in the technical sense of the term, as the entire body called the invisible church. No man can say with infallible certainty of any one, though baptized, that he is born of the Spirit. These regenerated and baptized persons do not compose the universal church of the Holy Scriptures; and the church that Christ loved and gave himself for, includes many who, like the penitent thief on the cross, never received baptism. They will form a part in the general ecclesia of the heavenly city; and God will be glorified in them by Jesus Christ, throughout all ages, world without end. This

---

[1] John iii. 5.

universal church is not limited to the baptized; and in no proper sense does the baptized part of it constitute an ecclesia. The true universal church includes the *whole* company of those who are saved by Christ; and their spiritual organization is not dependent on outward ceremony.

SECTION V.—PROGRESS AND DURATION.

THE CHURCH UNIVERSAL IS IN PROGRESS OF CONSTRUCTION, AND WILL BE COMPLETED AT THE END OF THE WORLD, AFTER WHICH IT WILL ENDURE FOR EVER.

The words of the Saviour, "On this rock will I build my church," prove that the building was not then completed. In another place, speaking of the church under the figure of a fold: "Other sheep I have, which are not of this fold: them also I must bring, and they shall hear my voice; and there shall be one fold, and one shepherd."[1] The calling of the gentiles, and the introduction of them into the privileges of the gospel, are here intended. By the ministry of the word accompanied with the influence of the Holy Spirit, great multitudes were converted in the days of the apostles. These converts are described by Peter as lively or living stones, built on Christ the living stone disallowed of men, but chosen of God and precious.[2] Paul uses the same figure; and both of these inspired writers speak of the edifice as a *growing* temple.[3] The work is still in progress; and innumerable multitudes are yet to be gathered, who are to complete the glorious structure. On the last day, when all the redeemed shall have been brought in, Jesus will present them to the Father: "Behold, I and the children which God hath given me."[4] This will be the church completed in number, sanctified and glorified, a glorious church, without spot, wrinkle, or any such thing. The church will remain throughout eternity: "Unto him be glory in the church by Christ Jesus throughout all ages, world without end."[5]

Some difficulty exists in determining the date at which the church of Christ may be properly said to have commenced. The

---

[1] John x. 16.   [2] 1 Peter ii. 4, 5.   [3] Eph. ii. 21.
[4] Heb. ii. 13.   [5] Eph. iii. 21.

same difficulty exists respecting the beginning of the gospel, and of Christ's mediatorial reign. Mark dates the beginning of the gospel of Jesus Christ from the ministry of John the Baptist;[1] but Paul says that the gospel was before preached unto Abraham.[2] The reign of Christ is dated from the time of his exaltation at the right hand of the Father; yet saints were saved by his mediation, and he was David's Lord, under the former dispensation. So Christ said, "on this rock will I build my church," as if the work was still future; and yet the edifice is said to be built on the foundation of the prophets, as well as of the apostles.[3] The Scriptures represent a gathering of all things under Christ, both in heaven and on earth,[4] at the time of his exaltation in human nature to supreme dominion. The Old Testament saints who had been saved by the efficacy of his blood before it was shed, and who had desired to understand what the Holy Ghost signified when it testified to their prophets concerning the sufferings of Christ, and the glory which should follow, were waiting in heaven for the unfolding of this mystery. Moses and Elias evinced their interest in this theme, when, during their brief interview with the Saviour on the mount of transfiguration, they discoursed of the decease which he was to accomplish at Jerusalem.[5] The angels had desired to look into this mystery, but the fulness of time for its disclosure did not arrive until the man Christ Jesus entered the heavenly court, and was crowned with glory and honor. Then the angels gathered around and worshipped the Son. Then the saints drew near, and adored him as their Lord and Saviour. The proclamation was made throughout the courts of glory, and every inhabitant of heaven rendered willing homage to the Mediator. The Holy Spirit brought the proclamation down to Jerusalem on the day of Pentecost, that it might go thence through all the earth. They who gladly received it, were received into his royal favor, made citizens of the heavenly Jerusalem, and members of the great ecclesia.

In the words of Christ before cited, the church is represented as a building. The beginning of an edifice may be dated back to the first movement in preparing the materials. In this view the

---

[1] Mark i. 1, 2.   [2] Gal. iii. 8.   [3] Eph. ii. 20.
[4] Eph. i. 10.   [5] Luke ix. 31.

church was begun, when Abel, Enoch, Noah, and Abraham first exercised faith. But in another view, the building was commenced when the materials were brought together in their proper relation to Jesus Christ. To the Old Testament saints, until gathered under Christ with the saints of the present dispensation, Paul attributes a sort of incompleteness, which may be not unaptly compared to the condition of building materials not yet put together: "These all, having obtained a good report through faith, received not the promise: God having provided some better thing for us, that they without us should not be made perfect."[1]

Section VI.—RELATION TO CHRIST'S KINGDOM.

The doctrine of the Scriptures concerning the kingdom of Christ, has been investigated in the Manual of Theology, pp. 221-229. The result of the investigation, so far as our present subject is concerned, may be briefly stated as follows:—

The kingdom of Christ is the kingly authority with which he, as mediator, is invested, and which he exercises over all things, for the glory of God and the good of his church. The peculiarities of this divine reign are, that it is exercised in human nature, and that it grants favor to rebels. An incomplete administration of it commenced, immediately after the fall of man; but the full development was not made till the man Christ Jesus was crowned with glory and honor, and seated at the Father's right hand. The subjects of his reign are divided into two classes; the obedient, and the disobedient. To the obedient, all the blessings of his reign are promised; and the disobedient, he will ultimately gather out of his kingdom, and banish to everlasting misery. The obedient subjects of his reign, are the same persons that compose the church universal, which has been defined "the whole company of those who are saved by Christ." For the benefit of this church, his kingly authority over all things is exercised.

As theological writers have maintained that there is a visible church catholic, distinct from the spiritual universal church of the Scriptures; so some of them have maintained that there is a visible kingdom of Christ, a society of external organization, into which

---

[1] Heb. xi. 39, 40.

men enter by baptism. But the kingdom of Christ is not a society of men, bound together by external organization, like a family, a nation, or a local church. This view of it is not authorized by the Holy Scriptures.

The kingdom of Christ is properly the kingly authority with which he is invested; and the phrase is used, by metonymy, to denote the subjects of his reign, and especially the obedient subjects on whom the blessings of his reign are conferred. But the tie which binds these obedient subjects to their king, and his reign, is internal. "Every one that is of the truth, heareth my voice."[1] These men constitute a holy nation, a nation bringing forth the fruits of the kingdom; but they are not made a nation by external organization.

Jesus said, "My kingdom is not of this world."[2] We are not to understand this declaration to imply, that his reign had nothing to do with the men and things of this world. The other sentence just quoted, which was spoken in connection with this declaration, "Every one who is of the truth, heareth my voice," claimed the men who receive and love the truth as the subjects of his kingly authority. Having all power in heaven and earth committed to him, he rules in the army of heaven, and among the inhabitants of the earth. Hence every relation among men, and all the duties arising from it, come under his authority. The family, the nation, and the local church, are all institutions in his kingdom, or under his reign; and the external organization of these institutions should be regulated according to the will of the sovereign king; but the kingdom itself exists, independent of all external organization.

Some passages of Scripture have been supposed to favor the opinion, that the kingdom of Christ is a society of external organization, including good men and bad. The kingdom of heaven is compared to a net cast into the sea, which brought good fish and bad to the shore;[3] to a sower, who sowed seed that fell in bad ground as well as in good;[4] to a field, which contained tares as well as wheat.[5] These parables are designed to illustrate important truths connected with the reign of Christ. The *gospel* of the kingdom was

---

[1] John xviii. 37.   [2] John xviii. 36.   [3] Matt. xiii. 47—50.
[4] Matt. xiii. 3—8.   [5] Matt. xiii. 24—30.

to be preached to every creature; and the commission to preach it, was accompanied with the declaration, "He that believeth, and is baptized, shall be saved; but he that believeth not, shall be damned."[1] However variously men may be affected by the word preached, and however difficult it may be to distinguish their true character, and separate the bad from the good in the present life. the separation will be made in the last day, and none will be admitted to enjoy the blessings of the reign but obedient subjects To suppose an organized religious society, including good men and bad, to be intended by the net which enclosed good fish and bad, or the field containing tares and wheat, is to overstrain and misapply the parables. The Saviour does not so explain them. The field is the world, and not an organized *society* in the world. The command was given that the tares and wheat should be permitted to grow together until the harvest, which is the end of the world. Then the King will sit in judgment on the whole world, and not on a particular society in it; and will separate the good from the bad, whom he has permitted to remain together in his kingdom. Then he will remove out of his kingdom all that offends; and will say concerning his enemies, in the midst of whom he now reigns, "Those mine enemies, which would not that I should reign over them, bring hither, and slay them before me."[2] Yet it is the will of the King that bad men and good should be permitted to remain together *in the world*; but instead of commanding that they should be permitted to grow together in religious association with each other, he commands his followers, "Come out from among them, and be ye separate."[3] Moreover, though the tares and the wheat grow together in the field, the tares are called the children of the wicked one; and the good seed, the children of the kingdom. The kingdom does not embrace the good and bad alike, as sustaining the same relation to it; but a society embraces all its members, irrespective of their moral character.

Families, nations, and local churches, are societies of external organization; and they are organized for the present world. At the end of the world, all these organizations will cease. The kingdom of Christ is not of this world; but at the end of the world, when earthly organizations shall have passed away, he will gather

---

[1] Mark xvi. 16. [2] Luke xix. 27. [3] 2 Cor. vi. 17.

the wicked out of his kingdom; and the kingdom itself, freed from all rebellious subjects, will continue for ever. Then shall the righteous, who alone are the children of the kingdom, shine as the sun, in the kingdom of their Father.

SECTION VII.—RELATION TO LOCAL CHURCHES.

If none but true believers were admitted into the churches, there would be an exact agreement between the character of the membership in the local churches, and in the church universal. And if all believers professed their faith without delay according to the law of Christ, and united with the local churches, the aggregate membership of the local churches, and that of the universal church, so far as it exists on earth, would be identical. Nothing but disobedience to the law of Christ gives occasion to distinguish between the church universal, and the great body of professing Christians united in the several local churches; and in a pure state of Christianity, the distinction might be overlooked. When the church universal was spoken of in the times of the apostles, the thoughts of men were naturally directed to the great body of professing Christians; and for all the ordinary purposes of speaking and writing, the distinction between this aggregate of professors and the true body of Christ was unnecessary. So when we speak of a wheat-field, we disregard the fact that tares may be here and there intermixed with the wheat. The name does not signify this intermixture, but is applied as if nothing but wheat were in the enclosure. In like manner, the name church was used in some cases for the aggregate of Christian professors, although in its strict signification, false professors are not included.

The fact that the same name ecclesia that is applied to local churches, is also applied to the church universal, is liable to mislead into the opinion that the membership must be strictly homogeneous; and, therefore, the universal church must include false professors as well as the local churches. So the name *brass*, denotes the same mixture of metals, whether it is applied to a large mass or a small one. The cases, however, are not analogous. The name brass denotes the metal without respect to its quantity, and is as applicable to a particle as to a mass. But the name ecclesia does not denote the material of which a church is composed, and is not applicable to a single member. It signifies the quantity rather than the quality. There may be an ecclesia of wicked men as well as of righteous. It applies to a local church, because the members of it actually assemble; and it applies to the church universal, because the members of it will actually assemble in the presence, and for the everlasting worship of God. The mere fact that the same name is applied, gives no ground for the conclusion that the membership in the two cases is strictly homogeneous. In the epistles to the local churches, the members are addressed as saints and faithful men in Christ. This was their character according to their profession, and what they ought to be according to the law of Christ. False professors who might chance to be among them, were not of them. When excluded, they were not deprived of rights which had belonged to them. Hence, the churches were addressed as if composed entirely of true Christians.

Though unconverted persons are not entitled to membership according to the law of Christ, they nevertheless obtain admittance into local churches through human fallibility. Membership in the church universal is determined by God himself. When Paul described the Hebrew saints as come "to the church of the first born," he described them as come also "to God, the judge of all." The infallible judge determines membership in the great ecclesia; but fallible men admit to membership in the local churches. Hence, a corrupt element finds entrance into local churches, and because of it they are not strictly homogeneous with the universal spiritual church. This want of homogeneousness existed in some degree, even in the purest age of Christianity; but it became much more manifest when corruption overspread the churches, and the evils attending it are now painfully felt by the lovers of Zion.

CHAPTER IV.

INFANT MEMBERSHIP.

WE have ascertained that believers in Christ are the only persons who have a Scriptural right to membership in the Christian churches. But this right has been claimed for infants; and the number, talents, and piety of those who make the claim, entitle the arguments by which they defend it, to a careful and thorough examination.

SECTION I.—DIRECT ARGUMENTS FOR INFANT MEMBERSHIP.

Argument 1.—In epistles written to church-members, Paul addresses children; and, at the same time, exhorts the parents to bring them up in the nurture and admonition of the Lord. It is clear, therefore, that young children were among the church-members to whom these epistles were written. If such children were in these churches, it cannot be doubted that they were in all the churches, and that they were admitted in infancy.

Because children were addressed in an epistle directed to a church, it does not necessarily follow that they were members of the church. As parents were required to bring up their children in the nurture and admonition of the Lord, the same epistle that enjoined this duty on the parents, might appropriately contain a direct command from the Lord, requiring the children to obey their parents. In performing the duty enjoined on them, the parents would naturally and properly take their children with them to the public worship of the church, where the apostolic epistles would be read in their hearing. The fact, therefore, that an apostolic command was addressed to them, proves nothing more than that the apostle expected it to reach them, and claimed the right of commanding them in the name of the Lord.

But the probability is, that the children whom Paul addressed were members of the church. The command, "Obey your parents *in the Lord*,"[1] is so expressed, as apparently to imply that the obligation was to be felt and acknowledged by them, because of their relation to the Lord. The children to whom Paul addressed this command must have possessed intelligence to apprehend its meaning, and piety to feel the force of the motive presented in these words, "For this is well pleasing unto the Lord."[2] Timothy, from a child, had known the Holy Scriptures. Intelligent piety has, in all ages, been found in children who have not yet reached maturity; and such children have a Scriptural right to church-membership.

The argument that the children were so young as to need the care and discipline of their parents to bring them up in the nurture and admonition of the Lord, does not prove that they were destitute of personal piety. Adult church-members need instruction and discipline adapted to their circumstances; and the instruction and discipline of wise and pious parents are of inestimable advantage to their pious children.

The argument contains a fallacy which deserves to be noticed, in the assumption, that the children who were commanded to obey, and the children who were to be brought up in the nurture and admonition of the Lord, were the same. Masters were commanded how to treat their servants, and servants were commanded to obey their masters; but it would be wrong to infer that no masters were so commanded but those who had pious servants, or that no servants were so commanded but those who had pious masters. On the contrary, those servants who had believing masters are distinguished from those whose masters were unbelievers; and yet the latter class were commanded to obey, as well as the former. The relation of master and servant existed, in some cases, when both of the parties were members of the church; and, in other cases, when one party was in the church and the other party out of the church. No proof exists, that the relation of parent and child may not have been divided in the same manner. Parents were not commanded to bring up their children in the nurture and admonition of the Lord because the children were church-members; and

---

[1] Eph. vi. 1.   [2] Col. iii. 20.

children were not commanded to obey their parents because the parents were church-members. The supposition, therefore, that the children in the two cases were the same, is an assumption without proof.

The inference that, if there were children in the primitive churches, they were admitted in infancy, and not because of personal piety, is illegitimate. It cannot be made to appear that they were destitute of personal piety; and, as this was the established condition of church-membership in all other cases, the fair inference is that their membership in the church stood on the common ground.

Argument 2.—The King of Zion has expressly declared, in Matt. xix. 14, that the privileges of his kingdom belong to infants; and, among these privileges, that of church-membership must be included. Children are to be received in the name of Christ, or because they belong to Christ;[1] and this must imply that they are members of his church.

In interpreting and applying the phrase, "Of such is the kingdom of heaven," an important question must be decided; whether the word "such" denotes literal children, or persons of child-like disposition. As the clause stands in our common version, it seems to import that the kingdom consists of such persons exclusively. Now, no one imagines that the kingdom is a community consisting of literal infants only; and, therefore, this rendering, if retained, greatly favors the other interpretation, according to which the whole community are properly described as persons of child-like disposition. The disciples of Christ are humble, confiding, teachable, and free from malice and ambition; and these qualities characterize all who have a part in the kingdom.

But the advocates of infant church-membership have proposed another rendering of the clause. They remark that it corresponds, in grammatical construction, with the clause in Matt. v. 3: "Theirs is the kingdom of heaven;" but, since the word "such" has no genitive in English corresponding to the genitive "theirs," the sense must be expressed thus: "To such belongs the kingdom of heaven." After a careful consideration, I am inclined to think that this rendering gives the true sense of the passage. It makes it analogous to the clause in Matt. v. 3; while the other rendering

---

[1] Mark ix. 37.

is, I think, without any analogy in the New Testament. The kingdom does not consist wholly of its subjects; but it has also its king, its laws, its privileges, and its enjoyments. We have Scripture analogy for saying, that the subjects receive the kingdom, enter into the kingdom, inherit the kingdom, and have part in the kingdom; but none for saying that they compose or constitute the kingdom. Hence the rendering, "To such the kingdom belongs," is recommended to our adoption, as the best interpretation of the Saviour's words. So much having been granted to the advocates of infant church-membership, we proceed to inquire into the true sense of the passage.

In the parallel passage, "theirs is the kingdom of heaven," the persons intended are "the poor in spirit;" and these include all the loyal subjects of the kingdom. If the parallelism between the passages is complete, the word "such" must, in like manner, include all the loyal subjects of the Redeemer's reign, and cannot therefore signify literal children. But if we take the word "such," to signify *a part* only of those to whom the kingdom belongs, we shall still be compelled to consider the declaration as importing that the kingdom belongs to *all* such. Nothing in the words, nothing in the context, nothing in the nature of the subject, leads to the supposition that the kingdom belongs to some infants, and not to others. But the most consistent advocates of infant church-membership, do not admit all infants indiscriminately. If the word "such" was intended to signify any qualifications for membership, peculiar to these children, and not found in all children, no clue whatever has been left us, in the whole context, for ascertaining what these peculiar qualifications were. If Jesus had designed to instruct his apostles how to discriminate between the children to be admitted, and all other children, it is unaccountable that he should have given his instruction with so much obscurity and indefiniteness.

The words demand an interpretation, which will make the term "such" include all who have a right to the kingdom, and no others; and this is precisely the interpretation to which the context leads. Immediately after uttering the words, Jesus explained them: "Whosoever shall not receive the kingdom of God as a little child, he shall not enter therein."[1] To be a little child, and

---

[1] Mark x. 15; Luke xviii. 17.

to act as a little child, are different things; and the latter, not the former, is what the Saviour intended. His explanation shows this clearly; and that the explanation was made, we are expressly informed by Mark and Luke. Matthew has omitted it; but he has recorded, in the preceding chapter, a discourse of Christ on the same subject, giving the same instruction fully and clearly: "At the same time came the disciples unto Jesus, saying, Who is the greatest in the kingdom of heaven? And Jesus called a little child unto him, and set him in the midst of them, and said, Verily I say unto you, except ye be converted and become as little children, ye shall not enter into the kingdom of heaven. And whoso shall receive one such little child in my name, receiveth me. But whoso shall offend one of these little ones which believe in me, it were better for him that a millstone were hanged about his neck, and that he were drowned in the depth of the sea."[1] Here, a child is made the representative of him who was to be greatest in the kingdom; and the phrase, "one such child," denotes one who possesses a child-like disposition. Jesus was accustomed to call his disciples "little children;"[2] and he here calls them, "these little ones which believe in me." In this discourse, no room was left for doubt as to the import of the phrase, "one such child," and this discourse had prepared the minds of the disciples to understand his meaning, when he afterwards said, "To such the kingdom belongs," even if no explanation had followed; but when he added an explanation, reiterating the very teaching which he had before given, no doubt ought to remain, that the same kind of qualification for his kingdom was intended—not literal childhood, but a child-like disposition.

A further demand for this interpretation is found in the nature of Christ's kingdom. Those who suppose literal children to be intended, assume that the kingdom is the visible church catholic; and they understand that membership in this body is here affirmed to belong to infants. Our inquiries in the last chapter have brought us to the conclusion, that Christ's kingdom is not identical

---

[1] Matt. xviii. 6.

[2] John xiii. 33. In the original text a different word is here employed, which seems to have been more appropriate for the expression of endearment. Its literal meaning agrees with that of the other term, and is properly given by our translators in the words "little children."

with the visible church catholic of theological writers; and that such a body as this does not in fact exist. In Christ's kingdom, there are two classes of subjects; the loyal, and the disobedient. To the former class exclusively, the kingdom belongs, according to the uniform teaching of the Scriptures; and the passage under consideration corresponds precisely with this teaching, if persons of child-like disposition be intended. But if the kingdom belongs to literal infants, who are such by natural birth, it must be a different kingdom from that of which Jesus discoursed to Nicodemus, when he said, "Except a man be born again, he cannot see the kingdom of God."

Some persons understand the clause under consideration to import that the kingdom of glory belongs to little children; and they argue that if they have a right to the church in heaven, they ought not to be shut out from the church on earth. But infants have not an unconditional right to the kingdom of glory. If they die in infancy, they are made fit for that kingdom and received into it; but if they remain in this world till they grow up, they cannot obtain that kingdom without repentance and faith. Since the right of children to the kingdom of glory depends on the condition, either that they die in infancy or that they become penitent believers, no inference can be legitimately drawn from it that they have a present and unconditional right to membership in the church on earth. Children are not taken to heaven without being made fit for it; but churches on earth are organized for the worship and service of God, and infants are not fitted for these duties. Even the privileges of the church on earth they are confessedly unfit for. A right to baptism is claimed for them, but a right to communion at the Lord's table is not; yet without this right, it cannot be said that the church or kingdom belongs to them. If by any mode of inference from the passage the right of infants to the church on earth can be established, it must include a right to communion at the Lord's table.

It has been objected to our interpretation of this passage, that the word "such," properly denotes the kind or quality of the thing to which it is applied, and not the resemblance which something else bears to it. In proof of this, such passages as the following have been cited: "Because they suffered such things."[1]

---

[1] Luke xiii. 2.

"With many such parables spake he unto them."[1] In the first example, *such things* means *these very things;* and in the second, *such parables* means *these parables and others like them.* In like manner it is argued, *such children* must mean either *these very children* or *these children and others like them.* Hence, it is alleged that an interpretation which excludes the children present from the import of the word "such," is inadmissible.

It is true that the word *such* denotes the kind or quality of the thing to which it is applied; but just so far as it does this, it denotes also the resemblance which another thing bears to it, if that other thing is of the same kind or possesses the same quality. It denotes the kind or quality of the thing, and not the thing itself. In this particular, it differs from *this* or *these*. If the first of the above examples had read "because they suffered *these things*," the identical sufferings would have been signified, and not their kind or quality. Hence, *such* does not mean *these*. So in the other examples "such parables" does not mean *these and other parables*, for it denotes the kind and quality of the parables, and this the phrase *these and other* would not do. The fact that "such things" in the first example, denoted the identical sufferings which had just been mentioned, is not determined by the meaning of the word *such*, but by the connection in which it is used. Any other sufferings of like kind would suit the meaning of the word equally as well. So any parables of like kind equally suit the meaning of the phrase "such parables." The fact that the sufferings and parables previously mentioned are denoted by the word *such*, or included in its meaning, is accidental. *Such* does not mean *these*, and does not include *these* in its meaning, unless by accident. However frequent this accidental use of the term may be, its essential meaning refers to kind or quality, and not to particular things. When it is said, "They which commit such things, are worthy of death;"[2] the particular things that had been mentioned are not necessarily intended or included; but any things of like kind are denoted. In the words of Paul, "I would to God, that not only thou, but also all that hear me this day, were both almost, and altogether, such as I am, except these bonds."[3] The word such neither intends nor includes "I," but merely denotes likeness;

---

[1] Mark iv. 33.   [2] Rom. i. 32.   [3] Acts xxvi. 29.

and that likeness is confined to spiritual endowments and privileges, and does not extend to the body or the external condition. So the word such in the case before us, does not intend or include the children present, but denotes a likeness to them; and that likeness does not respect the body or outward condition, but those mental qualities which made them fit representatives of converted men.

If we were unable to distinguish between the essential meaning of the word *such* and its accidental use, we might still be preserved from an erroneous conclusion in the present case by a due regard to Matt. xviii. 5. In this verse the same word is used by the same speaker with reference to the same subject, and in like circumstances, a little child being present as the children were present in the other case. Yet in this case, the word such does not intend or include the child present, but denotes those qualities in which that child was made a representative of converted persons. The verse preceding proves this: and the words which follow the use of the term *such* in the other case, prove the same. The analogy is complete, with the single exception that the explanation follows in one case, and precedes in the other. But it follows immediately as if uttered by the same breath, for it was spoken before Jesus laid hands on the children. If any importance can be attached to the order of time in which the explanation was given, it should be remembered that the whole of the discourse in the 18th chapter preceded the transaction recorded in the 19th, and prepared the minds of the disciples for understanding it. When all these facts are considered, we need not be staggered, though numerous examples be adduced in which *such* may appear to have a different meaning. True criticism will regard the analogy of the cases rather than their number; and if the word has different meanings, will prefer that which is supported by an analogy so remarkable and complete. But the truth is, criticism has no choice to make between different meanings of the word, for in every case the meaning of the word is the same.

If the criticism which we have set aside were just, it would fail to justify the conclusion that has been drawn from it. In the passage recorded in Luke ix. 47, 48, the word *such* is not used: "Jesus, perceiving the thought of their heart, took a child, and set him by him, and said unto them, Whosoever shall receive this child in my name, receiveth me; and whosoever shall receive me, receiveth him that sent me: for he that is least among you all, the same shall be great." Here the expression is, "this child;" but the meaning is not to be taken literally. The whole transaction was symbolical. The disciples had desired the highest place in their Master's kingdom. It was their ambition to sit on his right hand and on his left. But Jesus set the little child *by him*, and constituted that child his prime minister and representative: "Whoso shall receive," &c. All this was symbolical; and was designed to teach the disciples what they must be, to obtain the honor which they coveted. If criticism could convert the word *such* into *these*, and the clause, "of such is the kingdom," into *theirs is the kingdom;* there would be sufficient reason, even then, to regard the children as only symbols or representatives of converted or humble and child-like persons.

It has been further objected, that the clause, "for of such is the kingdom of heaven," could not, according to our interpretation, contain a reason for admitting into Christ's presence the children that were brought to him. We cheerfully grant, that the connection of this clause with what precedes would be quite obvious, if it could be shown to declare the right of infants to church-membership; and if it could also be shown that these infants were brought to Christ to be initiated into his church. This last has been supposed by some, but without any proof from the sacred narrative. The purpose for which they were brought to Jesus is thus expressed: "that he should put his hands on them, and pray;"[1] "that he should touch them."[2] If initiation into the church was the design, it is unaccountable that all the inspired writers should have failed to mention it, and that they should have described the act as performed with a different design. If it was usual for infants to be admitted to church-membership, the apostles must have known it; and their opposition, in the present case, is unaccountable. Moreover, if these infants were brought to be initiated into the church, and if Jesus declared their right to the privileges of his church, it cannot be supposed that they were sent away without the benefit desired. But were they initiated? If so, by what rite? Baptism has been considered the rite of initiation; but there is no evidence that these children were baptized. When Jesus made disciples,

---

[1] Matt. xix. 13.   [2] Mark x. 13; Luke xviii. 15.

they were baptized, not by himself, but by his disciples. There is no evidence that he put these children into the hands of the disciples, with a command to baptize them; but, on the contrary, he took them into his own arms, not to baptize, but to bless them.

On a careful examination of the passage, we discover that the conjunction "for" connects the clause which follows with the command, "forbid them not." This command was addressed to the disciples; and the reason which follows may be supposed to have been introduced for their sake, rather than for the sake of the children. He was displeased with his disciples, and designed to rebuke them. Now, to understand his rebuke, we must view it in connection with the fault of which the disciples had been guilty. They expected their Master to set up a temporal kingdom; and all his teachings to the contrary, and even his crucifixion at last, did not convince them that his kingdom is not of this world. They were ambitious to have the highest place in his kingdom; and this sinful ambition remained, till they ate the last passover with him. He had recently set a little child before them, and used it as a representative of the chief favorite in his kingdom. This discourse they had not understood. Like other discourses designed to explain the nature of the kingdom, and of the qualifications for it, the instruction which it contained was not properly received until after Christ's departure, when the Holy Spirit brought it to their remembrance. Ambition and worldly policy blinded their minds. How they understood the Saviour's discourse, we cannot certainly determine; but they seem, like the advocates of infant church-membership, to have understood the word *such* to refer to age, and not to moral qualities. Hence, the words, "Whoso receiveth one such child," placed little children before their minds as rivals for the highest place of dignity in the kingdom. Whether they feared that Christ would postpone the setting up of his kingdom until these young rivals should be of age, or whether they apprehended that he would, among the miraculous works which he performed, endow them supernaturally, even in infancy, for holding office in his kingdom, we have no means of ascertaining. But, whatever may have been their notions, they seem to have conceived a jealousy of these young rivals. The ministers of Eastern monarchs guarded the way of access to their sovereign. This right of guarding the way of approach to their Master, the disciples assumed on this occasion. Jesus, who never denied access to any that sought favor at his hands, was displeased with their conduct and the worldly ambition which instigated it. To them, and for their benefit, he said what may be thus paraphrased: "Suffer the children to come unto me, and forbid them not. Do not, by this usurpation of power, think to exclude these dreaded rivals from my presence and favor; for to such as these the privileges and honors of my kingdom belong, rather than to those who, like you, are actuated by worldly ambition. Instead of driving these children away, imitate their spirit; for whosoever shall not receive the kingdom as a little child, shall not enter therein."

Whether we have succeeded or not in discovering the true connection of the clause with what precedes, the clause itself does not affirm the right of infants to church-membership. The proofs which have been adduced on this point are clear and decisive.

What has been said, sufficiently explains Mark ix. 27, the other passage quoted in the argument. We admit that to receive one of such children in the name of Christ, is to receive him because he belongs to Christ; but the passage does not teach that literal infants are members of Christ's church. We have proved that the Saviour employed the phrase, *such children*, to denote persons of child-like disposition. Hence, the doctrine of infant church-membership cannot be inferred from the passage.

Some Congregationalists have held that children are members of the church universal, but not of local churches. This distinction may perhaps account for their admission to baptism, and exclusion from the Lord's supper; but it accounts in such a way as to show clearly, that the privileges of the kingdom do not belong to them. No one maintains that unregenerate infants are members of the spiritual church. If they are members of a universal church, it must be the visible church catholic. Now, if such a body exists, it never meets or acts; and the privileges of membership in it, to those who are denied membership in local churches—what are they? To the local churches belong the regular worship of God, a stated ministry, the benefits of discipline and mutual exhortation, and the communion of the Lord's table. The baptized children grow up, without the membership which entitles to these privileges. How, then, can it be said that the kingdom belongs to them?

Argument 3.—Paul declares, that the children of certain members of the Corinthian church were holy.[1] The word *holy*, or *saints*, was used by him to denote church-members, that is, persons consecrated to God. We have, therefore, ground for the conclusion, that these children were members of the church.

The passage referred to, reads as follows: "For the unbelieving husband is sanctified by the wife, and the unbelieving wife is sanctified by the husband: else were your children unclean; but now are they holy." This passage, if the holiness of which it speaks signifies church-membership, will prove too much. The word "sanctified," which is applied to the unbelieving husband and unbelieving wife, means *made holy*. These unbelievers, therefore, were also holy; and must, according to the interpretation, have been members of the church. The text is a process of reasoning; and the laws of reasoning require, that the term "holy" in the conclusion, should be used in the same sense as in the premises. If *holiness* implies church-membership, when predicated of the children, it must imply the same when predicated of the unbelieving husband and wife. But no one imagines that those unbelievers were members of the church; and, therefore, the holiness affirmed of the children, is not church-membership.

If it be asked, what holiness could be predicated of these children, or of the unbelieving husband and wife, which did not include church-membership—the answer is at hand. The Jews accounted gentiles unclean, and thought it unlawful to enter their houses, to keep company or eat with them, or to touch them. The Jewish Christians retained this opinion, as is manifest from Gal. ii. 12. According to this opinion, they with whom familiar intercourse was lawful, were considered holy; and all others were unclean. The question had arisen among the Corinthians, probably from the influence of Judaizing teachers, whether familiar intercourse with unbelievers is lawful.

In the fifth chapter of the epistle, Paul discusses this question, and decides that association in church-membership with such persons, was unlawful; but that ordinary intercourse with them must be admitted, or Christians "must needs go out of the world." As the principle which he opposed had produced a doubt among the

---

[1] 1 Cor. vii. 14.

Corinthians, whether it was lawful for Christians to live in familiar intercourse with unbelieving husbands or wives, Paul considers this case in the seventh chapter. He decides that, if this principle may disturb the domestic relations, it will separate parent and child, as well as husband and wife. If familiar intercourse with the unconverted is unlawful in one case, it is unlawful in the other also. This is the argument of the apostle; and it is precisely adapted to meet the difficulty. But this argument presupposes, that the children, like the unbelieving husband and wife, were not members of the church. The text, therefore, furnishes decisive proof, that infant church-membership was unknown in the time of the apostles.[1]

Argument 4.—The writers of the New Testament used words in the sense in which they were accustomed to read them in the Scriptures of the Old Testament. The Greek word Christ, corresponded to the Hebrew word Messiah; and both words denoted the same person. The Greek word *ecclesia*, was not a newly-invented term; but it was the word by which the LXX. had rendered the Hebrew *cahal*, of the Old Testament, and must therefore be understood to denote the same thing, the Congregation of the Lord. Hence the church was not a new organization. It was the Hebrew congregation, continued under the new dispensation; and, as children were included with their parents, in the former dispensation, the right of membership cannot now be denied to them. The identity of the church under both dispensations is further apparent in the fact, that the names Zion and Jerusalem, derived from the places where the Old Testament worshippers assembled, are given to the church of the New Testament.

It is true that the Hebrew word Messiah, and the corresponding Greek word Christ, denoted the same person; but it cannot be hence inferred as a universal truth, that identity, either of person or things, always attends identity or correspondence of name. The Hebrew name Joshua is applied in Scripture to different persons;[2] and the corresponding Greek name Jesus, is applied to persons different from these, and different from one another.[3] The English words assembly, convention, association, &c., are in common use as names of organized bodies; but the character of the organiza-

---

[1] For a more extended examination of 1 Cor. vii. 14, see a tract entitled "A Decisive Argument against Infant Baptism," published by the Southern Baptist Publication Society.
[2] Ex. xxiv. 13; Zech. iii. 1.   [3] Matt. i. 21; Col. iv. 11.

tion cannot be inferred from the name. The name Assembly sometimes signifies the legislative body of a state, and sometimes an ecclesiastical judicatory. With this name the Hebrew and Greek words for congregation and church very nearly correspond in signification; but were the correspondence perfect, it could not be inferred that organized societies denoted by them must be identical.

But the correspondence between the designations of the church and of the Hebrew congregation is not perfect. Two Hebrew words, קהל and עדה, were used to denote the Hebrew congregation, and neither of these is invariably rendered by the Greek word εκκλησια. In the sixth verse of Exodus 12, the chapter in which the Hebrew congregation first appears on the sacred page, both Hebrew words occur, and one of them the LXX have rendered πληθος, and the other συναγωγη. In Numbers xvi. 3, both words occur, and both are rendered συναγωγη. If any one should argue from hence, that whenever the New Testament writers use the words πληθος, and συναγωγη, they must mean the Hebrew congregation, he would err egregiously. The argument which would be so fallacious when applied to these words, cannot be valid when applied to εκκλησια.

The single words which we have noticed, are, when used to designate the bodies to which they are applied, often accompanied with adjuncts. The Hebrew congregation was called the Congregation of the Lord or Jehovah, and the Congregation of Israel. It was a congregation instituted for the worship of Jehovah as the God of the Hebrew nation. The church is called the church of God, and the church of Christ. These full designations of the two bodies are by no means coincident; but we have proof that the two bodies are not identical, which is far more to be relied on than a want of coincidence in their names.

When the New Testament church is first introduced in the sacred writings, Jesus calls it not the cahal or ecclesia of Israel, but my ecclesia. He moreover speaks of it as yet to be constructed: "On this rock will I build my ecclesia." It cannot be that he intended the cahal of Israel which was instituted in the time of Moses, and its organization completed in the most minute particulars. The next occurrence of the word ecclesia in the New Testament is still more remarkable: "Tell it to the ecclesia. If he will not hear the ecclesia, let him be, &c." Can it be true that the New Testament writer who recorded these words, understood the word ecclesia in the sense in which he had been accustomed to read it in the Scriptures of the Old Testament, as referring to the Hebrew cahal? Can it be that Jesus meant it to be so understood? Did he mean that his followers should refer their matters of grievance to the great congregation of Jewish worshippers, their enemies and persecutors, and be governed by their decision? Incredible! The next mention of the New Testament ecclesia is equally decisive: "The Lord added to the ecclesia such as should be saved." The time was the feast of Pentecost, when the worshippers of the Hebrew cahal were assembled at Jerusalem. From this assembly the converts to the new religion were made; and when made, they were added to the ecclesia. No proof more decisive can be desired; that the ecclesia to which they were added, was not the cahal to which they had previously belonged.

The argument from the name may be retorted with effect. When Jesus said, "Tell it to the church;" the Christian churches in which discipline was to be exercised had not yet been organized. The master of the family was still present to manage the affairs of the household by his direct authority; but he gave the command to be observed after his departure, as a perpetual rule of discipline. The unguarded manner in which he speaks of the ecclesia, furnishes proof of no inconsiderable force, that the word which he employed, was not at the time in familiar use as a name for the congregation of Jewish worshippers. Had it been, this application of the word would have been natural to the disciples, and some accompanying explanations would have been needed to guard them from mistake. When intending that which did not yet exist, of which they had no personal knowledge, and which never had existed, he would not, without explanation, have employed a term to denote it, with which they were familiar as the name of something that had long existed and was well known to them. The conclusion to which this argument tends, is strongly corroborated by the fact, that although the word ecclesia occurs in the New Testament more than a hundred times, it never, with but one exception, denotes the people of Israel; and in this single exception, "He that was in the ecclesia in the wilderness,"[1] it does not

---

[1] Acts vii. 38.

denote the people of Israel as an enduring organization, but refers to a particular time in their history, when they were assembled at Sinai to receive the law, and for this reason it should have been translated *assembly*. As an enduring body, they are called the house of Israel, the commonwealth of Israel, the people, the nation; but the ecclesia they are never called.

The passage, "In the midst of the ecclesia I will sing praise unto thee,"[1] is quoted from the Old Testament, where the word cahal is used, and where there is an allusion to the Hebrew congregation; but as used by Paul, the ecclesia intended consists of the "many sons" brought to glory, who are mentioned in the context. The same ecclesia is afterwards spoken of, "The church of the first born," with an apparent allusion to the assembly of Old Testament worshippers. This allusion may be readily accounted for by the fact, that the worship of the Old Testament dispensation was "a shadow of good things to come." Zion and Jerusalem were types of heaven, the future meeting place of the saints; and the congregation of Israel assembled for the worship of God, typified that future assembly in which the redeemed of the Lord shall come from the east, the west, the north, and the south, and shall sit down with Abraham, Isaac, and Jacob, in the kingdom of Heaven. This fully accounts for the use which the prophets have made of the names Zion and Jerusalem, in predicting the glory of the church.

The Hebrew cahal was an actual assembly. Three times in the year the tribes were required to meet for public worship in the place where the Lord would put his name.[2] This obligation continued as long as the ordinances of their worship were obligatory; and ceased when the handwriting of them was nailed to the cross of Christ. An intimation that the obligation to meet at Jerusalem was to cease, is given in the words of Christ to the women of Samaria: "The hour cometh, when ye shall neither in this mountain, nor yet at Jerusalem, worship the Father."[3] When men were no longer required to meet in Jerusalem, the cahal of Israel was dissolved.

The distinction between the church and the Hebrew congre-

---

[1] Heb. ii. 12.   [2] Deut. xii. 5.   [3] John iv. 21.

gation, may be further elucidated by an attentive consideration of the design with which the congregation was instituted.

Although, in the divine purpose, a sufficient sacrifice for sin had been provided from eternity, yet it did not seem good to Infinite Wisdom that it should be immediately offered, when sin first entered into the world. Four thousand years of ignorance and crime, God winked at, or overlooked as unworthy of his regard, or unfit for his purpose; and fixed his eyes on that period denominated "the fulness of time," when it would best display the divine perfections, for the Redeemer to atone for transgression; and repentance and remission of sins to be preached in his name, among all nations. As, in the exercises of an individual Christian, the discovery of salvation in Christ is withheld, until an anxiety is excited in his breast that makes the discovery welcome; so in the history of the world, the Messiah makes not his appearance, until mankind have felt the necessity of such a deliverer; then he comes, the desire of all nations. It pleased God that a full experiment should be made of man's power and skill to find a remedy for his moral disease, before God's remedy for the healing of the nations should be revealed and applied. "After that, in the wisdom of God, the world by wisdom knew not God, it pleased God, by the foolishness of preaching, to save them that believe."

The experiment which, in the wisdom of God, opened the way for the Redeemer's entrance into the world, was of a two-fold nature; or, rather, there were two distinct experiments, demonstrating distinct truths. When the bolder enemies of God and religion make their appeal from the volume of inspiration to the volume of nature, and assert the sufficiency of the latter to enlighten and direct them in the search after God; we can refer to actual experiment, to ascertain how far fallen man, without the oracles of God, can advance toward the knowledge of the Divine character. With the light of nature, the bright beams of science, and the keen eye of natural genius, the wisest men of antiquity still *felt* in the dark, after the unknown God.[1]

When those who profess to receive the truth, deny the doctrine of grace, and maintain that man has sufficient native virtue, if properly cultivated, to render him acceptable to God; that there are

---

[1] Acts xvii. 27.

influences of the Word or Spirit common to all men, which are sufficient, without any additional special influence, to bring him to know and enjoy the Most High; we have in the wisdom of God, another completed experiment, which decides against this doctrine, with as much certainty as is anywhere to be found within the limits of experimental philosophy. In the sacred record is the history of a people, who had the advantage over every other people much every way. They were not left to read the volume of nature only; but to them were committed the oracles of God. They were not left with unmeaning forms, and unauthorized rites of religion; but they had ordinances of divine service, instituted on the authority of God. "To them pertained the adoption, and the glory, and the covenants, and the giving of the law, and the service of God, and the promises." Nor were they without instructors in religion; but holy men were raised up among them, who spake as they were moved by the Holy Ghost. Neither were they without motives to obedience; but a covenant was made with them, containing every threat which might deter—every promise that might allure. The experiment was made fairly and completely. Jehovah himself said, "What could have been done more to my vineyard, that I have not done?" And what was the result? It was clearly demonstrated that man is totally depraved; that the best institutions, instructions, and motives, with all common influences of the Spirit, whatever such there may be, are altogether insufficient to restore his fallen nature; and that a direct special influence upon his heart, by the effectual working of Divine power, is indispensably necessary, in order to make him delight in the law of God, and render acceptable obedience to its holy requirements. See Heb. viii. 8, 9, 10.

That society of persons which was the subject of the last-mentioned experiment, is frequently denominated *the Congregation of the Lord.* It appears to have been the only divinely instituted society, organized for religious worship, that ever existed before the coming of Christ. That God designed by the Mosaic dispensation, of which this congregation was the subject, to give a clear demonstration of man's depravity, may be inferred from the end which has actually been accomplished, and from such declarations of Scripture as the following: "The law was added because of transgression until the seed should come. The law entered that the offence might abound." Since unto God all his works from the beginning are known, he well knew the imperfections of the Mosaic covenant, even from the time of its institution, and what would be the result of the experiment. He found fault with it long before its abrogation; and so prepared it at first, that it typified and foretold a better covenant that should succeed it, established upon better promises.

The first account that the Scriptures give of the Congregation of the Lord, we find in the twelfth chapter of Exodus. When a new order of things was introduced; when the year received a new beginning, and became, as it has been called, the ecclesiastical year; when God *took his people by the hand*, to lead them out of the land of Egypt;[1] when that code of laws for the regulation of religious worship, which the apostle means by the first covenant throughout his epistle to the Hebrews, began to be promulgated; and the Passover, as one of the ordinances of divine service pertaining to the first covenant, was instituted; then, first, are the Israelites recognised as a worshipping congregation. Before this, the word of the Lord had come to individuals, and individuals had performed religious rites; but now, the word is sent to a whole congregation, and that congregation, by divine appointment, perform a rite of divine worship simultaneously. Before this, the Israelites had indeed been distinguished from the rest of mankind; but not by the characteristics of a worshipping society. That there were persons among them who worshipped God in sincerity and truth, will not be disputed. But where were their public altars? Where was their sanctuary? Where were their public ministers of religion? Where were their appointed sacrifices? Where their statute book, the laws of their worship, the rules of their society, &c.? A worshipping society, without forms, and rites, and rules of worship, God never constituted.

The seed of Abraham were destined to be the subjects of special dispensations, throughout all their generations. This appears no less in their history since the Christian era, and before their deliverance from Egyptian bondage, than in the intermediate time. But, during all this intermediate time, they were the subjects of that peculiar, experimental, preparatory dispensation, which we

---

[1] Heb. viii. 9.

have been considering. They were constituted, and continued to be, the Lord's peculiar cahal, his only worshipping congregation.[1] But while the ordinances of their worship were wisely contrived to be types and prophecies of Christ, at the same time that they afforded to the world that experiment, which appears to have been so important a part of their design; in like manner, an instructive intimation of the future exclusion of the Jews from gospel privileges, and of the admission of the gentiles, appears to have been given, in the character of the members who composed this sacred congregation. The great body of its constituents were the descendants of Abraham; but provision was made in its charter, that Israelites in some cases should be excluded, and that gentiles might be admitted.[2] Nothing like this can be found in the covenant made with Abraham and his seed, as recorded in the 17th chapter of Genesis. This covenant received into its arms every circumcised son of Jacob (in whom the seed was ultimately called), without any exception; and thrust from its embrace every Gentile, without any distinction. It was, indeed, one of its stipulations that every Israelite should have all the males of his house circumcised; but there is no intimation that they were all thereby incorporated among the covenant seed, or that they had more right to the territory granted in the covenant, than had Ishmael, or the sons of Keturah. Jacob's servants were circumcised; but they did not become heads of tribes in Israel, as they would have been, had circumcision endowed them with the privileges of the covenant seed.

When the end for which any society was instituted has been accomplished, it is natural to expect its dissolution. The experiment for which the Congregation of the Lord had been organized, was completely made, when the Redeemer appeared, in the end of the world, "to take away sin by the sacrifice of himself." The first covenant, established upon conditional promises, was proved, upon due trial, to be faulty, weak, and unprofitable; and the necessity of a better covenant, whose better promises should be all yea and amen in Christ Jesus, was clearly demonstrated: "He taketh away the first, that he may establish the second." When "There was a disannulling of the commandment going before," in which was contained the charter of the Congregation of the Lord, the

---

[1] 1 Chr. xxviii. 8; Mic. ii. 5.   [2] Deut. xxiii. 1—8; Exod. xii. 43—47.

society was dissolved. Deprived of the character of a worshipping congregation, it lost its existence. The wall that had enclosed it from the rest of mankind, was broken down, when its ordinances were nailed to the cross of Christ.[1]

We have not insisted on the obvious difference between the church and the Hebrew congregation, as to the character of the members composing them. The congregation consisted mainly of Israelites; and these were admitted without regard to moral character, if circumcised, and free from ceremonial defilement and bodily defect. Gentiles were admitted, on conforming to the law of circumcision; but a Moabite, or Ammonite, could not be admitted until the tenth generation; and the most pious Israelite was prohibited, if he was ceremonially defiled, or the subject of a particular bodily defect.[2] In Christ Jesus, circumcision availeth nothing, but a new creature. Moabites and Ammonites are not excluded; but, in every nation, he that feareth God, and worketh righteousness, is accepted with him.[3] Ceremonial defilement and bodily defects constitute no obstacle to the fellowship of the saints. If the institution were the same, such radical changes in the membership could not well consist with the continued membership of infants. But the Mosaic institution has been abolished: "For there is verily a disannulling of the commandment going before, for the weakness and unprofitableness thereof."[4] "For if that first covenant had been faultless, then should no place have been sought for the second."[5] "He taketh away the first, that he may establish the second."[6]

Some advocates of infant church-membership, admit the temporary nature of the Mosaic institution; but maintain that there ran through it, and was contained in it, a spiritual and unchangeable covenant, which had been made with Abraham, and which is now in force. To this covenant, our attention will next be directed.

Argument 5.—The Lord promised Abraham, that in him all nations of the earth should be blessed; and entered into a covenant with him, constituting him the father of many nations, and engaging to be the God of him and his seed. Believers in all nations where the gospel is preached, are accounted the children of Abraham;

---

[1] Eph. ii. 14, 15.   [2] Deut. xxiii. 1—3.   [3] Acts x. 35.
[4] Heb. vii. 18.   [5] Heb. viii. 7.   [6] Heb. x. 9.

and admitted into this covenant, and become members of God's church. In this covenant, children have always been included with their parents; and their right to its privileges was recognised by Peter, on the day of Pentecost, in these words: "The promise is to you and your children." That believing gentiles were received into the same covenant which belonged to national Israel, is taught by these words of Christ: "The kingdom of God shall be taken from you, and given to a nation bringing forth the fruits thereof."[1] And still more clearly by Paul, under the figure of the good olive-tree, of which the people of Israel were the natural branches; but into which believing gentiles were grafted, so as to partake of the root and fatness of the olive-tree. In this way, the blessing of Abraham comes on the gentiles; and the covenant which secures the blessing, embraces their children with them.

In order to estimate the force of this argument, it will be necessary to review some events in the life of Abraham.

The first event that claims our attention, is thus recorded:—

"Now the Lord had said unto Abram, Get thee out of thy country, and from thy kindred, and from thy father's house, unto a land that I will show thee: and I will make of thee a great nation, and I will bless thee, and make thy name great; and thou shalt be a blessing; and I will bless them that bless thee, and curse him that curseth thee; and in thee shall all the families of the earth be blessed."[2] In this narrative, all is to be taken literally. The command was meant, and understood, and obeyed, according to the literal import of the words. The promise has thus far been fulfilled in its literal sense, and is still in progress of literal accomplishment. Abraham was personally blessed with eminent piety, and extraordinary tokens of the Divine favor. Though an humble man, dwelling in a tent, and not distinguished as a conqueror, statesman, or philosopher, he is one of the most renowned of all whose names have been transmitted to our times. The nation of Israel, descended from him, was great in number, and strength, and great in its influence on the world. To this nation, under God, mankind are indebted for the Bible, the gospel; and, above all, the Saviour of the world, who was, according to the flesh, of the seed of Abraham. This nation has given to the world the knowledge of the true God; which knowledge is ultimately to overspread the earth, and bless all nations. In this manner the

---

[1] Matt. xxi. 43. [2] Gen. xii. 3.

promise made to Abraham, that in him all the families of the earth should be blessed, will be fulfilled. This promise was repeated to the patriarch, after the birth of his son Isaac, in these words: "And in thy seed shall all the nations of the earth be blessed."[1] The source of blessing to mankind was originally in the person of Abraham, but was now transferred to the person of the son that had been born of him: and hence the language of the promise was changed, "In *thy seed*," &c. The same promise was afterwards repeated to Isaac,[2] and to Jacob.[3] This promise is frequently referred to in the Scriptures, and is called the covenant which God made with the fathers[4]—the word covenant being used according to its latitude of meaning, to denote a firm and stable promise; and it is once called, the gospel preached unto Abraham.[5] No doubt can exist, that this important and distinguished promise included spiritual blessings; but the language is not spiritual in the sense in which this epithet is sometimes used, to mark what is not literal. Every word of this "gospel to Abraham," is as literal as the gospel declaration of Paul: "Believe on the Lord Jesus Christ, and thou shalt be saved."

The second event which we shall notice, is stated thus:—

"And he brought him forth abroad, and said, Look now toward heaven, and tell the stars, if thou be able to number them; and he said unto him, So shall thy seed be. And he believed in the Lord; and he counted it to him for righteousness."[6]

Here, again, all is to be understood in the literal sense. The posterity promised to the patriarch, were literal descendants, persons born out of his bowels.[7] The great blessing of justification, bestowed on this eminent believer, is spiritual in its nature; but the language in which it is described, is as simple and literal as that which is used in the New Testament, to denote the same blessing: "By him, all that believe are justified from all things."

The third event which claims our consideration, gave existence to the covenant of circumcision. The record of this important transaction is found in the 17th chapter of Genesis:—

"And when Abram was ninety years old and nine, the Lord

---

[1] Gen. xxii. 18.   [2] Gen. xxvi. 4.   [3] Gen. xxviii. 14.
[4] Acts iii. 25.   [5] Gal. iii. 8.   [6] Gen. xv. 5, 6.
[7] V. 4.

appeared to Abram, and said unto him: I am the Almighty God; walk before me, and be thou perfect. And I will make my covenant between me and thee, and will multiply thee exceedingly. And Abram fell on his face, and God talked with him, saying, As for me, behold my covenant is with thee."

Thus far all is to be taken as literally as any other historical record.

"And thou shalt be a father of many nations."

This has been supposed by some, to be more than was true of Abraham, in the literal sense; but they err. From Jacob, the grandson of Abraham, was descended the nation of Israel—the great nation intended in the promise, "I will make of thee a great nation." From Esau, another grandson, sprang the Edomites, a great and powerful nation. From Ishmael, the son of Abraham by Hagar, twelve nations were descended.[1] These several nations were less great and powerful than the Israelites, or Edomites; but, nevertheless, each of them was called a nation, according to the use of the word in those times. Besides Isaac and Ishmael, Abraham had six sons by Keturah.[2] If these were as prolific as the other two, the whole number of nations descended from Abraham was fifty-six. No reason, therefore, exists for abandoning the literal sense of the clause. We have no right to insist on such a sense for the word "nation," as will correspond with its use in modern history. What it meant, when the covenant was made, is what it means in this clause; and in this sense, the promise has been literally fulfilled.

"Neither shall thy name any more be called Abram, but thy name shall be Abraham."

This change of name has been thought to imply that there is something mystical in the covenant. The change was doubtless significant; but the supposition that it had any signification which militates against the literal construction of the covenant, is wholly unfounded. The posterity of the patriarch, including the many inspired prophets whom God raised up among them, the first preachers of the gospel, and the writers of the New Testament, were accustomed to use this new name Abraham to signify their literal ancestor.

---

[1] Gen. xxv. 16.   [2] V. 1—3.

"For a father of many nations have I made thee. And I will make thee exceeding fruitful; and I will make nations of thee, and kings shall come out of thee."

The first of these clauses explains the change in the patriarch's name. It was not in some mystical sense that God made him exceedingly fruitful; and, therefore, the phrase, "I have made thee a father of nations," does not need a mystical interpretation. God "made Abraham fruitful," not by some mystical appointment, but by literally multiplying his seed; and in this literal sense he made him the father of many nations. The promise, "and kings shall come out of thee," was literally fulfilled; and this clause, a mystical interpretation of which no one has ventured to insist on, binds down the covenant to the literal construction.

"And I will establish my covenant between me and thee, and thy seed after thee in their generations, for an everlasting covenant."

All this is to be understood according to the meaning which common usage assigned to the words. A difficulty would attend the interpretation, if the term "everlasting" always denoted unlimited duration; but this was not its only signification. The grant of the land of Canaan afterwards made in the covenant, could not extend beyond the duration of the present world; and, if the covenant was to continue in force to the end of time, or even till that state of things should cease, for which the covenant was designed to provide, the epithet "everlasting" was properly applied to it. In various passages of Scripture the word is used in this sense.

"To be a God unto thee, and to thy seed after thee."

These words were not designed to be a promise of spiritual grace, or eternal life, to all the descendants of Abraham. A new covenant predicted by the prophet Jeremiah, contained the stipulation: "I will be their God; and they shall be my people."[1] This promise secured spiritual grace; but it would not have been a new covenant if the same grant had been made in the covenant with Abraham. As contained in this covenant, the promise engaged a special divine care over Abraham and his descendants; and particularly over the nation of Israel, the seed to whom the grant of

---

[1] Jer. xxxi. 33.

Canaan was made in this covenant. In this sense, the promise was literally fulfilled. He separated them from all other nations, and acknowledged them to be his people: "You only have I known of all the families of the earth."[1] His providence over them, and his revelations to them, were all peculiar. In all his dealings with them, he acted in the relation of a God. He rewarded as a God, and punished as a God. He made himself known to them as a God, while other nations were permitted to remain in ignorance of him; and as a God, while he granted to this nation means of grace and salvation unknown to the rest of the world, he used the nation as the channel for conveying spiritual blessings to all the nations of the earth.

"And I will give unto thee, and to thy seed after thee, the land wherein thou art a stranger, all the land of Canaan for an everlasting possession."

All this was meant literally, and was literally fulfilled. The import of the word "everlasting," has been explained in the remarks on the phrase "everlasting covenant." Whether the word everlasting, either in application to the covenant or to the possession of Canaan, was limited to the dispensation that preceded the time of Christ, or extended into the present dispensation, and still stretches forward into future time, will be a subject of future inquiry. But whatever may be true on this question, the use of the word militates nothing against the literal construction of the covenant.

"And I will be their God."

This promise, as has already been explained, was literally fulfilled.

"And God said unto Abraham, thou shalt keep my covenant therefore, thou and thy seed after thee in their generations. This is my covenant, which ye shall keep, between me and you, and thy seed after thee; every man child among you shall be circumcised. And ye shall circumcise the flesh of your foreskin; and it shall be a token of the covenant betwixt me and you. And he that is eight days old shall be circumcised among you; every man child in your generations, he that is born in the house or bought with money of any stranger, which is not of thy seed. He that is born

---

[1] Amos iii. 2.

in thy house, and he that is bought with thy money, must needs be circumcised; and my covenant shall be in your flesh for an everlasting covenant. And the uncircumcised man child whose flesh of his foreskin is not circumcised, that soul shall be cut off from his people; he hath broken my covenant."

The precept enjoining circumcision was intended to be understood literally, and it was understood and obeyed literally. An important, very important part of God's design in making this covenant, was to distinguish and separate the descendants of Abraham from the rest of mankind; and this design would have been frustrated if this part of the covenant had not been taken literally. The whole history of the Hebrew nation, and almost every page of the New Testament, testify in favor of the literal construction.

"And God said unto Abraham, as for Sarai, thy wife, thou shalt not call her name Sarai, but Sarah shall her name be. And I will bless her, and give thee a son also of her: yea, I will bless her, and she shall be a mother of nations; kings of people shall be of her."

The new name Sarah, like the new name Abraham, was significant; but neither of them signified anything contrary to the literal construction of the covenant. Abraham was the father of many nations, because he had sons by other wives; but his only son by Sarah was Isaac, the father of Jacob and Esau; and the only nations descended from Sarah, were the Israelites and the Edomites. It was promised that Sarah should be a mother of "nations," not of "many nations;" and this adaptation of the language to what became literally true, proves that the covenant was made in the literal sense of the words. In the literal sense kings came out of Sarah; the kings of Edom, and the long line of kings in Israel and Judah.

Our examination of the covenant has proved conclusively, that it was designed to be understood literally; but a question arises whether it does not admit another and more spiritual sense.

The precepts which enjoined the ceremonies of worship to be observed by the Hebrew congregation, were all designed to be understood and obeyed literally. Literal bulls and goats were to be sacrificed; literal fire was to be used, and all the directions given were to be observed in their literal import. But the various ceremonies of this worship were shadows of things to come; and a large part of the epistle to the Hebrews is employed in explaining their spiritual signification. Persons and events of the Old Testament which appear in their proper connection as subjects of literal history, are in the New Testament made to represent spiritual things, and spiritual instruction is drawn from them. The history of Hagar, as given in the book of Genesis, is literally true; but Paul calls it an allegory, and uses it to represent spiritual things. In the same manner the covenant of circumcision is made a source of spiritual instruction. The chief particulars in the covenant which are made representatives of spiritual things, are three:

1. The literal descendants of Abraham are made to represent believers, who are called his children in a different sense of the word. The metaphorical use of the terms which denote the paternal and filial relations, is frequent in the Scriptures. One who appears at the head of a class of persons as a father appears at the head of his family or tribe, is called the father of that class; and the individuals composing the class, are called his children. Thus, "Jabal was the father of such as dwell in tents, and of such as have cattle: and Jubal was the father of all such as handle the harp and organ."[1] These persons called fathers, were inventors of arts; and the class of persons who practise these arts are regarded as their children. So those who practise the piety of which Abraham was an illustrious example, and walk in the footsteps of his faith, are called his children. In this tropical sense of the term, Jesus said to the wicked Jews, "If ye were Abraham's children, ye would do the works of Abraham."[2] Since the men whom Jesus addressed were children of Abraham in the literal sense, the distinction between the literal and the metaphorical sense is plainly marked; and the latter sense is made to depend on imitation of Abraham in the works for which he was eminent. Paul has distinguished between the literal Jew and the metaphorical Jew;[3] between the children according to the flesh, and the children of promise.[4] The latter, he says, "are counted for the seed;" that is, they are accounted the seed of Abraham when the covenant is viewed as an allegory.

---

[1] Gen. iv. 20, 21.   [2] John viii. 39.   [3] Rom. ii. 29.
[4] Rom. ix. 8.

2. Circumcision is made to represent regeneration, the spiritual change by which men become new creatures. Hence it is said, "In Christ Jesus neither circumcision availeth any thing, nor uncircumcision; but a new creature."[1] A tropical use of the word circumcise to denote a moral change, is found in the Old Testament: "The Lord thy God will circumcise thine heart, and the heart of thy seed, to love the Lord thy God with all thine heart, and with all thy soul, that thou mayest live."[2] Paul distinguishes between the literal and the spiritual circumcision; thus, "Neither is that circumcision which is outward in the flesh. . . . . Circumcision is that of the heart, in the spirit, and not in the letter."[3] This circumcision of the heart is in another passage called the "circumcision of Christ."[4] While the literal circumcision which marked the literal seed of Abraham avails nothing in Christ Jesus, the spiritual circumcision marks those who belong to Christ, and who are, in the spiritual sense, the seed of Abraham. "If ye be Christ's, then are ye Abraham's seed, and heirs according to the promise."[5]

3. Canaan, the land promised to Abraham and his literal seed, is made to represent heaven, the future inheritance of those who have like faith with the patriarch. Abraham at the command of God left his native country, and sojourned in the land of Canaan; but though the land was his by promise, he never obtained possession of it. Paul makes a spiritual use of this fact: "Confessed that they were strangers and pilgrims on the earth. But now they desire a better country, that is, an heavenly."[6] The literal Canaan was present to the sight of the patriarch, as a desirable possession secured by covenant to him and his seed; but the eye of his faith was directed to a better country, of which this was but a type. His spiritual seed are like him in faith, and their faith directs its eye to the same heavenly inheritance.

The allegorical interpretation of the covenant is beautifully harmonious in all its parts. Abraham, the most illustrious example of faith found in the Old Testament, appears at the head of a class of persons who are like him in faith; and he is hence called the father of the faithful. As he was marked by the circumcision

---

[1] Gal. vi. 15. [2] Deut. xxx. 6. [3] Rom. ii. 28, 29.
[4] Col. ii. 11. [5] Gal. iii. 29. [6] Heb. xi. 13, 16.

of the heart, and distinguished thereby from the rest of mankind, so are they. As he looked beyond the earthly possession granted to him, and sought a heavenly inheritance, so do they.

The spiritual truths which the covenant represents in its allegorical use, were not brought into existence by the covenant, and are not dependent on it. They are above it, as the things which the Mosaic ceremonies typified are superior to the ceremonies; or as a substance is superior to its shadow, and independent of it. In the third chapter of Galatians, Paul teaches that believers are the children of Abraham, and are blessed with him; and he dates back their connection with him to a time that preceded the covenant of circumcision. He says, that "the law was four hundred and thirty years after." Now, reckoning back four hundred and thirty years from the giving of the law, we arrive at the time when Abraham received the first promise. This preceded the covenant of circumcision by twenty-four years. This promise, first made with reference to Abraham himself, and afterwards renewed with reference to his seed, is the covenant to which this passage evidently refers. Hence, believers hold their connection with Abraham receiving the great gospel promise, and not with Abraham receiving the covenant of circumcision; with Abraham as first distinguished by the circumcision of the heart, and not with Abraham as afterwards distinguished by the circumcision of the flesh. Precisely the same view is presented in the fourth chapter of Romans, in which it is taught that believers are connected, not with the circumcised, but with the uncircumcised Abraham, in obtaining the blessing of justification.

The judaizing Christians taught, "Except ye be circumcised and keep the law, ye cannot be saved." This was the current doctrine of the Jews. They gloried in the covenant of circumcision, and their connection with the circumcised Abraham; and for the purpose of securing a title to the earthly Canaan, literal descent from Abraham, and the circumcision that is outward in the flesh, were sufficient. But Paul opposed the doctrine of the judaizing teachers, and opened a different view of the Holy Spirit's teachings in the Old Testament. He taught that to secure the spiritual blessings which Abraham enjoyed, we must seek them in the way in which Abraham obtained them. He did not obtain the favor of God by circumcision and keeping the law; but enjoyed this blessing four hundred and thirty years before the law, and while he was yet uncircumcised. He received the blessing by faith; and every one who would be blessed with him, must seek it in this way. These arguments of Paul, in which he deduced the true doctrine of the gospel from the Scriptures of the Old Testament, were powerful in opposition to the judaizing theory.

The covenant of circumcision in its literal sense, included in the covenant seed none but the literal descendants of Abraham. The patriarch and his sons were commanded to circumcise all the males of the household, including the servants born in the house, and those bought with money; but these servants did not thereby become incorporated with the covenant seed. None of the servants in the families of Abraham, Isaac, and Jacob, had this privilege conferred on them; and it cannot be supposed that the servants of their descendants were more highly favored than the servants of the patriarchs themselves. On the contrary, those servants, though circumcised, are expressly said in the covenant itself, to be "not of thy seed." When the Congregation of the Lord was instituted, provision was made for gentiles to be admitted to the privileges of its worship on conforming to the law of circumcision; but they were nevertheless strangers within the gate, and not a part of the covenant seed, or entitled to a part in the land of Canaan. Genealogical records were kept distinguishing the seed proper from the proselytes of the gate; and hence Paul was able to call himself "a Hebrew of the Hebrews;" that is, a Hebrew by original extraction.

As the covenant of circumcision in its literal sense, admitted none into the covenant seed but literal descendants of Abraham; so in the allegorical sense, none are included in the spiritual seed but true believers. This is clear from many passages of Scripture:— "So then they which be of faith are blessed with faithful Abraham.[1] .... If ye be Christ's, then are ye Abraham's seed, and heirs according to the promise."[2] The following passage is perfectly decisive on this subject, and shows conclusively that genuine faith is intended, and not the mere profession of it: "Therefore it is of faith, that it might be by grace; to the end the promise might be sure to all the seed."[3]

---

[1] Gal. iii. 9. [2] V. 29. [3] Rom. iv. 16.

One among the promises made to Abraham was, "I will make of thee a great nation." In the covenant of circumcision, it was promised that he should be the father of many nations; and the nation of Israel was contemplated as one of these. The covenant in its literal sense, instituted no ecclesia or worshipping congregation. A cahal for the worship of God, was instituted by Moses; and laws and ceremonies for that worship were instituted with it. The covenant then made with Israel had ordinances of divine service and a worldly sanctuary; but he who looks for these in the covenant of circumcision will look in vain. It contains no sanctuary, no ordinances of divine worship, no priesthood, no assembly. We have shown that the cahal instituted by Moses has been dissolved; and, if the covenant of circumcision still survives, it exists as it did before the days of Moses—a national covenant, made with the literal descendants of Abraham, admitting no others to be incorporated with the covenant seed, and making no provision for the public worship of God. Surely, the Christian church is not founded on this covenant.

Since the covenant of circumcision instituted no ecclesia, and cannot admit gentile infants among the covenant seed, the doctrine of infant church-membership cannot be affected by the question, whether the covenant has been abrogated, or is now in force: and, for any purpose of our present inquiry, we are under no obligation to decide this question. Since this covenant existed before that which was made by Moses, the abrogation of the latter may have left the former just as it had previously been. In it, the land of Canaan was given for an everlasting possession; and the covenant is styled "an everlasting covenant." We may hence infer, that the covenant will continue in force as long as the Israelites shall possess the land of Canaan. If the general expectation be well founded, that they will return to their land and repossess it, the covenant must be still in force. The facts that, since the abrogation of the Mosaic covenant, they have been called the people of God;[1] that they have the promise of being restored again to his favor;[2] and are declared not to be cast off, because the gifts and calling of God are without repentance;[3] confirm this view. To all this we may add the remarkable fact, that, when the apostles

---

[1] Rom. xi. 1 2.   [2] V. 23—30.   [3] V. 29.

declared converts from among the gentiles to be under no obligation to be circumcised, they did not release Jews from this obligation. For a gentile to be circumcised, is an admission that the Congregation of the Lord is still in being, and the Mosaic law still in force; and for any one, whether Jew or gentile, to be circumcised as a means of salvation, is to set aside Christ and render him unprofitable. But can any one prove that it is inconsistent with the gospel for a Jew to retain circumcision, as a token of his connection with Abraham, and his interest in that remarkable people, through whom he still expects God to display the riches of his grace in the most wonderful manner?

Is the covenant of circumcision in force, in its allegorical sense? This question is about as unmeaning as if it were asked, whether a portrait exists in the person of him whom it resembles. The portrait and the man exist independently of each other. The man may die, and leave the portrait; or the portrait may be destroyed, while the man lives. If the covenant of circumcision is in force at all, it is in force in that only sense in which it is a covenant—namely, the literal. No one would say that the ceremonial law is now in force, because the spiritual truths which the ceremonies prefigured abide for ever. Whether the covenant is abrogated, or is now in force, the spiritual instruction derived from it is the everlasting gospel.

While the covenant, literally construed, gives no sanction to infant church-membership, the spiritual use which is made of it in the Scriptures incidentally decides that all the members of the primitive churches were believers. Paul says to the Galatians: "Now *we*, brethren, as Isaac was, are the children of promise." ..... "*Ye* are all the children of God by faith in Jesus Christ. If *ye* be Christ's, then are ye Abraham's seed." These texts prove that the members of the Galatian churches were all accounted the children of Abraham, in the spiritual sense—that is, were true believers—and what was true of those churches, must have been true of all other churches instituted by the apostles.

A portrait is not more distinct from the man whom it resembles, nor a shadow more distinct from the substance which casts it, than is the covenant of circumcision from the spiritual truth which it represents, in the allegorical interpretation of it. We ought never to confound things so distinct; but this is done by the doctrine of infant church-membership. It follows the literal sense, from Abraham down to the introduction of the gospel, and accounts the literal seed, during this period, to be the church: it then follows the spiritual sense, and introduces gentile believers among the covenant seed: it then returns to the law of literal descent, and follows this for one generation, and then abandons it. By this unaccountable mixture of interpretations, the immediate literal descendants of those who are, or ought to be, according to their profession, the spiritual seed of Abraham, are supposed to be brought within the covenant, and incorporated with the covenant seed: but, alas! they are a seed which inherit neither the literal nor the spiritual promises made to the patriarch. They do not inherit the literal promises, because they are gentiles; nor the spiritual promises, because these are secured only to believers.

It remains that we examine the other texts of Scripture, which the argument that we are considering, cites in its support.

"For the promise is unto you, and to your children, and to all that are afar off, even as many as the Lord our God shall call."[1]

The word which is here rendered "children," denotes posterity, immediate or remote, without respect to age. The same word is used in the sentence, "Children shall rise up against their parents, and shall cause them to be put to death;"[2] and in the phrase, "children of the flesh,"[3] when used to denote all the natural posterity of Abraham. The promise here referred to appears, from the words which immediately precede, to be the promise of the Holy Spirit; but, whether it be this, or the promise made to Abraham as the argument supposes, it must be understood to include spiritual blessings. Three classes of persons are mentioned, to whom the promise is given; the Israelites of that generation, their posterity, and the gentiles: "you, your children, and all that are afar off." To neither of these classes is the promise given without condition or limitation. When it is said, "Repent, for the promise is to you," the receiving of the promise is evidently suspended on the condition of repentance. The same condition applies equally to the other two classes. This is fully established by the limiting clause, "even as many as the Lord our God shall call." The promise is not absolute to all who are externally called by the

---

[1] Acts ii. 39.   [2] Matt. x. 21.   [3] Rom. ix. 8.

gospel, but to those only who are effectually called to repentance. This limitation applies equally to all the three classes. Though the word "children" may sometimes be used with exclusive application to infants, there is no reason to suppose that such use of it is made here, but the whole posterity are intended; and it cannot be that spiritual blessings were promised to all those, without condition or limitation. The mention of the posterity, in this case, was peculiarly appropriate. Peter had charged them with the crime of crucifying the Lord Jesus. When this crime was committed, in calling on Pilate to crucify him, they had said: "His blood be on us, and on our children." This fact rendered the information suitable and welcome, that the same means of salvation that were granted to them, would be granted to their posterity.

"The kingdom of God shall be taken from you, and given to a nation bringing forth the fruits thereof."[1]

The name of a type is sometimes applied to the thing typified. Regeneration is called circumcision; but, to show that literal circumcision is not intended, it is called the circumcision of the heart, or the circumcision of Christ. Heaven is called a country, in allusion to the country promised to Abraham, which typified it; but, for the sake of distinction, the epithets "better" and "heavenly" are applied: "a better country, that is, a heavenly." The nation of Israel, marked by the literal circumcision, and heirs of the earthly Canaan, typified those who are circumcised in heart, and are heirs of the heavenly country. These last are on this account called a nation; but, to distinguish them from the nation which typified them, they are called "a nation bringing forth the fruits" of the kingdom; that is, the fruits of holy obedience to God as their king. Peter calls them "a chosen generation, a royal priesthood, a holy nation, a peculiar people." They are not a nation, in the literal sense of the term, as the nation of Israel was. Earthly nations included infants, but this spiritual nation consists of those who bring forth the fruits of the kingdom; and who, according to Peter, "show forth the praises of him who hath called them out of darkness into his marvellous light." These things cannot be predicated of infants. It follows, therefore, that, in this transfer of the kingdom, infants are not its recipients.

---

[1] Matt. xxi. 43.

The precise sense in which the kingdom is said to be taken from the nation of Israel, it is not necessary, for our present purpose, to determine. The government of that nation has been called a theocracy. God was their king; and various benefits resulted to them from being under his reign. To these benefits the text may refer; and the sense may be, that the peculiar privilege of having God to reign over them, should no longer distinguish them from other nations of the earth; but this privilege would henceforth be confined to a spiritual people, to be selected out of all nations. But, as the phrase, "kingdom of God," was commonly used by Christ to denote the new kingdom which he was establishing, the reference may be exclusively to this. He was born "King of the Jews," and was crucified with this title. He was sent, as he himself declared, not to the gentiles, but to the lost sheep of the house of Israel. The first proclamation of his reign was made to this people; and the beginning and first benefits of his reign were confined to them. Their rejection of his reign was made the occasion of its extension to the gentiles: "It was necessary that the word of God should first have been spoken to you: but seeing ye put it from you, and judge yourselves unworthy of everlasting life, lo, we turn to the gentiles."[1] The blessings of the Messiah's reign were expected by the nation to be theirs, and the first offer and bestowment of them accorded with this expectation: but the peculiar privilege was taken from them when they rejected their king; and it is now enjoyed by those who obey him in every nation. These, and these only, bring forth the fruits of the kingdom; and, however the transfer to them may be understood, it cannot prove the church-membership of infants.

The last Scripture cited in the argument has been much relied on, as proof that the Christian church is a continuation of an organized society which existed in the Old Testament dispensation. Under the figure of the good olive-tree, Paul is supposed to teach that the church sprang from Abraham, and that it has continued to the present time.

In the passage which contains this figurative representation, the following things may be observed:—

1. The olive-tree underwent an important change when many of

---

[1] Acts xiii. 46.

the natural branches were broken off. The reason for their separation is expressly given: "Because of unbelief, they were broken off." Since the unbelieving branches were taken away by this act, none were left but believing branches. These are the remnant before spoken of; "the remnant according to the election of grace:" the seed intended when it is said, "Except the Lord of Sabaoth had left us a seed, we had been as Sodoma, and been made like unto Gomorrha."[1]

2. A second change took place when branches were engrafted from the wild olive-tree. The character of these branches is made known by the words with which Paul addresses them: "Thou standest by faith." We are hence assured that these also were believing branches. This accords with what is elsewhere taught: "That the blessing of Abraham might come on the gentiles through faith."

3. Another important change is still expected when the natural branches which were broken off shall be "graffed in again." The condition on which it will be done is expressly stated: "They also shall be graffed in again, if they abide not in unbelief." They are recognised as natural branches, and the olive-tree is called "their own;" but neither of these facts will suffice to effect their restoration. If they come in again, they must come as believing branches.

These three comprehend all the changes which the olive-tree is said to undergo; and as a consequence of these, none but believing branches have a present, or can have a future connection with the tree. The design for which this figurative illustration was introduced, and the explanations which accompany it, clearly show that the natural branches were designed to represent the natural seed of Abraham; and the changes which the tree undergoes, are precisely such as substituted the spiritual seed for the natural, the children by faith for the children according to the flesh. The whole scope of the apostle's teaching in connection with the passage, if attentively considered, leaves no reasonable doubt that this was the design of the figure.

Types, parables, and allegories, are founded on similitude; but when spiritual things are likened to natural, the likeness is neces-

---

[1] Rom. ix. 29.

sarily imperfect. He who seeks to extend the likeness beyond its proper limit, is in danger of mistake. In the present case it would be unprofitable, and perhaps worse than unprofitable, to inquire what may be signified by the trunk of the tree, its leaves, and the various other parts of which botanists could tell us. In the sketch which the apostle's pencil has drawn, imperfect indeed, but sufficient for all his purpose, we see nothing of the tree but its branches, its root, and its fatness, unless its fruit may be referred to in v. 16. The chief question before the apostle's mind, related to the branches; and what these signify he has sufficiently informed us. What the root and fatness of the olive-tree signify, we are left to learn from the connection of the passage; and from this we may infer that Abraham, and the promises made to him, are intended.

Some have supposed that Christ is the root of the olive-tree; and that the figure corresponds with that of the vine in the 15th chapter of John. The strongest argument in favor of this opinion, is furnished by the words, " Thou bearest not the root, but the root thee." Since Christ is the only name by which we must be saved, the believing soul is borne or supported by him, and not by Abraham. But such support as this, is not intended by the word "bearest" in this passage. The word is used with evident allusion to the figure, and signifies only what the figure signifies by the dependance of the branches on the root. The natural descendants of Abraham, who are the natural branches of the olive-tree, do not depend on their illustrious progenitor as the believing soul depends on Christ; and, therefore, such dependence is not implied in this passage. Paul, though he was the minister of the uncircumcision, was careful to teach the gentiles their indebtedness to the Jews. He urged the obligation of contributing to relieve the poor saints at Jerusalem by this consideration: "Their debtors they are. For if the gentiles have been made partakers of their spiritual things, their duty is also to minister unto them in carnal."[1] So in the present case, he urges on the gentiles, " Boast not against the natural branches; for if thou boast, thou bearest not the root, but the root thee." The religion which blesses the gentiles was obtained from the Jews. Jesus Christ was a Jew. The Old Testa-

---

[1] Rom. xv. 27.

ment was a Jewish book; and the New Testament is the gospel written by Jews. In the comprehensive words of Christ, "Salvation is of the Jews." The promise to Abraham, "In thee shall all the families of the earth be blessed," contemplated the Hebrew nation to whom the oracles of God were committed, and from whom, according to the flesh, Christ came, as yet in the loins of the patriarch. In this view, Abraham is presented in the figure as the root of the olive-tree; and the spiritual blessings are its fatness of which gentile believers partake.

An objection presents itself, that in the substitution of the spiritual for the natural seed, such a change is supposed as destroys the identity of the olive-tree, and the more so, because the fatness of which the two kinds of branches partake, cannot be the same. To this objection it is a sufficient reply, that figures cannot be expected to hold good in everything. But another reply may be given. The nourishment which proceeds from the root of a tree to its various parts, is assimilated to each according to its nature, and becomes woody fibre, bark, leaf, or fruit. Even the fruit may vary, though deriving nourishment from the same root; for that which is produced by a grafted branch will differ from that produced by a natural branch. All this is found in a natural tree; and yet the change of its branches by grafting, and the variety of nourishment which the root yields, do not affect the identity of the tree in a general view of it. It can, therefore, be no objection to Paul's figure, that it represents natural and spiritual branches as connected with the same root and deriving benefits of different kinds from it. This mode of meeting the objection is proposed merely to show that it has not a solid foundation to sustain it; but we cannot suppose that Paul, in sketching out this figure, had reference to abstruse principles of vegetable physiology. He informs us that the distinction represented by the two classes of branches existed in the days of Elijah, when God informed the prophet that he had reserved to himself seven thousand men who had not bowed the knee to the image of Baal. "Even so," he adds, "there is at this time a remnant according to the election of grace." Besides the natural branches who were bowing to Baal, there then existed a remnant who were faithful and enjoyed spiritual blessings. All these together, the advocates of infant church-membership tell us, composed the visible church of that day, and were branches of the same olive-tree; and the same constitution of things, uniting natural and spiritual branches on the same trunk, they suppose continues to the present time. According to the view which we have taken, the great Husbandman has broken off the natural branches, and but one species of branches now remains. It follows, therefore, that the objection, whatever may be its force, is applicable rather to the opinion which we oppose, than to that which we defend.

The question whether the passage teaches the church-membership of infants, may be approached aside from the objection which we have been considering, and from all perplexing inquiry as to what the root and fatness of the olive-tree signify. It relates wholly to the branches of the tree; and with respect to these, we have the unerring Spirit to guide our interpretation. His express teaching determines, that the branches now connected with the olive-tree, are all believing. Here a landmark is fixed, which must not be removed. If we leave the plain teaching of the Spirit, and follow the guidance of our own fancy, until we become involved in error, it must be our own fault.

Infant membership is argued from the identity of the olive-tree; but, unfortunately for the argument, the changes which the apostle has described, infringe on the identity of the tree, exactly in the wrong place. All these changes respect the branches, and are made on one principle—the substitution of faith for natural descent; as the bond of connection between the branches and the root. Infant membership depends on natural descent; and the one principle on which all the changes are made, by taking away natural descent, leaves infant membership to hang on nothing.

Section II.—ARGUMENTS FOR INFANT BAPTISM.

The arguments which were considered in the last section, aim directly to establish the right of infants to church-membership. Other arguments, tending indirectly to establish the same point, have immediate respect to the docrine of infant baptism.

The Holy Scriptures contain no precept or example for infant baptism; and the qualifications which they uniformly describe, as necessary to baptism, infants do not possess. With these facts before us, we are compelled to reject infants from the ordinance, unless a special claim in their behalf can be well established. We shall now proceed to consider the chief arguments which have been used, in support of their claim.

Argument 1.—Repentance and faith are as much required by the Scriptures, in order to salvation, as in order to baptism; but as infants may be saved without them, so they may be baptized without them. From the nature of the case, these qualifications are required of adults only. The commission does indeed place *believing* before *baptizing*, but it equally places it before *being saved;* and it even declares, in express terms, "He that believeth not shall be damned." If, therefore, we may infer from it, that infants ought not to be baptized, we may, with as much certainty, infer that they cannot be saved.

This argument has no force, to establish infant baptism. Because infants may be saved without repentance and faith, it does not follow that they are entitled to every privilege which may be claimed for them. The utmost extent to which the argument can go, is to weaken the force of the opposing argument; and this it does in appearance only. How are we to reconcile the declaration, "He that believeth not shall be damned," with the doctrine of infant salvation? The answer is obvious. When Christ commissioned his disciples to preach the gospel to every creature, he meant every creature capable of hearing and understanding it. "He that believeth not," means—he that, having heard the gospel, rejects it. In this obvious meaning of the phrase, it affirms nothing contrary to infant salvation. Adopting the same mode of exposition, in the preceding clause, it signifies—he that hears the gospel, believes it, and is baptized, shall be saved. The commission does not say, whether infants will be saved, or whether they ought to be baptized; for the simple reason, that it has no reference to them. The argument before us, drives us to this exposition of the commission; but what does infant baptism gain by it? We learn from it, that, in the great commission which Christ gave to his apostles, by which baptism was established as a permanent institution to be observed among all nations to the end of time, he had no reference to infants.

Argument 2.—Though the Scriptures contain no positive precept for infant baptism, the same is true with respect to female communion, and the Christian Sabbath. The Lord's Supper is a positive institute; and yet we admit females to partake of it, without a positive precept. The change from the seventh day of the week to the first, in the observance of the Sabbath, has no express command for it in the Scriptures, and is, in part, a repeal of the fourth commandment; yet we admit it on satisfactory inference, supported by the practice of the early churches. In like manner the observance of infant baptism may be vindicated, though not prescribed by positive precept.

We do not exclude all reasoning with respect to positive institutes. No one on earth can point to a positive precept in the Scriptures, requiring him in particular to be baptized. Paul was directly commanded to be baptized; and so were those whom Peter addressed, on the day of Pentecost, and in the house of Cornelius. From these facts, we think it lawful to infer, that persons of like character, and in like circumstances, ought now to be baptized. The commission did not directly command any one to be baptized: but it commanded the apostles to baptize; and from the obligation to baptize laid on one party, we infer the obligation of another party to be baptized; and we infer the perpetuity of the obligation, from the fact that the commission was manifestly designed to be perpetual. Such inferences we hold to be legitimate and necessary; but we maintain, that positive institutes originating in the will of the lawgiver, cannot be determined by mere reasoning from general principles. The obligation to baptize believers, can be referred to express divine command; and if an obligation to baptize infants exists, it cannot be made out by any process of reasoning from the parental and filial relations or general principles of morals; but must be referred, in like manner, to some divine command. We ask for this command. Whatever reasoning may be necessary, to unfold the command, and show that infant baptism is contained in it, we consent to undertake; but we must know that it is the will of Christ, before we can observe it as an institution of his religion.

The necessity for divine command is rendered the more urgent, because infant baptism interferes with the divine institution of believers' baptism, and would, if universally practised, banish it from the earth. God commands a believer to be baptized;—is he released from the obligation by the fact that his parents had him baptized in infancy? Is he now chargeable with the sin of anabaptism, if he obeys the divine command? For proof of all this, some divine authority for infant baptism is needed, as clear and certain as that by which believers' baptism is established.

For female communion, we have divine authority in the command of Christ, "this do," "drink ye all of it." The Scriptures interpret this command. Women were among the disciples mentioned in the first chapter of Acts, verse 8,—and all these, with the three thousand who were added, continued in the breaking of bread.[1] In the same number were included the widows, who were neglected in the daily ministration. Women were in the church at Corinth, when the whole church assembled to celebrate the Lord's supper.[2] In the command, "Let a man examine himself, and so let him eat,"[3] the word rendered man, signifies a human being, of either sex. It is evident, from these facts, that female communion is practised on divine authority; and it, moreover, sets aside no other divine command. If such authority for infant baptism can be produced, we ought to practise it: but even then we might question the propriety of its superseding believers' baptism.

But it is alleged, that the Christian sabbath does supersede the observance of the seventh day prescribed in the decalogue; and therefore, presents a case analogous to the one before us. Is it then true, that our inferences can in any case set aside the express commands of God? We think not. The decalogue requires the observance of the seventh day, regularly returning after six days of labor; and not the seventh day of the week. As thus interpreted, the Christian practice literally conforms to it. If the seventh day in the commandment means the seventh day of the week, it is our duty to obey strictly; and if we can learn, by legitimate inference, that the first day of the week ought to be observed, our course of duty is plain—we ought to observe both days: so, if infant baptism can be made out by legitimate inference, instead of permitting it to supersede believers' baptism, we ought to observe both. We open our minds, therefore, to the inferential reasoning by which infant baptism is to be sustained.

Argument 3.—Christ's commission is, "Teach or make disciples of all nations, baptizing them." Children form a part of all nations; and the commission, therefore, contains authority for baptizing them.

The word "nations" in the original, is of the neuter gender, and the word "them" is masculine. It has been concluded, hence,

---

[1] Acts ii. 42.   [2] 1 Cor. xi. 5—20.   [3] V. 28.

that the pronoun stands properly, for the masculine noun " disciples" understood. But, without the aid of this criticism, the connection of the clauses shows that this is the true meaning. The sense is the same as in the passage, "Jesus made and baptized disciples." If the commission authorizes to baptize every one in the nation, adult unbelievers must be included, contrary to what all admit.

Argument 4.—The commission requires to baptize disciples. A disciple is one engaged to receive instruction from a teacher. In secular matters, parents select teachers for their children, and make engagements for their instruction. In religion, they are under the highest obligation to place them in the school of Christ, that they may be brought up in the nurture and admonition of the Lord. The commission requires, that these young disciples should receive the mark of discipleship. The propriety of considering them disciples, may be proved by the passage, "Why tempt ye God, to put a yoke on the neck of the disciples, which neither our fathers nor we were able to bear?"[1] The yoke of circumcision is here referred to. And every one knows that this fell chiefly on infants. The import of the word used in the commission, and its applicability to infants may be proved by a passage in Justin Martyr, who wrote near the middle of the second century. Among those who were members of the church, he says, "there were many of both sexes, some sixty, and some seventy years old, who were made disciples to Christ from their infancy." The word he uses is $ἐμαθητεύθησαν$, the same word that is used in the commission. It is evident, therefore, that Justin understood the command of Christ to make disciples and baptize, as applicable to little children. And he wrote only about one hundred years after Matthew, who records that command. This testimony is important, as showing the early prevalence of infant baptism, since these persons must have received the mark of discipleship within a few years after Matthew wrote. But it is cited here, to show the sense of the Greek word which Christ employed in the commission.

In secular concerns, it is possible, though not usual, for parents to engage their children, from early infancy, to some teacher, by whom they may be afterwards instructed; but the *usus loquendi* will scarcely allow us to call them his disciples, until they begin to learn from him.

In the Scriptures, we read of John's disciples, the disciples of the Pharisees, the disciples of Jesus; and such is the current use of the term, that, in these several applications of it, the idea of

---

[1] Acts xv. 10.

infancy is never suggested. We read, "The number of the disciples was multiplied in Jerusalem." * * * "And the apostles called the multitude of the disciples to them, and said, 'Wherefore, brethren, look ye out.' * * 'And the saying pleased the whole multitude: and they chose," &c.[1] If the infants of all the believers in Jerusalem were disciples, they must have been included in the multitude here mentioned; but the things stated in the narrative forbid the supposition. Another passage in the same chapter shows that to be a disciple, and to have faith, are descriptive of the same person: "The number of the disciples multipled in Jerusalem greatly; and a great company of the priests were obedient to the faith."[2] The same is proved by another passage in a subsequent chapter: "Finding certain disciples, he said unto them, Have ye received the Holy Ghost since ye believed?"[3] But we have still clearer proof on this subject;—Christ himself expressly declared the qualifications necessary to constitute a disciple: "If any man come to me, and hate not his father, and mother, and wife, and children, and brethren, and sisters, yea, and his own life also, he cannot be my disciple. And whosoever doth not bear his cross, and come after me, cannot be my disciple."[4] Against such declarations of the divine Master, the inference from a merely possible use of the term in secular concerns, can be of no avail.

But the argument alleges that we have Scripture example for the application of the term to infants. In the case referred to, Judaizing teachers had taught, "Except ye be circumcised, and keep the law, ye cannot be saved." The yoke which they imposed on the gentile converts was not circumcision merely, but the whole burden of the legal ceremonies. Circumcision was not, in itself, the intolerable yoke referred to, "which neither our fathers nor we were able to bear." These were circumcised in infancy, and did not afterwards account circumcision a grievous burden. But the burdensome law received from Moses is manifestly the thing intended; and the burden did not fall on infants. The passage therefore contains no proof that infants were intended by the word disciples.

The words of Justin Martyr, απο παιδων, are incorrectly translated *from infancy.* The name *Pedobaptist,* which is given to those

---

[1] Acts vi. 1—5. [2] V. 7. [3] Acts xix. 1, 2.
[4] Luke xiv. 26, 27.

who practise infant baptism, and which is derived in part from the Greek word παις, seems to countenance this rendering: but, in truth, παις does not signify *an infant*. It is used, in either the masculine or feminine gender, for one who has not reached maturity; and is applied to the young man who fell from the loft while Paul was preaching;[1] and is used by Justin, in another place, for the boys or young men who were the objects of unnatural lust.[2] A diminutive, παιδιον, formed from this word, is frequently used for infants; but even the diminutive is applied to a person twelve years of age.[3] In classic usage, the primitive word is rendered applicable to infants by a word added—νηπιος παις—*an infant boy*.[4] If the word itself denoted infancy, this addition would not be necessary. Once in the second chapter of Matthew it is applied to infants; but it is remarkable that the diminutive, παιδιον, is used nine times, in the same chapter, for infants. Why did the inspired writer adopt another word in this one case? We have the explanation in the note of Dr. Campbell on the passage: "The historian seems purposely to have changed the term παιδιον, which is used for *child*, no less than nine times in this chapter; as that word being neuter, and admitting only the neuter article, was not fit for marking the distinction of sexes; and to have adopted a term, which he nowhere else employs for infants, though frequently for men servants, and once for youths or boys." This application of παις to infants may be illustrated by a familiar usage in our own language. The words *boy* and *girl* do not signify an infant; and yet we ask whether an infant is a boy or a girl, if we wish to know its sex. Justin had no need to distinguish the sex of the persons whom he referred to, for he says, "There are among us persons of both sexes." Had Justin designed to say that these persons had been made disciples in infancy, the Greek language had words to express the idea; but what he did say amounts to nothing more than that these persons, now sixty or seventy years of age, had become disciples of Christ before they had arrived at maturity. This was the pedo-

---

[1] Acts xx. 12.

[2] Γυναικας εμοιχευσαν, και παιδας διεφθειραν. Justin's Works, London Edition, A. D. 1722, p. 10.

[3] Mark v. 39, 40, 42.   [4] Parkhurst's Lexicon, under the word νηπιος.

baptism which existed in the days of Justin; and to such pedobaptism there can be no objection.

Argument 5.—The commission may be rendered, "Go proselyte all nations, baptizing them." Christ was a Jew, and addressed these words to Jews. The Jews had been accustomed to make proselytes to their religion from among the gentiles. When these proselytes were received, they were circumcised and baptized, together with their children. Had Christ commissioned his apostles to proselyte the nations to Judaism, circumcising and baptizing them, they must have understood that children were to be circumcised and baptized with their parents. Being accustomed to this mode of receiving proselytes, they would naturally conclude that their Master intended them to adopt it in executing his command.

The proposed translation, "Go proselyte all nations," is not correct; for a proselyte and a disciple are not the same thing. If for the sentence, "Thou art his disciple, but we are Moses' disciples," we substitute, "Thou art his proselyte, but we are Moses' proselytes," every one will perceive that an important change is made in the meaning. A proselyte to Judaism abandoned his former religion; but when John and Jesus made disciples, these disciples did not cease to be Jews. Paul claimed to be a Jew,[1] and even a Pharisee,[2] after his conversion. The fishermen of Galilee were indeed Jews, but they knew little, in all probability, of those efforts in which some of their nation compassed sea and land to make one proselyte; and they could not have understood their Lord to refer to those efforts in the commission under which they were to act. Some of them had been disciples of John; and all of them had been associated with Christ in making and baptizing disciples from among the Jews. Had they witnessed the admission of a proselyte from heathenism to Judaism, they knew well that the ceremonies which he underwent did not make him a disciple of Christ. They could not, therefore, understand the Saviour to refer to this process. The making and baptizing of disciples was a process to which they were accustomed, and by it they would naturally interpret the commission. Even if their Jewish prejudices had led to the supposed interpretation, it would have been unauthorized. These prejudices caused them to misinterpret the commission in another particular; and, in consequence,

---

[1] Acts xxi. 39. [2] Acts xxiii. 6.

they did not, for some time, preach the gospel to the uncircumcised gentiles. It was their duty, in interpreting the commission, to look more to the Saviour's words, and less to their Jewish prejudices: and the same obligation rests on us, and deserves the attention of those who urge the argument which we are considering.

The question whether the custom of baptizing proselytes to Judaism existed as early as the time of Christ, has engaged the attention of learned men, who have been divided respecting it. Prof. Stuart has given the subject an extended investigation, and finds no evidence that the custom existed before the destruction of Jerusalem.

Argument 6.—Infants were admitted to church-membership by circumcision, the initiatory rite under the former dispensation; and baptism now takes its place, being the same seal in a new form; and therefore ought to be administered to infants.

The arguments for the church-membership of infants were considered at large in the preceding section of this chapter. In this discussion, it was shown, that the church is not identical with the great nation descended from Abraham, and distinguished by the mark of circumcision. Since baptism was designed for those only who are spiritually qualified for membership in the church, no valid argument for the application of it to infants can be drawn from the fact, that the infant descendants of Abraham were marked by circumcision, as entitled to membership in the commonwealth of Israel.

If baptism is merely a new form of the same seal, the subjects to whom it is to be applied remaining the same, it ought still to be applied to infants on the eighth day. This day was fixed by express divine command. No authority inferior to that which made the covenant, can abrogate or change this precept. Moreover, the seal, as anciently administered, was not confined to descendants of the first generation; and baptism, if it is the same seal under another form, ought to be extended in its application to all the descendants of those who are admitted within the covenant.

It is an argument against the identity of baptism and circumcision, that baptism was administered to those who had previously received the seal in the other form, according to the command of God. They who were baptized under the ministry of John and of Jesus, were children of the covenant, and had been previously marked with the proper seal according to divine command in the covenant. Why was the seal necessary in another form? For some time after the ascension of Christ, the gospel was preached to the circumcised only; and no others were baptized. These persons were addressed as children of the covenant; and had the seal of the covenant in their flesh, affixed when that form of the seal was not only valid, but obligatory. Why was the repetition of the seal in another form necessary?

The command to circumcise, was positive; and every one who did not receive this token of the covenant in his flesh, was to be cut off from among God's people. If the church is founded on the covenant of circumcision, it becomes a deeply interesting inquiry, whether any but circumcised persons can be members. The theory is, that baptism takes the place of circumcision; but how can this theory annul the express command of God? We need authority for changing the form of the seal, as great, and as express, as that by which the original form was instituted; but we look for it in vain in the Holy Scriptures. Instead of finding an express precept for changing the form, or an express declaration that it has been changed, we find decisive proof, that the inspired apostles did not understand baptism to be a new form of the old seal. They discussed the question, whether gentile converts ought to be circumcised, and they decided in the negative; but they did not so decide, on the ground that baptism had taken the place of circumcision, and rendered the continued use of the old form unnecessary. This, according to the pedobaptist theory, was the true ground of their decision, being the true and only sufficient reason for laying aside the old form of the seal. That the apostles did not assign this reason, is decisive proof that they were strangers to the theory. With this evidence before us, how can we hold ourselves bound by the Abrahamic covenant, and expect the blessings which it is understood to promise, if we refuse its only divinely authorized seal?

In describing the completeness of Christians, Paul states, in one verse, that they are " circumcised with the circumcision that is made without hands;" and in the next, that they are " buried with Christ in baptism."[1] From the connexion in which these things

---

[1] Col. ii. 12.

are mentioned, some have argued that baptism takes the place of circumcision: but the passage does not justify the inference. Literal circumcision is not the duty of gentile believers; and is therefore no part of Christian completeness. Literal baptism is a duty of all Christians; and is therefore necessary to their completeness. The adjuncts with which circumcision is mentioned in the passage, shows regeneration to be intended. This, in the order of Christ's appointment, precedes baptism; and in this order Paul mentions both as distinct parts of Christian completeness. Nothing in the passage justifies the confounding of baptism with circumcision. Whatever analogy there may be between the two rites, their identity is not taught in these verses.

Argument 7.—Without insisting on a strict substitution of baptism for circumcision, it may be assumed as unquestionable, that a striking analogy exists between the two rites. Both are initiatory, both are religious, both are outward signs of inward grace, and seals of the righteousness of faith. The parental relation is one of exceeding importance. God has distinguished it greatly in his Word, and uses it, in his providence, as a chief means of perpetuating his church in the world. This relation is the same in all ages, and the essential principles of religion are the same. As, therefore, the relation was marked by a religious rite in the former dispensation, the immutable principles of the divine government make it proper that it should be marked by a religious rite now. Whatever may be said of the Abrahamic covenant as a whole, the stipulation which it contains, that the Lord would be a God to him and his seed, includes spiritual blessings, and is substantially the covenant which God now makes with every believer. As the parent and the child were admitted into the covenant by the same religious rite formerly, so they ought to be admitted by the same religious rite now. In this sense, baptism takes the place of circumcision; and ought, therefore, to be administered to infants.

This argument is objectionable, on the ground that it rests the proof of a positive institute, on reasonings from general principles. If immutable principles require the parental relation to be marked with a religious rite, why was it not so marked from the beginning of the world? And why, when it became marked, was the relation to male descendants only, affected by the immutable principle? In the family of Abraham, the relation of the patriarch to all his descendants, remote as well as immediate, was marked by the rite then instituted: and if immutable principles require the relation to be marked by a religious rite now, it ought to be applied to remote descendants.

The promise to Abraham, to be a God to him and his seed, is contained in the covenant of circumcision, and is to be understood according to the tenor of that covenant. It extended to remote descendants, contemplated them as a nation, and brought the nation into a peculiar relation to God. It did not absolutely engage the spiritual blessing of justification which had been previously bestowed on the believing patriarch personally. The covenant now made with believers is personal, and secures personal spiritual blessings. "This is the covenant that I will make with the house of Israel: after those days, saith the Lord, I will put my laws into their minds, and write them in their hearts; and I will be to them a God, and they shall be to me a people."[1] The promise of this covenant is absolute, and secures the putting of the law in the heart. This, the promise in the Abrahamic covenant did not secure; and, on this account, the covenant established on better promises, is called a new covenant. So different is its nature, from the national covenant made with Abraham, that, if it were right to infer positive institutes from general principles, we could not, with propriety, draw the inference which infant baptism requires.

The agreement between baptism and circumcision, as *initiatory* rites, is urged to no avail, if the bodies into which they initiate are differently constituted. They may both be called religious rites, because religion has to do with whatever God commands; but we need God's command, to instruct us in the proper use of these rites. They have also been called *sealing* rites: but in what sense they seal, is involved in obscurity. Abraham received the sign of circumcision,—a seal of the righteousness of the faith which he had, yet being uncircumised. His *receiving* of circumcision seems to imply more than merely his being circumcised. It signifies that circumcision began with him. This fact was viewed by Paul as a proof that he was already in the favor of God; and the apostle regards it as a confirmation or seal of what had been previously said. "Abraham believed in the Lord, and he counted it to him for righteousness."[2] Paul does not say that circumcision was a seal to all to whom it was administered. The case of Abraham, and the faith

---

[1] Heb. viii. 10.   [2] Gen. xv. 6.

of Abraham, are all that his argument had in view, in the use of the word seal.

Baptism is nowhere in the Scriptures called a seal. Believers are said to be sealed by the Holy Spirit; and the validity of this seal God will ever acknowledge; but many receive baptism who are not sealed by the Holy Spirit unto the day of redemption.[1] We need to understand in what sense, and by what authority, the two rites are called sealing, and what engagements they, as seals, confirm, before we can argue, that because one of them was applied to infants, the other must, in like manner, be applied to infants. When we view the nature and design of the two rites in the light of the Holy Scriptures, we discover that circumcision was intended for the literal descendants of Abraham, but that literal descent from Abraham, without faith, gave no title to baptism. Whatever agreement may be traced between the two ceremonies in other respects, their difference in this particular destroys the analogy, at the very point where alone it can be of use to the cause of infant baptism.

The argument proves too much. We have seen that it extends the application of the religious rite to remote descendants. Besides this, it applies it, not to infant children only, but to children of whatever age, provided they belong to the household. Moreover, it requires that the relation of master and servant be marked in the same way. This also is an important relation, which God has used in extending his church; for servants have often been converted by being brought into pious families. The precept given to Abraham, extended to the whole household; and was given in very explicit language. The argument requires that every believer should put himself in the place of the patriarch, and consider himself bound by this command. At this point, the subject may be viewed advantageously in connection with the following argument.

Argument 8.—The three households of Lydia, the jailer, and Stephanas, are said in Scripture to have been baptized. It is improbable that there were three entire households without any infants in them. The manner in which the facts are recorded, especially in the case of Lydia's household, indicates that it was the prevailing custom to baptize the household, when the head of it became a believer. No intimation is given, that the members

---

[1] Eph. iv. 30.

of the household were all believers, and admitted to baptism on their personal faiths; but their baptism followed, of course, on the admission of Lydia herself into the church. Were such a statement published, in the journal of any modern missionary, every one would understand the missionary to be a pedobaptist. No one expects to read an account of household baptisms, in a history of Baptist missions.

Mention is made in the New Testament, of several households, which appear to have consisted entirely of Christian believers.[1] Such instances are not uncommon in modern times, even among Baptists: and, in times of religious revivals, whole households are not unfrequently baptized on profession of faith. The probability of such occurrences in the slow progress of modern missions in a heathen nation, is far less; and it would be unfair to estimate from a history of missions, the probability that whole households were converted at once, under the ministry of the apostles. A modern missionary sometimes labors for years, and scarcely reports a single convert; but, in primitive times, three thousand were converted in one day, and the Holy Spirit fell on the whole congregation assembled in the house of Cornelius. In this state of things, it is not surprising that three households should have been converted and baptized. We are told that the nobleman of Capernaum "believed, and his whole house;"[2] that Crispus "believed with all his house;"[3] and that Cornelius "feared God with all his house." Here are three households, which consisted entirely of pious persons; and the probability that these three had infants in them, must be as great as in the case of the three households that were baptized. Besides, in the accounts given of these last households, circumstances are mentioned which strongly indicate the absence of children. 1. In the case of the jailer's household, "they spake unto him the word of the Lord, and to all that were in his house;"[5] "he rejoiced, believing in God with all his house."[6] Who would expect to read such statements as these in the journal of a pedobaptist missionary, who, on receiving a convert from heathenism, baptized him with his infant children? 2. In the case of the household of Stephanas we are informed, "that they *addicted*

---

[1] 2 Tim. iv. 19; Acts x. 2; Acts xvi. 34; 1 Cor. xvi. 15, 19; John iv. 53.
[2] John iv. 53.   [3] Acts xviii. 8.   [4] Acts x. 2.
[5] Acts xvi. 32.   [6] V. 34.

ARGUMENTS FOR INFANT BAPTISM. 197

themselves to the ministry of the saints."[1] It has been said that this was some years after their baptism, when the infants might have grown up. But, in most families, while some infants grow, other infants are added; and in replying to an argument dependant on probability, we are at liberty to assume, that the probability of finding infants in the house of Stephanas was as great at one time as at the other. We may also notice, that the baptism of this household is not mentioned in connection with the baptism of the head. Paul baptized the household of Stephanas;[2] but who baptized Stephanas himself, we are not informed. So far as appears, the two baptisms were performed at different times, and were independent of each other. 3. In the case of Lydia's household we have the following facts: Lydia was "a seller of purple of the city of Thyatira."[3] No mention is made of husband or children. She had a house at Philippi, which she called "my house;" and the business in which she was engaged, appears to have been under her own management. When Paul and Silas were released from prison, it is said, "they entered into the house of Lydia; and when they had seen the brethren, they comforted them, and departed."[4] The connection of the clauses in this verse, renders it probable, that the brethren here mentioned, belonged to the house of Lydia, and were the persons baptized with her. This probability ought to be admitted, in an argument founded on probability; and it is at least as great, as that Lydia, the apparently single proprietor and manager of her own house and business, should have had infant children. So far as to the argument about probability.

The second part of the argument is, that the narrative states the baptism of the household as following, of course, on the faith and baptism of the head. But this, as we have seen, is not the case, with respect to the household of Stephanas and the jailer. All the weight of the argument rests on the single case of Lydia; and it is merely an argument from the silence of Scripture. We are not expressly informed that Lydia's household were believers; but the silence on this point does not prove that they were not. It is stated, in another place, that "Crispus, the chief ruler of the synagogue,

---

[1] 1 Cor. xvi. 15. [2] 1 Cor. i. 16. [3] Acts xvi. 14.
[4] V. 40.

believed, with all his house." No mention is made of their baptism: but the silence of Scripture on this point, does not prove that they were not baptized. Faith and baptism are everywhere throughout the narrative so connected with each other, that the mention of both, in every instance, was unnecessary. The faith of the household is not mentioned in the case of Lydia; neither is it mentioned in Paul's address to the jailer:—"Believe on the Lord Jesus Christ, and thou shalt be saved, and thy house."[1] Here the promise of salvation is made to the household, without an express requirement of faith from them,—the command, "believe," being in the singular number. We know, from the whole tenor of Scripture, that the jailer's household were not saved on his faith; and we have the same reason for knowing that Lydia's household were not baptized on her faith.

If any one should maintain that, when households are said to *believe* and to *fear God*, infants may have been overlooked in the statement, because known to be incapable of religious affections, we admit the possibility of what is supposed, and we maintain, in turn, that the same may have been true with respect to baptism. In all the sacred volume, and in all the usage of primitive times, faith was a qualification for baptism; and it may be that, in the mention of household baptism, no account was taken of infants, because it was universally known that they were never baptized. Our cause admits this hypothesis; but is not dependent on it.

A distinction ought to be made, between household baptism and infant baptism. The preceding argument, if it proves either, proves household baptism; and the same is true of the argument now before us. Children of various ages, even to adult years, and servants, are included in the proper import of the word household. It was so, when the covenant of circumcision was made with Abraham; for his son Ishmael, and his servants, were circumcised. It is so in the Acts of the Apostles: for in the household of Cornelius, " two household servants" are mentioned.

It deserves to be carefully noticed, that almost every argument for infant church-membership and infant baptism, tends to prove, so far as it proves either, not the church-membership and baptism of infants, but of whole households. The covenant of circumcision

---

[1] V. 31.

required the rite to be administered to the whole household. Under the Mosaic covenant, when a stranger was admitted, he was required to be circumcised with all his household; and the same law was applied to him, in the keeping of the passover, as to those born in the land. When proselyte baptism was practised, it was applied to all the household. No example of infant baptism can be found in the Bible; but the three examples which have been relied on to prove it, are all examples of household baptism. Now, according to a hypothesis stated in the last paragraph, it may be that the infants of a household may be overlooked, when something is affirmed of the household, which is incompatible with infancy; but it can never be supposed, that the term household signifies infants only, to the exclusion of older members. If household baptism has been proved, who will practise it? The admission of ungodly youths and servants to baptism and church privileges, when the father and master becomes converted, is so contrary to the spirit and tenor of the gospel, that no one ventures to advocate it. Yet this is the point to which almost every argument tends, which has been advanced in support of infant baptism. These arguments are numerous: and if each one could bring a ray of light, however feeble, we might expect the combined illumination to render the subject visible; but we have traced the direction of the rays, and find that their concentrated force, whatever may be its illuminating power, falls elsewhere, and leaves infant baptism still in the dark.

Argument 9.—Learned men have searched the writings of the Christian fathers, and have found evidence as abundant, and specific, and certain, as history affords of almost any fact, that infant baptism universally prevailed from the days of the apostles, through four centuries. This ought to satisfy us, that the practice originated in the apostolic churches.

Other learned men have examined the same writings, and have arrived at the conclusion, that infant baptism was wholly unknown, until about the close of the second century;—that it originated in Africa, and in the third century became prevalent there, but did not supplant the primitive baptism in the Oriental churches, until the fifth century.

Amidst this conflict of opinions, derived from the same source, it is a happy privilege which we enjoy, to leave the muddy streams of tradition, and drink at the pure fountain of revelation. The aim of the present work is, to ascertain what the Scriptures teach on the subject of church order; and it does not accord with the design, to enter into an investigation of questions appertaining to ecclesiastical history; but I will state, very briefly, what appear to me, so far as I have been able to investigate the subject, the chief facts to be gleaned from the early fathers, relative to the origin of infant baptism.

No trace of infant baptism can be found, previous to the time of Justin Martyr. The passage of his writings, which is quoted on page 174, has been regarded as the first clear testimony on the subject; but we have shown that this, when properly interpreted, means nothing more than that some persons, then sixty or seventy years of age, had been made disciples of Christ before they were fully grown. In another part of Justin's writings, he purposely gives an account of the usages which existed among Christians, respecting baptism; and, in doing this, he describes the baptism of believers, without any intimation that infants were concerned in the rite. Had infant baptism been the universal practice, his purpose would have required a description of it.

The primitive practice required each candidate for baptism to profess his faith personally. But a custom arose, of permitting the profession to be made by proxy: the candidate being present, and signifying his assent. This custom made it easy for very young persons to be admitted to the rite, and the opinion, which had now become prevalent, that baptism possessed a saving efficacy, produced a tendency to extend the application of it to children. Tertullian, who wrote about A. D. 200, opposed this tendency; and insisted that, instead of granting baptism on the candidate's asking for it, and making profession through his sponsors, the baptism should be deferred until he had become instructed respecting its nature and design. Thus far, it does not appear that the rite was ever administered to children incapable of asking for it; but Cyprian, A. D. 250, interpreted the cries of new-born babes to be an asking for the grace which baptism was supposed to confer. The propriety of giving it to infants was now extensively admitted, but the practice was not universal.

The late Neander, who is esteemed the greatest of ecclesiastical historians, says: "Baptism was administered at first only to adults, as men were accustomed to conceive baptism and faith as strictly connected." "Immediately after Irenæus, in the last years of the second century, Tertullian appears as a zealous opponent of infant baptism: a proof that the practice had not as yet come to be regarded as an apostolical institution; for, otherwise, he would hardly have ventured to express himself so strongly against it."[1]

"For these reasons, Tertullian declared against infant baptism; which at that time was *certainly not a generally prevailing practice;* was not yet regarded as an apostolical institution. On the contrary, as the assertions of Tertullian render in the highest degree probable, *it had just begun to spread;* and was therefore regarded by many *as an innovation.*"[2]

Jacobi, a learned friend of Neander, says: "Infant baptism was established neither by Christ nor the apostles." "Many circumstances conspired early to introduce the practice of infant baptism."[3]

Mosheim, in his account of the Second Century, says: "The sacrament of *baptism* was administered publicly twice every year, at the festivals of Easter and Pentecost, or Whitsuntide, either by the *bishop,* or the *presbyters,* in consequence of his authorization and appointment. The persons that were to be baptized, after that they had repeated the creed, confessed and renounced their sins, and particularly the *devil* and his pompous allurements, were immersed under water, and received into Christ's kingdom by a solemn invocation of Father, Son, and Holy Ghost, according to the express command of our Blessed Lord. After baptism, they received the *sign of the cross,* were *anointed,* and, by *prayers* and imposition of hands, were solemnly commended to the mercy of God, and dedicated to his service; in consequence of which they received *milk* and *honey,* which concluded the ceremony. The reasons of this particular ritual coincide with what we have said in general concerning the origin and causes of the multiplied ceremonies that crept from time to time into the church.

"Adult persons were prepared for baptism by abstinence, prayer, and other pious exercises. It was to answer for them that spon-

---

[1] History of Christian Religion and Church, pp. 311, 312 (Torrey's Translation.

[2] Spirit of Tertullian, p. 207. Quoted from Christian Review, Vol. xvi. pp. 517, 520.

[3] Kitto's Cyclopedia; Art. Baptism.

sors or godfathers were first instituted, though they were afterwards admitted also in the baptism of infants."

The use of sponsors is retained in the Episcopal Church. The officiating minister addresses the child as if he were an intelligent candidate; and the sponsors give what is regarded as the answer of the child. In these forms, we may see the remains of primitive usage, the lifeless corpse of the ancient baptism, which was once animated with piety, and profession strictly personal.

CHAPTER V.

COMMUNION.

SECTION I.—PERPETUITY OF THE LORD'S SUPPER.

THE RITE USUALLY CALLED THE LORD'S SUPPER WAS INSTITUTED BY CHRIST, TO BE OBSERVED IN HIS CHURCHES TILL THE END OF THE WORLD.

On the night which preceded the Saviour's crucifixion, he ate the passover with his disciples. At the close of the meal, the ceremony called the Lord's Supper was instituted. The account of the institution is thus given by Matthew: "As they were eating, Jesus took bread, and blessed it, and brake it, and gave it to the disciples, and said, Take, eat; this is my body. And he took the cup, and gave thanks, and gave it to them, saying, Drink ye all of it: for this is my blood of the new testament, which is shed for many for the remission of sins. But I say unto you, I will not drink henceforth of this fruit of the vine, until that day when I drink it new with you in my Father's kingdom."[1] Mark's account is in nearly the same words.[2] Luke's narrative differs in several particulars. He mentions a previous cup, which seems to have concluded the proper paschal supper. At the distribution of the bread, he adds these words, omitted by the other evangelists: "This do in remembrance of me." In the giving of the second cup, he states explicitly that it was "after supper;" and, by this expression, distinguishes it from the preceding cup, which was a part of the supper.[3] In the eleventh chapter of the first epistle to the Corinthians, Paul gives an account of the institution, agreeing substantially with the accounts given by the evangelists. At the

---

[1] Matt. xxvi. 26—29.   [2] Mark xiv. 22—24.   [3] Luke xxii. 17—20.

distribution of the bread, he adds the words: "This is my body, which is broken for you: this do in remembrance of me." And, at the giving of the cup, he adds: "This cup is the new testament in my blood: this do ye, as oft as ye drink it, in remembrance of me." To all this he subjoins, "As often as ye eat this bread and drink this cup, ye do show the Lord's death till he come. Wherefore whosoever shall eat this bread, and drink this cup of the Lord unworthily, shall be guilty of the body and blood of the Lord. But let a man examine himself, and so let him eat of this bread and drink of this cup. For he that eateth and drinketh unworthily, eateth and drinketh damnation to himself, not discerning the Lord's body."

From these several accounts taken in connection, we learn that after Jesus had concluded the last passover with his disciples, he used the bread and cup for a purpose unknown in that supper; and commanded the disciples to use them in the same manner, in remembrance of him. The time during which this memorial of Christ was designed to be kept, we might infer from the words of the evangelist. Jesus directed the minds of the disciples from the feast which he then kept with them to a future feast, to be enjoyed together in the Father's kingdom. During the interval this new institution was to be observed as a memorial of the past, and a pledge of the future. But Paul has drawn the inference for us, "As often as ye eat this bread, and drink this cup, ye do show the Lord's death till he come." The time for the observance is here definitely marked out as extending to Christ's second coming. Baptism was instituted to be observed "till the end of the world," and the supper has the same limit prescribed for its duration.

The institution of the supper described by Paul, he states that he had received from the Lord Jesus, and had delivered to the Corinthian church. These facts show that Christ designed his apostle to inculcate the observance; and that the apostle was not negligent in this particular. He praised the church for keeping the ordinances as he had delivered them; but censured an abuse which had arisen among them in celebrating the supper. He does not, because of this abuse, dissuade from the further observance of it, but he labors to correct the abuse; and he renews the command, "Let a man examine himself, and so let him eat." The proof thus furnished is abundant and decisive, that the observance was designed to be established and perpetuated in the churches.

We have further proof in the Acts of the Apostles. The church at Jerusalem continued steadfastly in the apostles' doctrine and fellowship, and in breaking of bread, and in prayers;[1] and the disciples at Troas assembled on the first day of the week *to break bread.*[2]

The Scriptural designation of the rite in the passages just cited, is *the breaking of bread.* The name *Eucharist* is often given to it, derived from the Greek word ευχαριστεω, and referring to the thanksgiving which preceded the distribution of the elements. This name is not used in the Scriptures. Some remarks have been made in another place (pp. 57, 58) respecting the name *Lord's Supper.* It is not clear that we have Scripture authority for using this name to designate the rite. But, considering the rite as a memorial of our Lord's last supper with his disciples, the name is significant—like the name *passover* applied to the rite which kept in memory the fact, that the destroying angel *passed over* the habitations of the Israelites. The name may also refer to the spiritual feast which believers enjoy with their Lord, who graciously *sups* with them. The name *Trinity*, and the name *person*, applied to the three-fold distinction in the Trinity, are used without Scripture authority, merely as convenient terms; and the names *Eucharist* and *Lord's Supper*, may be used in the same way, but we must always be careful to found no article of faith on any use of terms for which we cannot produce divine authority.

The Quakers object to the perpetuity of the supper, as they do to that of baptism. Their chief objections, we shall proceed to consider.

Objection 1.—The bread and the cup belonged to the passover; and the evangelists state, that it was while eating this feast that the bread and cup were used, which constitute the supposed new institution. The breaking of bread is frequently mentioned as customary in ordinary meals. We ought, therefore, to consider it as a common occurrence at table, and to interpret the words of Christ as a command that in all our eating and drinking we should remember him, according to what is said elsewhere, " Whether ye eat or drink, or whatsoever ye do, do all to the glory of God."[3]

---

[1] Acts ii. 42.   [2] Acts xx. 7.   [3] 1 Cor. x. 31.

The simplicity of the rite, is no valid objection against it; but rather a recommendation. Bread and the cup were in common use; but they were not, on this account, less adapted to the purpose for which Christ employed them. Water is a common element, and *immersion* in it was common among the Jews; but these facts did not render immersion in water less fit for a Christian ordinance. The rites are new, not because new elements are used, but because they are used for a new purpose. The whole of the paschal services commemorated the deliverance from Egypt. The new institution was designed to commemorate a different deliverance, by the broken body and shed blood of Christ. No one will maintain, that the breaking of bread in ordinary meals, was designed for this purpose. So distinctly marked was this new purpose, that Paul says, "He that eateth and drinketh unworthily, is guilty of the body and blood of the Lord." If he did it, "not discerning the Lord's body," he overlooked the great design of the institution, and was guilty. This fault the objection commits, in confounding the bread and wine of the eucharist with ordinary food.

Objection 2.—The Acts of the Apostles mention only two instances in which the breaking of bread was observed by the disciples; and both of these manifestly refer to ordinary meals. The church at Jerusalem continued in the breaking of bread; and this is explained in the words, "Breaking bread from house to house, did eat their meat with gladness, and singleness of heart."[1] The disciples at Troas met to break bread; and what is hereby meant, may be learned from what is afterwards said: "When he therefore was come up again, and had broken bread, and eaten, and talked a long while, even till break of day, so he departed."[2] This is clearly an ordinary meal, preparatory to Paul's departure. We see, therefore, that the Acts of the Apostles record no instance of the eucharistic observance; and the silence cannot be accounted for, if the observance had been customary.

No doubt exists that the phrase, *breaking of bread*, sometimes describes what occurred at ordinary meals. Jesus manifested himself to the two disciples at Emmaus, in the breaking of bread, when they had sat down to an ordinary meal; and Paul broke bread to those who were with him in the ship, to terminate their long fast. In the second chapter of Acts, the phrase occurs twice. In the first instance, the connection shows that the eucharistic

---

[1] Acts ii. 46.   [2] Acts xx. 11.

observance is intended. "They continued in the apostles' doctrine, and fellowship, and breaking bread, and prayers." In the second instance, the connection shows that ordinary meals are intended. The repetition, instead of proving the same thing to be intended in both instances, proves rather the contrary. Distinct facts are described.

Did the disciples at Troas meet for an ordinary meal? Was this the meeting which the sacred historian so particularly mentions? The character of primitive Christianity forbids the supposition. These disciples were accustomed to meet for the worship of God; and the important design of their assembling together could not have been forgotten or overlooked on this occasion, when they had the presence of Paul. It was appropriate to mention the eucharist, as a part of public worship, in speaking of the purpose for which they assembled; but to describe them as having assembled for an ordinary meal, is inconsistent with their character, and inconsistent with the occasion. If, as is most probable, the breaking of bread next morning, at the break of day, was an ordinary meal preparatory to Paul's departure, it was a different breaking of bread from that which had brought the disciples together on the preceding day.

These are the only two cases in which the observance of the Lord's supper is mentioned in the Acts; but they are sufficient to prove the existence of the observance. The church at Jerusalem continued steadfastly in the breaking of bread. It could have been no commendation of them, that they continued steadfastly in eating ordinary meals; but their steadfast continuance in the divine institution, is historical proof that it was observed by the first church as a part of their public worship. This fact explains what is said about the disciples at Troas, and the two statements make the historical evidence, in this book, as satisfactory as is necessary. The observance of the rite by the church at Corinth, makes the historical proof complete.

Objection 3.—The Jewish worship consisted of meats, and drinks, and divers baptisms, and carnal ordinances; but these are not adapted to the spiritual worship of the Christian dispensation. Paul teaches that "the kingdom of God is not meat and drink; but righteousness, peace, and joy in the Holy Ghost."[1] The Lord's

---

[1] Rom. xiv. 17.

supper comes under the denomination of meats and drinks, and is therefore not appropriate to the new economy. Paul expressly commands, "Let no man judge you in meat or in drink;"[1] and urges believers to leave those things which perish in the using, and set their affections above.

This objection substantially agrees with Objection 5 to the perpetuity of baptism; and what is there said in reply, is applicable here. The meats and drinks of the former dispensation were shadows of good things to come; but the body is of Christ. So Paul teaches, in connection with the text last quoted in the objection; and, in this way, he explains what meat and drink he refers to. The Jewish ceremonies were typical of Christ to come; but the Lord's supper is a memorial of Christ already come. It is, therefore, not included in the meat and drink intended by the apostle. The passover was included in these abrogated meats and drinks; which ceased to be obligatory after Christ, our passover, was sacrificed for us. At the very time when he was about to put an end to this old ceremony, he instituted the Lord's supper; and it is, therefore, incredible that he meant this to expire with the other. Paul says, "Let no man judge you in meat or in drink." The abrogated ceremonies are now without divine authority; and, therefore, he calls *these meats and drinks* the commandments of men. But the bread and wine of the supper, are commandments of the Lord; and therefore Paul says, with reference to these: "Let a man examine himself, and so let him eat."

The numerous and burdensome rites of the Old Testament would not be adapted to the more spiritual dispensation which we are under; but it does not follow that the two simple ceremonies, baptism and the Lord's supper, are incompatible with it. We are yet in the flesh, and need the use of such memorials. In the proper use of them, believers have found them greatly profitable, and well adapted to promote spirituality. Besides the benefit which they yield to the individual believer, these two ceremonies stand, like two monuments, reared up in the time of Christ, and testifying to the world concerning Christ and his doctrine. Their use, as evidences of Christianity and its cardinal doctrines, the Trinity and the atonement, is incalculably great, and displays the wisdom which instituted them.

---

[1] Col. ii. 16.

In addition to the direct arguments which have been adduced, some allusions are found in the New Testament, showing, in an interesting manner, that baptism and the Lord's supper were contemplated as parts of Christianity. In the next chapter to that in which Paul corrects the Corinthian abuse of the supper, he says, " By one Spirit are we all baptized into one body, and have all been made to drink into one Spirit."[1] The allusion to both the ordinances, is manifest. In another part of the same epistle, he speaks of baptism unto Moses, and of their eating and drinking in the wilderness, in a manner which shows an allusion to the two Christian rites.[2]

Objection 4.—At the same supper in which Christ is supposed to have instituted the eucharist, he washed his disciples' feet, and commanded them to wash one another's feet. The command is equally as positive, as that which enjoined the use of bread and wine; yet Christians are generally agreed, that the command does not require to be obeyed literally. The thing signified by the outward form is what demands regard; and the same rule of interpretation ought to be applied to the eucharist.

The command ought, in both cases, to be obeyed strictly, according to the design of Christ. If Christians generally fail to render strict obedience to Christ's command respecting the washing of feet, we ought to begin a reform, and not make one neglect a precedent and argument for another. In the next chapter we shall inquire into the obligation to wash one another's feet. In this, we have ascertained, that Christ designed a literal use of bread and wine, and, this point being ascertained, our duty is determined; whatever doubt and obscurity may remain respecting any other subject.

SECTION II.—DESIGN.

THE LORD'S SUPPER WAS DESIGNED TO BE A MEMORIAL OF CHRIST, A REPRESENTATION THAT THE COMMUNICANT RECEIVES SPIRITUAL NOURISHMENT FROM HIM, AND A TOKEN OF FELLOWSHIP AMONG THE COMMUNICANTS.

The rite is commemorative. The passover served for a memorial of deliverance from Egypt; and, year after year, as the pious

---

[1] 1 Cor. xii. 13.   [2] 1 Cor. x. 2, 3, 4.

Israelites partook of it, they were reminded of that marvellous deliverance, and were required to tell of it to their children. The passover was instituted on the night of that deliverance. The Lord's supper was instituted on the night when Jesus was betrayed to be crucified; and serves for a memorial of his sufferings and death. When we remember him, we are to remember his agonies, his body broken, and his blood shed. In preaching the gospel, Paul determined to know nothing but Jesus Christ, and him crucified. So, in the eucharist, Christ is presented to view; not as transfigured on Mount Tabor, or as glorified at his Father's right hand, but as suffering and dying. We delight to keep in memory the honors which they whom we love have received; but Jesus calls us to remember the humiliation which he endured. To the lowest point of his humiliation, the supper directs our thoughts.

The simple ceremony is admirably contrived to serve more than a single purpose. While it shows forth the Lord's death, it represents at the same time the spiritual benefit which the believer derives from it. He eats the bread, and drinks the wine, in token of receiving his spiritual sustenance from Christ crucified. The rite preaches the doctrine that Christ died for our sins, and that we live by his death. He said, "Except ye eat the flesh of the Son of Man, and drink his blood, ye have no life in you."[1] These remarkable words teach the necessity of his atoning sacrifice, and of faith in that sacrifice. Without these, salvation and eternal life are impossible. When Christ said, "My flesh is meat indeed, and my blood is drink indeed,"[2] he did not refer to his flesh and blood, literally understood. He calls himself the living bread which came down from heaven.[3] This cannot be affirmed of his literal flesh. To have eaten this literally, would not have secured everlasting life; and equally inefficacious is the Romanist ceremony, in which they absurdly imagine that they eat the real body of Christ. His body is present in the eucharist in no other sense than that in which we can "*discern*" it. When he said, "This is my body," the plain meaning is, "This represents my body." So we point to a picture, and say, "This is Christ on the cross." The eucharist is a picture, so to speak, in which the bread represents the body of Christ suffering for our sins. Faith discerns what the

---

[1] John vi. 53.   [2] John vi. 55.   [3] John vi. 51.

picture represents. It discerns the Lord's body in the commemorative representation of it, and derives spiritual nourishment from the atoning sacrifice made by his broken body and shed blood.

A third purpose which this ceremony serves, and to which it is wisely adapted, is, to signify the fellowship of the communicants with one another. This is taught in the words of Paul: "The bread which we break, is it not the communion of the body of Christ? For we, being many, are one bread, and one body: for we are all partakers of that one bread."[1] A communion or joint participation in the benefits of Christ's death, is signified by the joint partaking of the outward elements. "What communion," says he, "hath light with darkness; and what concord hath Christ with Belial?" "Ye cannot be partakers of the Lord's table, and of the table of devils."[2] In these words of Paul, to sit at the same table, and drink of the same cup, are regarded as indications of communion and concord. Believers meet around the table of the Lord, in one faith on the same atonement, in one hope of the same inheritance, and with one heart filled with love to the same Lord.

A notion has prevailed extensively, that a spiritual efficacy attends the outward performance of the rite, if duly administered. Some mysterious influence is supposed to accompany the bread and wine, and render them means of grace to the recipient. But, as the gospel, though it is the power of God unto salvation, does not profit unless mixed with faith in those who hear it; much less can mere ceremonies profit without faith. In baptism, we rise with Christ through the faith of the operation of God; and in the supper, we cannot partake of Christ, and receive him as our spiritual nourishment, but by faith: "That Christ may dwell in your hearts by faith."[3] The contrary opinion makes these sacraments as they have been called, saving ordinances, and substitutes outward ceremony for vital piety.

---

[1] 1 Cor. x. 16, 17.   [2] 1 Cor. x. 21.   [3] Eph. iii. 17.

Section III.—COMMUNICANTS.

THE LORD'S SUPPER WAS DESIGNED TO BE CELEBRATED BY EACH CHURCH IN PUBLIC ASSEMBLY.

Intelligence is necessary in order to the proper receiving of the supper. When infant baptism arose, infant communion arose with it. The superstitious notion that the sacraments possessed a sort of magical efficacy, prevailed extensively; and parental affection desired for the children the grace of the supper, as well as that of baptism. The argument was as good for the one as for the other; and infant communion had as much authority from the apostles as infant baptism. But the practice of infant communion is now generally laid aside. It is generally conceded, that infants are incapable of receiving the rite according to its design. They cannot remember Christ, or discern the Lord's body; and they cannot perform the self-examination which is required previous to the communion. If the rite conveyed a magical influence, infants might receive it; but correct views have so far prevailed, as to restrict this ordinance to persons of intelligence.

Faith is also a requisite to the receiving of the supper. If mere intelligence were a sufficient qualification, men who partake of the table of devils, might partake also of the Lord's table. Paul decides that this cannot be, and therefore that none can properly partake of the Lord's table but those who have renounced the devil, and devoted themselves to the Lord. The outward ceremony cannot, of itself, yield profit to those who receive it. They cannot please God in it, without faith; and without faith they cannot derive spiritual nourishment from the body and blood of Christ.

The rite was designed to be social. Of the three purposes which it serves, as enumerated in the last section, the third requires that it be celebrated by a company. It could not serve as a token of fellowship between the disciples of Christ, if it were performed in solitude. To perpetuate a social rite, society is necessary; and the disciples of Christ, by his authority, organize the societies, called churches. As these are the only divinely instituted Christian societies, we might judge beforehand, that the supper would be committed to these, for its observance and perpetuation. This we find to be true. Paul says to the church at Corinth, "I praise you that ye keep the ordinances as I delivered them to you." "I have received of the Lord that which also I delivered unto you."¹ He then proceeds to mention the institution of the supper, and speaks of it as observed by the whole church assembled. Of some other matters, he says, in this connection, "We have no such custom, neither the churches of God;"² but everything in his account of the Lord's supper, accords with its being a church rite; and with this, all that is recorded of its observance at Jerusalem and Troas, perfectly harmonizes. The administration of the rite to a dying individual, as is practised by some, has no sanction in the Word of God.

The rite should be celebrated by the church, in public assembly. It is said, "As often as ye eat this bread, and drink this cup, ye do show the Lord's death till he come."³ To show his death, requires that it be done in public. It should be held forth to the view of the irreligious, who may be willing to attend in the public assembly. In another part of the same epistle, Paul speaks of the effect produced on unbelievers who came into the public assembly of the church.⁴ As it is right to hold forth the word of life to them, so it is right to show the Lord's death before them, in the divinely appointed manner.

By the Jews it was held unlawful to eat with the uncircumcised. Paul has taught us, that familiar intercourse with unconverted persons, is not unlawful to Christians; but he says, "If any man, that is called a brother, be a fornicator, or covetous, or an idolater, or a railer, or a drunkard, or an extortioner, with such a one, no not to eat."⁵ In this prohibition, eating at the Lord's table with such a wicked person, if not specially intended, is certainly included. Though such an one may have been called a brother, it was wrong for the church to retain him in fellowship, and continue to eat with him, in the peculiar manner by which fellowship was indicated. In the words of Christ, every such wicked person was to be accounted as an heathen man and a publican.

In primitive times, the members of different local churches associated with each other, as members of the great fraternity. Paul was doubtless welcomed at the Lord's table, by the disciples at

---

[1] 1 Cor. xi. 2, 23. [2] V. 16. [3] 1 Cor. xi. 26.
[4] 1 Cor. xiv. 24, 25. [5] 1 Cor. v. 11.

Troas. This transient communion is now practised. The Lord's supper is properly a church ordinance; but an individual, duly qualified to be admitted to membership in a church, may be admitted for the time as a member, and received to transient communion, without any departure from the design of the institution.

Section 4.—OPEN COMMUNION.

We have seen that the Lord's supper has been committed to the local churches for observance and perpetuation; and that local churches, if organized according to the Scriptures, contain none but baptized persons. It follows hence, that baptism is a pre-requisite to communion at the Lord's table. The position which baptism holds in the commission, determines its priority to the other commanded observances therein referred to, among which church communion must be included. This is the doctrine which has been held on the subject by Christians generally, in all ages; and it is now held by the great mass of Pedobaptists. With them we have no controversy as to the principle by which approach to the Lord's table should be regulated. We differ from them in practice, because we account nothing Christian baptism, but immersion on profession of faith, and we, therefore, exclude very many whom they admit. But there are Baptists, who reject the principle that baptism is a prerequisite to communion, and maintain that nothing ought to be a condition of communion, which is not a condition of salvation. They hold that all pious persons, baptized or unbaptized, have a right to the Lord's supper. Their practice is called open or mixed communion, and the arguments in defence of it will now claim our attention.

Argument 1.—The Lord's supper, when instituted by Christ, was given to persons who had never received Christian baptism, and therefore baptism cannot be a prerequisite.

The first supper was administered to the apostles. Some of these had been baptized by John; and, since the disciples made by Jesus in his personal ministry, were also baptized, we are warranted to conclude, that all the apostles had been baptized. If it be denied that John's baptism, and the baptism administered under the immediate direction of Christ during his personal ministry, were Christian baptism, we call for proof. Until the distinction is established, the argument has no foundation.

But there is another way in which the argument may be met. We have every certainty, which the nature of the case admits, that the apostles were not baptized after the institution of the Lord's supper. From this time to the ensuing Pentecost, when they entered fully on the work assigned them, their history is so given as to exclude all probability that they were baptized in this interval; and, if they were qualified to enter fully on their work, without another baptism, another baptism was unnecessary; and was therefore never afterwards received. Mr. Hall, the ablest advocate of open communion, says: "My deliberate opinion is, that, in the Christian sense of the term, they were not baptized at all."[1] When Paul was made an apostle, before he entered on his work he was commanded to be baptized. From some cause, the other apostles were not under this obligation. We account for the difference, by the supposition, that they had already received what was substantially the same as the baptism administered to Paul. But, if we are mistaken on this point, it is still true that the eleven apostles were not under obligation to receive any other baptism; and their case, therefore, differed radically from that of persons who are under obligation to be baptized, and are living in neglect of this duty. The latter may be required, and ought to be required, to profess Christ according to his commandment, before they are admitted to church-membership and communion; but the eleven apostles, from some cause, whatever it may have been, were under no such obligation. The cases are not parallel; and, therefore, the argument fails.

Argument 2.—The argument for strict communion, from the position of baptism in the commission, proves too much. If it proves that we ought not to teach the unbaptized to commune at the Lord's table, it proves also that we ought not to teach them the moral precepts of Christ included in the words, "all things whatsoever I have commanded you."

The apostles were commanded to preach the gospel to every creature. In executing their commission, it became their duty to instruct the ignorant and them that were out of the way. They adapted their instructions to every man's character and circum-

---

[1] Hall's Works, Vol. i., p. 303.

stances To the impenitent, they said: "Repent, and be baptized." To the unbaptized disciple, they said: "Why tarriest thou? Arise, and be baptized." The baptized disciple they taught, according to the requirement in the commission, to observe all things whatsoever Christ had commanded. The impenitent were not to be taught to observe *all* things which Christ had commanded. The advocates of open communion deny that they have a right either to baptism, or the Lord's supper; but why? The same moral precepts which are to be taught to the baptized disciple, may be taught to the impenitent. We may, therefore, retort, that if they exclude the impenitent from baptism and the Lord's supper, their mode of reasoning will prove too much, and will equally exclude them from instruction in the moral precepts of Christ. If it be just to argue from the order prescribed in the commission, that baptism belongs to those *only* who have been made disciples; that order equally proves, that the baptized only ought to be taught to observe *all* things that Christ had commanded. Some things that Christ commanded might be taught to the unbaptized, and to the impenitent; but the full observance of *all* Christ's commands, was to be enjoined on the baptized disciples. Had the commission read, "Make disciples of all nations, and teach them to observe all things whatsoever I have commanded you," baptism and the supper would have been included together among the things commanded, and no inference could have been drawn from the commission as to the proper order in which they should be observed. But the separation of baptism from all the other things which Christ had commanded, gives it a peculiar relation to the other things enjoined in the commission; and the order in which it is introduced cannot but signify the proper order for our obedience.

Argument 3.—The fact that, in the primitive times, none but baptized persons were admitted to the Lord's table, is not a rule to us, whose circumstances are widely different. Then, no converted person mistook his obligation to be baptized. Had he refused baptism, the refusal would have proved him not to be a disciple; and now nothing ought to exclude from communion, but that which disproves discipleship.

The argument admits that, if all understood their duty, baptism would always precede the communion, as it did in apostolic times. How far it is our duty to tolerate disobedience to Christ's commands, and produce a church order unknown in the days of the apostles, in accommodation to error or weakness of faith, is an inquiry which will come up hereafter.

Argument 4.—The supper commemorates the death of Christ: baptism represents his burial and resurrection. The order of the things signified is the reverse of that in which they are observed. Hence, the order of observance ought not to be considered necessary.

Baptism represents the burial of Christ, but not to the exclusion of his death: "Know ye not, that as many of us as were baptized into Christ, were baptized into his death? Therefore, we are buried with him by baptism into death." The supper represents the death of Christ; but not to the exclusion of his burial and resurrection. Without the resurrection, the sacrifice would have been unaccepted, and the memorial of it useless. Moreover, the supper directs the thoughts to the second coming of Christ, and therefore supposes his resurrection. The same great facts of Christianity are represented by both rites, though in aspects somewhat different; and, therefore, no valid argument can be drawn, from their objective signification, to determine the proper order of their observance.

But while both rites direct our faith to the accepted sacrifice of Christ, they do not signify our relation to it in the same manner. Baptism represents a believer's dying to sin, and rising to walk in newness of life. It signifies the change by which he becomes a new creature. The supper represents the believer's continued feeding on Christ; and therefore presupposes the change which is denoted by baptism. It follows, that the subjective signification of the rites, so far as any valid argument can be drawn from it, determines the priority of baptism.

If there were anything in the objective signification of the rite furnishing ground for an argument in favor of its preceding baptism, it would tend to establish that precedence as universally necessary, rather than occasionally justifiable.

Argument 5.—Communion at the Lord's table is a token of brotherly love. To refuse it to any true disciple of Christ, is contrary to the spirit of brotherly love, and to the command of Christ which enjoined it.

Christ has commanded us to love every true disciple; but not to give to every one this particular token of love. Neither the law nor the spirit of brotherly love, can require us to treat our brethren otherwise than he has enjoined. We give them the love, and withhold from them the token, in obedience to the same authority, and in the exercise of the same fraternal spirit. If a right participation of the communion were the appointed means of salvation, and if baptism were necessary in order to this right participation, it would be the highest manifestation of brotherly love, to maintain firmly the practice of strict communion. Our firmness might correct an error in our brethren, which, in the case supposed, would, if persisted in, be ruinous to their eternal interests. A false tenderness might incline us not to disturb their misplaced confidence; but true Christian love would direct to a contrary course. Now, we are bound to perform every duty with the same careful regard to the divine will, as if salvation depended on it; and the true spirit of Christian love will incline us to guard our brethren against what is sinful, as well as against what is ruinous. Hence, the argument from brotherly love utterly fails to justify the practice of mixed communion, if that practice can be shown to be contrary to the mind of Christ.

Further, the argument from this topic must be inconclusive, until it be proved that brotherly love cannot subsist without a joint participation of the Lord's supper. But there are surely many modes of testifying and cherishing the warmest affection toward erring brethren, without participating in their errors. We may be ready, in obedience to Christ, to lay down our lives for our brethren—though we may choose to die, rather than, in false tenderness to them, violate the least of his commandments.

Argument 6.—A particular church differs from the church universal, only as a part differs from the whole; and, since Pedobaptist Christians are parts of the true church, they ought to be admitted to membership and communion in the particular churches.

That particular churches differ from the church universal, only as a part differs from the whole, is assumed by Mr. Hall, in his defence of mixed communion. This assumption, made without proof, is the fundamental error of his scheme. It begs the question. We call the atmosphere of a place, that part of the whole atmosphere which chances to be at the place; and if a local church is, in like manner, that part of the universal church which chances to be at the place, the question about communion is virtually decided. We cannot argue that the communion of a church shall be denied to any who have the full right of membership.

We have seen elsewhere, that the universal church is not the aggregate of the local churches, and is not strictly homogeneous with them. Hence the assumption which is fundamental to mixed communion, is erroneous.

Argument 7.—To exclude a Pedobaptist brother from communion, is substantially to inflict on him the punishment of excommunication, the punishment inflicted on atrocious offenders. Such is not the proper treatment of a fellow disciple, whose error of judgment the Lord graciously pardons.

When an advocate of open communion excludes from the Lord's table an amiable neighbor, who does not give evidence of conversion, the exclusion is not regarded as a punishment. Neither ought our exclusion of the unbaptized; much less is it right to speak of it as the punishment inflicted on atrocious offenders. The churches have no scale of penalties adjusted to different grades of crime. When they excommunicate, they withdraw their fellowship, and this may be done for wrongs of very different magnitude. There is no necessity to class the error of pedobaptism with the most atrocious of these wrongs. The church which excludes a Pedobaptist from the Lord's table, does not design to inflict a punishment on him, but merely to do its own duty, as a body to which the Lord has intrusted one of his ordinances. The simple aim is, to regulate the observance according to the will of the Lord.

Argument 8.—To reject from communion a Pedobaptist brother whom God receives, is to violate the law of toleration laid down in Romans xiv. 1-3.

The application of this rule to the question of receiving unbaptized persons to church-membership, has been considered, p. 96. The result of the examination was unfavorable to the admission of such persons; and the reasons which exclude them from church-membership, exclude them from church communion. Regarding the Lord's supper as an ordinance committed to the local churches, to be observed by them as such, the question, who are entitled to the privilege of communion, is decided by a simple principle. None are to be admitted but those who can be admitted to the membership of the church.

The argument does not claim that persons do right in communing while unbaptized, but it pleads for a toleration of their error. Since this is the plea which open communion Baptists chiefly rely on, it deserves a full examination.

It is a difficult attainment in religion, to preserve one's purity untarnished, while mingling with the men of the world, and exercising towards them all that benevolence and forbearance which the gospel enjoins. Our duty to mankind requires that we should not retire from the world, nor cherish a morose and misanthropic temper. In avoiding the error on this hand, there is danger of falling into the opposite one, and becoming too much conformed to the world. Vice is apt to appear less hateful in those whom we greatly love; and even the frequent sight of it, if we are not on our guard, will make its deformity less in our view. Hence arises a great need of much watchfulness and prayer, in those who practise that pure and undefiled religion, which requires them, on the one hand, to visit the fatherless and the widows in their affliction, and to go about doing good to all men; and, on the other hand, to keep themselves unspotted from the world.

There is a still severer trial of Christian principle. We meet it in our intercourse with Christian brethren, who love our Lord Jesus Christ, and in general obey his commandments; but walk disorderly in some matters which are deemed of minor importance. If these brethren are supposed by us, to have more spiritual knowledge than ourselves, there is much danger, lest, through the confiding nature of Christian love, and the readiness to esteem others better than ourselves, we be betrayed into their errors. Had their violations of duty been greater, a suspicion of their piety might have been awakened, and we might have been put on our guard. The man of God, who prophesied against the altar at Bethel, could not be induced, by the wicked king of Israel, to eat bread, or drink water, in the place; yet the old prophet, who came to him in the name of the Lord, found it easy to prevail. Had even he proposed some deed in itself highly criminal, the truth of his pretended message from God would have been suspected. But to eat bread and to drink water were things in themselves lawful; and the man of God too readily yielded to the old prophet, as his superior in the knowledge of the divine will, and ate and drank in violation of God's prohibition.

If we ought to guard against being led into error by our intercourse with good men, when no wrong is suspected, much more ought we, when the existence of wrong is known. But toleration implies wrong; and, if mixed communion be defended on the plea of toleration, the very defence admits that there is wrong somewhere. It becomes us, therefore, to take good heed, lest we be implicated in the wrong. The very names, toleration, forbearance, are commended to us by our sense of God's forbearance and long-suffering toward us; and the motives for their exercise are irresistible when their object is a brother in Christ. Towards such an one, how can we be otherwise than tolerant and forbearing? Shall we persecute him? God forbid. We would rather lay down our lives for him. Shall we indulge in any bitterness, or uncharitableness towards him? We will love him with pure heart fervently. Shall we, in any manner, prevent him from worshipping and serving God according to the dictates of his conscience? The very thought be far from us. Even if he err, to his own Master he standeth or falleth. We, too, are fallible and erring; and we will fervently pray that the grace which pardons our faults may pardon his also. What more do toleration and forbearance require?

When a church receives an unbaptized person, something more is done than merely to tolerate his error. There are two parties concerned. The acts of entering the church and partaking of its communion are his, and for them he is responsible. The church also acts when it admits him to membership, and authorizes his participation of the communion. The church, as an organized body, with power to receive and exclude members according to rules which Christ has laid down, is responsible for the exercise of this power.

Each individual disciple of Christ is bound, for himself, to obey perfectly the will of his Master. Whatever tolerance he may exercise towards the errors of others, he should tolerate none in himself. Though he may see but a single fault in his brother, he ought, while imitating all that brother's excellencies, carefully to avoid this fault. He may not neglect the tithing of mint, though he should find an example of such neglect accompanied with a perfect obedience of every moral precept.

In like manner each church is bound, for itself, to conform, in all its order, to the divine will. How much soever it may respect neighboring churches, which may have made high attainments in every spiritual excellence, it must not imitate them, if they neglect or corrupt any of Christ's ordinances. No argument is needed to render this clear.

The members of a church, who understand the law of Christ, are bound to observe it strictly, whatever may be the ignorance and errors of others. For them to admit unbaptized persons to membership, is to subvert a known law of Christ. Though there be unbaptized persons surpassing in every spiritual excellence, and though the candidate for admission excel them all, yet the single question for the church is, shall its order be established according to the will of God, or shall it not.

It may be asked, whether the persons whom we admit to membership and communion are not, in many cases, guilty of omitting duties more important than baptism. It may be so: and if a church sanctions these criminal neglects, it partakes in the guilt of them. Shall it, to escape the charge of the greater guilt, voluntarily assume that which is less? If Christ has given a law for the organization of churches, we have no right to substitute another, because it would be, in our judgment, more accordant with the proper estimate of moral actions. If the members of the universal church had been left to congregate into small societies, according to their spiritual instincts, if I may use the expression, and not according to a revealed law, these societies might be left to determine, by moral excellence merely, who ought to be admitted. But since it has seemed good to the Christian lawgiver, to prescribe rules for church organization, these rules should be observed. Each church should aim, in its church order, to exhibit a model of perfection to the world, though its several members may be conscious of imperfections in themselves. They should aim, as individuals, to come up to the full measure of their individual responsibility, and strive, each one, to exhibit a model of perfect obedience. If the organization and discipline of the church are not perfect, yet each member should aim to be perfect. If each member is not perfect, this lessens not the obligation to render the organization and discipline of the church perfect.

But may not each individual be left to his own conscience, and his own responsibility? He may be, and ought to be, so far as it can be done without implicating the consciences and responsibilities of others. If each were left wholly to himself, the discipline of the church would be nothing, and the power to exercise it would be attended with no responsibility. But the church is under an obligation, which cannot be transferred, to regulate its organization and discipline according to the word of God, which enjoins, on the one hand, to be tolerant and forbearing towards weak and erring brethren; and on the other hand, to keep the ordinances of God as they were delivered.

The argument for toleration is founded on the words, "Him that is weak in the faith, receive ye. * * * For God hath received him." It is a full reply to this argument, that God's receiving of the weak in faith furnishes the *rule*, as well as the reason, for our receiving of them. That God receives a man in one sense, can be no reason that we should receive him in a sense widely different. God receives an unbaptized weak believer as a member of his spiritual church, and we ought to receive him in like manner. We ought to regard him as a brother in Christ, and a fellow heir of the same inheritance. His interests should be near to our hearts, and we should welcome him to all that spiritual communion which belongs to the members of Christ's body. So, when God has received a baptized weak believer to local church-membership, we are bound to receive him in like manner, and allow him to sit with us at the table of the Lord; a privilege which, through the imperfection of church discipline, the vilest hypocrite may obtain. Unless we keep in view this important distinction, in applying this rule for toleration, it will indeed admit the unbaptized weak believer to ceremonial communion, but it will, with equal certainty, admit the hypocrite to that communion which is spiritual.

Argument 9.—The advocates of close communion are accustomed to invite Pedobaptist ministers to preach in their pulpits. To hold this pulpit communion with them, and at the same time to deny them a place at the Lord's table, is a manifest inconsistency.

If we admit the conclusion of this argument, it does not prove close communion to be wrong. Some Baptists admit the validity of the argument; and avoid the charge of inconsistency by refusing to invite Pedobaptist ministers into their pulpits. Their views will be examined hereafter, Chapter X., section 5, and we shall then attempt to show that what has been called pulpit com munion, may be vindicated in perfect consistency with the principles on which strict communion at the Lord's table is maintained.

Argument 10.—The communion table is the Lord's; and to exclude from it any of the Lord's people, the children of his family, is an offence against the whole Christian community.

There is a table which the Lord has spread, and to which every child of his family has an unquestionable right. It is a table richly furnished with spiritual food, a feast of fat things, full of marrow, of wine on the lees well refined. This table the Lord has spread for all his children, and he invites them all to come: "Eat, O friends; drink, yea drink abundantly, O beloved." Any one who should forbid their approach would offend against the community of God's children. The guests at this table have spiritual communion with one another; a species of communion which belongs of right to every member of the church universal.

There is another table which the Lord has commanded his people to spread in each local church. It is not, like the other, covered with spiritual good things, but with simple bread and wine. It is not, like the other, designed for the whole family of the Lord, but for the particular body, the local church, by whom, in obedience to divine command, it has been spread. Though human hands have set out the food, yet the table is the Lord's, because it is designed for his service, and prepared at his command; and the will of the Lord must determine who ought to partake. He knows best the purpose for which he commanded it; and, whatever may be the feelings of the guests, they have no right to invite to his table any whom the Lord has not invited.

We are aware that the practice of strict communion is considered offensive by a large part of the Christian community. We lament this fact; and if the arguments which have been adduced in defence of our practice, have failed to produce a conviction of its propriety, we would still crave from our brethren the forbearance and toleration for which they plead in behalf of the weak in faith. We conscientiously believe that we are doing the Lord's will; and we would gladly invite every child of God to unite in our simple ceremonial observance, if we had the divine approbation. But we believe that the purpose for which the observance was instituted, and the divine will by which it ought to be regulated, require the restrictions under which we act.

Does not the offence taken at our course indicate that the offended party estimate ceremonial communion too highly? To the rich feast of spiritual good which the Lord has spread, we rejoice to welcome every child of God; and we gladly accept an humble seat with them at the bountiful board. When with open hearts and hands we give this welcome, why will they be offended, if we do not also give them a crumb of our ceremonial bread, and a drop of our ceremonial wine? If the elements possessed some sacramental efficacy, there would be an apparent reason for their complaint; but regarding them as a token of union in a church organization to which our brethren object, and into which they are unwilling to enter, the ground and consistency of their complaint do not appear.

When Pedobaptists complain of our strict communion, we would remind them that they hold the principle in common with us, and practise on it in their own way. If they have aught to object, let it be at that in which we differ from them, and not at that in which we agree. The contrary course is not likely to produce unity of opinion, or to promote that harmony of Christian feeling which ought to subsist among the followers of our Lord.

When Baptists object to strict communion, we would propose the inquiry, Whether they do not attach undue importance to the eucharist, in comparison with baptism. Mr. Hall calls the eucharist a principal spiritual function.[1] In this view of it, he complains that the privilege of partaking in it should be denied to any. Is it more spiritual than baptism? If not, why should baptism be trodden under foot, to open the way of access to the eucharist? When both ceremonies were supposed to possess a saving efficacy, the proper order of their observance was still maintained; much more should it be maintained, if both are mere ceremonies. If baptism were a mere ceremony, and the eucharist a principal spiritual function, the arguments for open communion would have a force which they do not now possess: but our brethren will not defend this position.

---

[1] Vol. i. p. 322.

CHAPTER VI.

WASHING OF FEET.

WHEN JESUS REQUIRED HIS DISCIPLES TO WASH ONE ANOTHER'S FEET, HE DESIGNED, NOT TO INSTITUTE A RELIGIOUS CEREMONY, BUT TO ENFORCE A WHOLE CLASS OF MORAL DUTIES.

The requirement on the subject is contained in the following words: "If I then, your Lord and Master, have washed your feet, ye also ought to wash one another's feet."[1]

Every word of Jesus Christ is important, and every command which he has left as a rule of our conduct ought to be punctiliously obeyed. The words quoted above may be regarded as a part of his dying instructions to his apostles. Every circumstance connected with the time and manner of their being uttered, tends to invest them with interest. No one deserves the name of his disciple, who could knowingly neglect a duty recommended by such unparalleled love and condescension.

What, then, was the Saviour's meaning? "If ye know these things," says he,[2] "happy are ye if ye do them." We must know, in order to do; and if we mistake his design, how honest soever our intention may be, we shall not have fulfilled his command. If, on this memorable night, when he partook of the last passover with his disciples, and when he instituted the breaking of bread as the memorial of "Christ, our Passover, sacrificed for us," he designed to institute the washing of feet as another religious rite, till his second coming, together with baptism and the breaking of bread; then, this institution should be observed with punctilious carefulness; and no plea should be admitted from the neglect of it, to justify

---

[1] John xiii. 14.   [2] V. 17.

the neglect of any other divine command. But, if it was the Saviour's design, not to institute a religious ceremony for the observance of his disciples, but to enjoin on them a whole class of moral duties of the very highest importance, it would be a lamentable mistake, if we should substitute for these duties a mere external rite which he never meant to institute.

To ascertain the Saviour's design, let the following things be attentively considered:—

1. The particular duty enjoined is *moral*, as distinguished from those which are *positive*.

Baptism and the Lord's supper are positive institutes, because the obligation to observe them could not be inferred from any utility or apparent fitness in the things themselves. On the contrary, the washing of feet was not a mere ceremony, but a necessary act of hospitality which had been in use since the days of Abraham;[1] and it is accordingly reckoned by the Apostle Paul, in connexion with other moral duties of like kind, as the proper foundation of a reputation for good works. "Well reported of for good works, if she have lodged strangers, if she have washed the saints' feet, if she have relieved the afflicted, if she have diligently followed every good work."[2] It is the utility of the act which gives it a place among the "good" works here enumerated. In those days, when travelling was so generally performed on foot, and when the feet were shod with mere sandals; to wash the feet of the wayworn stranger was not a mere ceremony, but one of those "good works which are profitable unto men," and to be maintained "for necessary uses."[3]

2. The example of the Saviour recommends the act on the ground of its *utility*.

When Peter wished his hands and his head to be washed, "Jesus saith unto him, He that is washed needeth not, save to wash his feet." The two words here rendered *wash*, are different in the original: the former, denoting a washing of the whole body; and the latter, which is the word used elsewhere throughout the narrative, a partial washing, as of the hands or feet. The sense is—he that has been bathed, needs only to wash his feet, which may have

---

[1] Gen. xviii. 4; xix. 2.   [2] 1 Tim. v. 10.   [3] Titus iii. 8, 14.

been defiled in walking from the bath.[1] The apostles had bathed themselves before sitting down to the paschal supper, and therefore did not need any washing except of the feet. On this *need*, small as it may appear, the Saviour placed the fitness and propriety of the act which he performed. He was willing to set an example of performing the least possible act of real kindness; but he would not extend that act a whit beyond the line of necessity and utility. Beyond this line, it was no longer an act of kindness. But Jesus performed it as a good work for a necessary use; and since he therein gave to his apostles an example that they should do to each other as he had done to them,[2] it is manifest that he designed to enforce on them mutual service of practical utility.

3. It was not a *single* duty which the Saviour intended to enjoin:

This is apparent from verse 17: "If ye know *these things*, happy are ye if ye do *them*." Duties were manifestly intended beyond the single act of washing of feet. Of these duties this act was a mere specimen by which they might know the rest; and knowing, practise them.

A proof that the washing performed by our Saviour was a part and specimen of a whole class of duties, may also be derived from verse 8: "Peter saith unto him, Thou shalt never wash my feet. Jesus answered him, If I wash thee not, thou hast no part with me." The true import of this answer seems to be this: "*If I may not wash thy feet*, (so the word here used implies), *I may not, on the same ground, render to thee any of the great benefits resulting from my humiliation, in which I came not to be ministered unto, but to minister, and to give my life a ransom for many. If I may not perform to thee acts of condescending kindness, thou hast no part with me*. As in this declaration, the washing of Peter's feet

---

[1] Some interpreters take the first word to mean, not a bathing of the whole body, but a washing of the hands and face, which the disciples are supposed to have performed before taking their places at supper. "He who washeth his face and hands is considered sufficiently clean, and needs no other washing unless this mark of civility, that his feet be washed by a servant. This civility I exhibit to you, thus acting the part of a servant." This interpretation, though less satisfactory, because less conformed to the ordinary signification of the terms employed, will, nevertheless, serve equally well for sustaining the argument above presented.

[2] John xiii. 15.

was made by the Saviour a specimen and representative of all his acts of condescending kindness; so the washing of feet, enjoined upon Peter and his fellow-apostles, was intended to include all the acts of condescending kindness which they could perform towards their brethren. "A new commandment I give unto you, That ye love one another: as I have loved you, that ye also love one another: by this shall all men know that ye are my disciples, if ye have love one to another."[1]

4. It is an argument of weight against regarding the washing of feet as a religious ceremony instituted in the church, that it does not, like baptism and the Lord's supper, *typify* Christ.

The Lord's supper, in a lively figure, shows forth the death of Christ; and baptism, his burial and resurrection. These standing ordinances of the Christian church lead the mind directly to the great Author of our salvation, and to the atoning sacrifice by which that salvation had been effected. These ordinances teach us the grand doctrine of redemption, in a language which infinite wisdom has invented for the purpose. To this great doctrine these witnesses bear their testimony, in a voice, long and loud, through all the revolutions of centuries, and above all the tumults of heresy. What does the washing of feet teach us of Christ, or of redemption by Him? Does it lead the believer away from himself, and all his own works of righteousness, to the atoning sacrifice or the justifying righteousness on which he must rely for salvation? It might serve, as a religious rite, to remind those of a duty to be performed, whose faith rests upon such duty for righteousness; but of him who is the end of the law for righteousness to every one that believeth, of his suffering and death as the means of our salvation, it tells nothing.

5. The washing of feet was not practised as a religious rite by the primitive Christians.

That baptism and the Lord's supper were so practised we have the clearest evidence, both from the Scriptures and the writings of the Christian fathers; but not so with regard to the washing of feet. It is not necessary to pursue this subject beyond the clear light of Scripture, into the comparatively dark field of investigation which ecclesiastical history presents, as the testimony which

---

[1] V. 34, 35.

this less satisfactory source of evidence affords, though entirely consistent with the testimony of Scripture, is not needed, either for elucidation or confirmation. On opening the inspired history of the church, we read, at the very beginning, "They that gladly received his word were *baptized:* and they continued steadfastly in the apostles' doctrine, and fellowship, and in breaking of bread, and in prayers." Baptism is frequently mentioned in the subsequent history, and in the 20th chap. 7th verse express mention is made that "the disciples came together to break bread." But not a chapter, not a verse, in all the Acts of the Apostles, contains an intimation that any church, or any company of disciples, ever assembled to celebrate the washing of feet. In the Epistle to the Romans,[1] a reference is made to baptism, and an explanation given of its import. The first chapter of the next epistle (the first to the Corinthians), contains an account of several baptisms; and the 11th chapter a very particular account of the institution of the supper, and of abuses in its observance, which had already crept into the church of Corinth. But in these epistles, and in all those which follow, no allusion whatever is found to the washing of feet, as a rite observed by the churches.

There is, indeed, one passage, and only one, in which the washing of feet is mentioned; and this passage, 1 Tim. v. 10, furnishes decisive proof that it was not practised as a church ordinance, as were baptism and the Lord's supper. To demonstrate this, we have but to substitute, in the passage, the mention of these acknowledged ordinances, and the incongruity of such a connexion will immediately appear: "Well reported of for good works; if she have brought up children, if she have lodged strangers, if she have been baptized, or received the Lord's supper, if she have relieved the afflicted, if she have diligently followed every good work." As it must be supposed of every widow in the church that she had been baptized, and had received the Lord's supper; no "if," with respect to these ordinances, could be admitted, and no one widow could, on account of her having observed them, be more entitled to honor than any other. The same would have been true concerning the washing of feet, if this also had been a religious rite in common use in the churches; and it would have been a manifest absurdity to state the fact of any church member hav-

---

[1] Chap. vi.

ing performed the rite, as a reason for regarding him or her as specially entitled to reputation for good works, or to honor from the church.

There is, therefore, not only a total want of proof that such a religious rite was anciently observed, but there is (what few cases in controversy furnish) a proof of the negative, which is as clear and satisfactory as any such proof can be expected to be.

These considerations show clearly that it was the Saviour's design to enforce a whole class of moral duties, and not to institute a religious ceremony; and that he was so understood by his apostles. He who washes the feet of a saint, when those feet do not need washing, is as if he gave a cup of cold water to a disciple who is not thirsty. He may indeed make a show of voluntary humility, but he does not fulfil the command of Christ, nor imitate his example. He ought to remember that Christ declined to wash the hands and head of Peter; not because there would have been less show of humility in so doing, but because those parts did not need washing. He, therefore, who washes the feet of a saint when these feet do not need washing, instead of obeying or imitating Christ, does that which Christ refused to do. And he who washes the feet of a saint merely as a religious rite, without considering or caring whether the act which he performs is necessary and useful, is just as far as the other from obeying or imitating the Redeemer.

If, after a careful consideration of the subject, we have satisfactorily ascertained that our Saviour designed his disciples should perform towards each other every needful act of condescending kindness, even the smallest and the most servile, let us be ready with promptness and pleasure to fulfil his will. If we know these things, happy are we if we do them. If we have the spirit of Christ, we shall be ready, when need requires, to lay down our lives for our brethren, or give them a cup of cold water, or wash their feet, or render them any other comfort. In so far as by any of these means we seek to promote the happiness of a disciple of Christ, our good deeds will be remembered; and the great Judge, in the last day, omitting all mention of our most labored religious ceremonies, will bring that act of kindness to mind, and will say, "Inasmuch as ye did it to one of the least of these my brethren, ye did it unto me."

CHAPTER VII.

PUBLIC WORSHIP.

Section I.—TIME.

The first day of the week is the Christian sabbath, and is specially appropriate for the public worship of God.

The computation of time by weeks, appears to have prevailed at a very early period. It may be traced back to the time of Laban, who said to Jacob: "Fulfil her week."[1] A less visible trace of it may be seen in the account given of Noah, who waited "seven days:" and afterwards "another seven days,"[2] in his attempts to discover whether the deluge had subsided. The hebdomadal division of time existed very early in the gentile world; and no account of its origin is so probable, as that it was received from Noah, the father of the new world. No evidence appears, that Noah received it as a new institution from God; or that it originated with him. The statement of Scripture is, "God rested on the seventh day: wherefore God blessed the seventh day, and sanctified it."[3] This is the origin of the institution. When the decalogue was promulgated from Sinai, it did not speak of the sabbath as an institution before unknown. The command, "Remember the sabbath day,"[4] implies a knowledge of its existence; and this is confirmed by the previous historical fact, that the fall of manna had ceased on the sabbath day.

Since the sabbath originated at the creation, and was known before the giving of the law to the Israelites, it cannot be one of the abrogated Jewish ceremonies. The sabbath was made for man; and not exclusively for the Hebrews. The reason for it is

---

[1] Gen. xxi. 27. [2] Gen. viii. 10, 12. [3] Gen. ii. 2, 3.
[4] Ex. xx. 8.

taken from God's rest on the seventh day, after six days' work in creating the world; and not from anything that pertained specially to the nation of Israel. The institution is adapted to the nature of man, as a religious being, and the relation which he sustains to his Creator.

The decalogue was given as a law to the Israelites. Its preface shows this: "I am the Lord thy God, which have brought thee out of the land of Eygpt." It is further proved by the promise annexed to the fifth commandment: "That thy days may be long in the land which the Lord thy God giveth thee." But, though given to the Israelites, it was given to them as men. The ceremonial law was given to them, as the Congregation of the Lord; and the judicial law was given to them as the Nation of Israel. But the decalogue was adapted to the relations which they bore to God and one another, as men. The same relations are in human society everywhere; and therefore the same obligations bind everywhere. This part of the Mosaic code possesses universal and perpetual obligation; and this part, God specially distinguished from all the rest. He pronounced it audibly from Sinai, and twice engraved it in stone, in token of its perpetuity. In writing to gentiles at Rome, and at Ephesus, Paul refers to the decalogue, as a law which they were bound to obey;[1] and has thus decided that it was not peculiar to the Jews, or confined to the abrogated covenant. The ministration of the law in the letter, he distinguishes from the ministration of the Spirit, and declares it to be done away when the veil is taken away from the heart;[2] but the change then wrought does not consist in making a new law, but in transferring the writing from the tables of stone, to the fleshly tables of the heart.

Among the precepts of the decalogue, we find the command: "Remember the sabbath day." As the whole decalogue binds us, so does this commandment. No man has a right to separate it from the rest, and claim exemption from its obligation. Christians, therefore, must observe the sabbath; and, as a day which God has hallowed, it is specially appropriate for the public worship of God.

Some Baptists, in a conscientious regard to the divine com-

---

[1] Rom. xiii. 8—10; Eph. vi. 2.   [2] 2 Cor. iii. 6—12.

mands, observe the same day for their sabbath that the Jews observe, and are thence called Seventh Day Baptists. But they mistake, as we conceive, the true import of the precept. They interpret it, as if it had been expressed "The seventh day *of the week* is the sabbath," and as if the Jewish division of the week were recognised and fixed; whereas the language is, "Six days shalt thou labor, and do all thy work; but the seventh day is the sabbath of the Lord thy God." The seventh day, is that which follows six days of labor; and the words of the precept express no more. From the nature of the case, the regular return of the sabbath, at equally distant intervals of time, must be expected to follow. We may have light thrown on the true meaning of the language employed, by comparing it with that which enjoined the observance of the sabbatical year. The comparison may be advantageously made for this purpose, by examining a passage in which the sabbatical day and the sabbatical year are both enjoined.[1] "Six years thou shalt sow thy land, and shalt gather in the fruits thereof; but the seventh year thou shalt let it rest, and lie still." "Six days thou shalt do thy work, and on the seventh day thou shalt rest." As the seventh year is not determined by a natural division of time into weeks of years; so the seventh day is not determined by a natural division of time into weeks of days. No one thinks of the seventh year otherwise than as the year which follows six years of regular toil in the cultivation of the earth, and as regularly returning at equal intervals. The precise similarity of the command enjoining the observance of the seventh day sabbath, proves that the same method of interpretation must be applied to it. If an obligation exists to observe Saturday, or Sunday, rather than any other day of the week, it cannot be found in this precept of the decalogue, and must be made out in some other way.

The decalogue, in its admirable adaptedness to the relations in human society, displays the wisdom of its Author. We may see this wisdom in the adaptedness of the fourth commandment to universal observance. Since the rotundity of the earth has been demonstrated, it has become apparent, that a precept requiring the observance of the seventh day of the week, could not be

---

[1] Exodus xxiii. 10, 12.

obeyed universally, unless some meridian were established by divine authority for the universal computation of time. A few years ago it was stated in some of our missionary intelligence, that a practical question of duty in the observance of the sabbath had arisen between some missionaries, who had met at their field of labor on the other side of the globe, having sailed to it by different routes, some by the eastern and others by the western. On comparing their computation, their sabbaths differed; and what was Saturday to one party was Sunday to the other. If the seventh day *of the week* had been commanded, these missionaries could not have obeyed without becoming sabbath-breakers to each other; and if no higher wisdom than that of Moses, who was ignorant of the earth's true form, had dictated the decalogue, its admirable adaptedness to the condition and circumstances of men, in every age and country, and under every meridian, would not have been secured.

Another objection to the interpretation which supposes the seventh day of the week to be prescribed, may be seen in the fact that it makes Scripture dependent on tradition. Had the observance of the new moon, or of the full moon, been commanded, the means of ascertaining the time intended would have been within the reach of every one; but had the Scripture commanded to observe the seventh day of the week, who could know the day required? No banner is hung out in the sky, to distinguish it from the other days of the week. The revolution and boundaries of the week are not determined, like the revolution of the seasons, by any natural phenomena. The precept, once engraven in stone, and now indelibly recorded in God's book, would stand before us, binding each individual conscience to obedience; and yet the precept itself would give no clue by which to ascertain its true meaning. How could each individual know that he did not mistake the time, and profane the very day that God had hallowed? He has no other means of knowledge than tradition. The right sabbath may have been handed down without mistake, from the time of the creation, or from the time of Moses; but what proof have we? None but tradition. God has wisely decided to make known his will to men by Scripture, rather than by tradition; but what is the advantage, if the meaning of Scripture must be determined by tradition?

Another argument for our interpretation of the precept, may be drawn, from the word employed in the New Testament, to denote a week. It is the same word that is rendered sabbath, appearing sometimes in the singular form, sometimes in the plural. Take, for an example, the phrase "the first day of the week,"[1] which, literally rendered, is, "the first day of the sabbath or sabbaths." This may be explained, the first day according to the computation of the sabbath or sabbaths. But, however explained, it indicates that the sabbath determined the week, and not the week the sabbath.

According to the view which we have taken of the fourth commandment, Christians obey it, as literally as the Jews. The latter derive their series of weeks by tradition from the time of Moses; we derive ours by tradition from the time of Christ. We see with pleasure, the beginning of our series, in the brief accounts of Scripture, where the day on which Christians met for worship, is specified. On the first day of the week our Lord rose from the dead. This day was filled with the tidings and proofs of his resurrection, and with the admiration and joy of the disciples, and was closed with a meeting of the disciples, in which Jesus appeared in person. In his account of this meeting, the evangelist is careful to repeat that it was on *the first day of the week*.[2]

Another week rolled around, and a meeting of the disciples was held, in which Jesus was again present. A Jewish sabbath had intervened; and if it had been the Lord's design to perpetuate this sabbath, as the day of public worship for his disciples, why did he allow it to pass, and reserve the second joyful interview with his assembled people, to the ensuing day? The evangelist's statement is, "After eight days again his disciples were within, and Thomas with them; then came Jesus, the doors being shut, and stood in the midst."[3] When the chief priests applied to Pilate to have the sepulchre guarded, they said, "that deceiver said, while he was yet alive, after three days will I rise again. Command, therefore, that the sepulchre be made sure until the third day."[4] Here the phrase "after three days," is equivalent to "until the third day." If the phrase, "after eight days," in the above quotation from John, be

---

[1] John xx. 1.   [2] John xx. 19.   [3] John xx. 26.
[4] Matt. xxvii. 63, 64.

interpreted in the same manner, it will bring Christ's second interview with his disciples just one week after the first, and therefore on the first day of the week. The feast of Pentecost occurred according to the law,[1] on the day following the Jewish sabbath. It was therefore on the first day of the week, that the Holy Spirit was poured out, and three thousand converted under the preaching of Peter.

The disciples at Troas met together to break bread;[2] and the inspired historian is careful to tell us, that it was on "the first day of the week." In writing to the Corinthians, Paul directed them, in making their religious contribution for the poor saints at Jerusalem, "On the first day of the week, let every one of you lay by him in store, as God hath prospered him."[3] In describing the wonderful revelation which he received on the isle of Patmos, John says, "I was in the Spirit on the Lord's day."[4] By this phrase, he seems to designate the day on which our Lord arose, and which had been consecrated to his worship.

As the Mosaic revelation displays divine wisdom, in its mode of exhibiting the fourth commandment; so does the Christian revelation, in its mode of recommending the first day of the week to our observance. The old covenant, with its priesthood, and forms of worship, had passed away, and there was a fitness in instituting a new form of worship to be introduced, and it was fit that the resurrection of our Lord should begin the new computation, and be commemorated by it. But while the first day of the week is expressly mentioned, had the observance of it been expressly commanded, the same difficulties would have originated, that would have attended the observance of the seventh day of the week. It would have rendered the Christian Scriptures dependent on tradition for their interpretation, and the Christian sabbath impossible to be observed throughout the world, in strict obedience to the requirement. As the matter has been left, the decalogue is transmitted to us, requiring the consecration of one day in seven; and the New Testament teaches us, that no times are holy in themselves; and that the regard which the Jews demanded, for the day on which they kept their weekly sabbath, and for their other holy days, so far from

---

[1] Lev. xxiii. 16.   [2] Acts xx. 7.   [3] 1 Cor. xvi. 2.
[4] Rev. i. 10.

being obligatory on Christians, is inconsistent with the nature of the Christian economy.[1] The proportion and the succession of time, as prescribed in the fourth commandment, are obligatory; but no particular periods of duration have in themselves special sanctity. We are bound by the example of the apostles, to observe the first day of the week as the Christian sabbath; but not in such a sense as to fetter the conscience with insuperable difficulty, in such a case as that of the missionaries before mentioned.

The worship, adapted to the day, requires to be social; and each individual Christian may unite with his brethren, in the worship of God, on the day set apart for it, with the full conviction that, in so doing, he is honoring the Author of Christianity, and strictly obeying the decalogue.

Section II.—MODE.

PUBLIC WORSHIP SHOULD INCLUDE PRAYERS, SONGS OF PRAISE, AND THE READING AND EXPOUNDING OF GOD'S WORD.

Prayer is a natural duty of man, confined to no particular condition of life, or dispensation of religion. It may be performed in private, in the family, in companies accidentally brought together, or designedly convened for the purpose; and in public assemblies for divine worship, it ought always to make a part of the service.

In public prayer, one of the worshippers leads the service, speaking audibly, as Solomon did at the dedication of the temple, and the rest unite in heart in the devotions and supplications. The leading part in the service may be performed by the ministers of the word. The first Christians continued steadfastly in the apostles' doctrine, fellowship, breaking of bread, and prayers. All these, including the prayers, were directed by the apostles; and, when the apostles were relieved from ministering to tables, it was that they might give themselves to the word of God and to prayer. Private prayer cannot be exclusively intended here; for the obligation to this belonged equally to the deacons elected, and to all the members of the church. But, though the ministers of the word may, in general, most advantageously lead in public prayer,

---

[1] Col. ii. 16; Gal. iv. 10, 11; Rom. xiv. 5, 6.

other male members of the church may do it with propriety and benefit. "I will that men pray everywhere."[1] The word rendered "men," properly denotes persons of the male sex, and is distinguished from "the women" mentioned in the next verse. The intimation plainly made, is, that females are not expected to lead in public prayer. This accords with the words of Paul: "It is a shame for women to speak in the church," or public assembly. But there is great propriety in the separate meeting of females for prayer, and much benefit results to themselves and the cause of God.

The Saviour gave a form of prayer to his disciples, for a help and general directory; but it is manifest that the disciples never understood that they were restricted to this form, either in private or in public. Prescribed forms of prayer are objectionable, because they restrain the emotions of the heart, discourage dependence on the Holy Spirit, tend to produce formality, and are not adapted to all circumstances and occasions.

Praise may be mingled with the petitions and thanksgivings offered in prayer; and is then, like these, expressed in prose, and with the ordinary voice. But poetry and music are specially appropriate in the expression of praise. They were used in early times, and formed an important part of the temple worship. In the New Testament, we find frequent use of singing; and it is expressly commanded in several passages.[2] The phrase "admonishing one another in psalms," &c., being addressed to a church, sufficiently indicates that singing was designed to be a part of the church's public worship.

The book of Psalms was composed for the temple worship. It serves as a help and general directory in this part of the public service; but there is no proof that our praises ought to be expressed in no words but those found in this book. We have no book of prayers in the Bible; and we learn from this that a book of prayers is not needed in our public worship; but we have a book of Psalms, because, in a service in which many are to speak together, they cannot speak the same things without previous preparation. We learn hence the lawfulness of using hymn-books; and experience has proved their great utility.

---

[1] 1 Tim. ii. 8. [2] Col. iii. 16; Eph. v. 19; James v. 13.

Instrumental music formed a part of the temple worship; but it is nowhere commanded in the New Testament; and it is less adapted to the more spiritual service of the present dispensation.

In public worship, we not only address God in prayer and praise, but we honor him by reverent attention to his word, in which he speaks to us. The reading of the Scriptures formed an important part of the synagogue service, and was sanctioned by the Saviour, when, in the synagogue at Nazareth, he read from the prophet Isaiah. In Paul's direction to Timothy, "Give attendance to reading, to exhortation, and to doctrine,"[1] as the exhortation and doctrine or teaching were to be parts of the public service to be performed for the benefit of others, there is no reason to suppose that the reading which is commanded was to be exclusively private. The public reading of God's word appears to be at least included. In the days of Ezra, when the Scriptures were read, the sense was shown to the people.[2] When Christ read in the synagogue at Nazareth, on closing the book, he expounded and applied the passage which had been read. The direction to Timothy required that exhorting and teaching should be added to reading. God is honored when his word is so expounded to the people, that they not only hear the sound with the ear, but receive the meaning of it in their understandings, and feel its power in their hearts. God has graciously provided men who are able so to expound and exhort; and every church ought to seek the help of such gifts.

---

[1] 1 Tim. iv. 13.   [2] Neh. viii. 8.

CHAPTER VIII.

THE MINISTRY.

SECTION I.—MINISTRY OF THE WORD.

THE MINISTERS OF CHRIST ARE A SEPARATE CLASS OF PERSONS, DISTINGUISHED BY A SPECIAL DIVINE CALL TO PREACH THE WORD.

A DISTINCT CLASS.

The ministers of Christ are, like ordinary Christians, separate from the world. They are partakers of the heavenly calling, by which men are brought out of the world, and made the servants of Christ. In all his epistles to the churches, Paul claims to be a fellow-saint with them, a member of the same spiritual family, and an heir of the same heavenly inheritance. Throughout the Scriptures, the ministers of Christ are spoken of as persons who love Christ, and are from the heart devoting themselves to his service. They must therefore be of the number who are "called to be saints."

The ministers of Christ are also separate from ordinary Christians. They are one with ordinary Christians, as being called in one hope of their calling; but, besides the call to repentance and faith, which they have received in common with their brethren, they have been called to special service in the Lord's cause. It is clear, from the Holy Scriptures, that there were, among the first Christians, persons to whom the work of the ministry was specially intrusted. Paul says, concerning these, God "hath given to us the ministry of reconciliation."[1] "Giving no offence, that the ministry be not blamed."[2] "Who hath made us able ministers of

---

[1] 2 Cor. v. 18. [2] 2 Cor. vi. 3.

the new testament."[1] He speaks of himself, as counted faithful, and put "into the ministry;"[2] and of the special grace given to him, that he should preach among the gentiles the unsearchable riches of Christ.[3] The bestowment by the Holy Spirit of special qualifications for special service in the Lord's cause, is plainly taught in 1 Cor. xii., and Eph. iv. The inquiry, "Are all apostles? are all prophets?"[4] &c., shows that the offices designated did not belong to the whole body of the saints.

The separation of the ministry from the mass of ordinary Christians, is not like the separation of Christians from the world. In the latter case, they cease to be of the world, and become strangers and pilgrims in the earth. But men who enter the ministry, do not cease to be saints. Saul and Barnabas were separated unto the work to which the Holy Ghost had called them; but this separation did not take from them a place among the saints and faithful in Christ Jesus. John speaks, concerning the whole company of the saints: "We are of God; and the whole world lieth in wickedness."[5] Here is a strong line of division, like that which separates land and water. But the ministry appears, among the people of God, like the mountains on a continent, forming a part of it, and closely united with surrounding lands. Eminent spiritual gifts distinguish the ministers; but the same spirit that actuates them, pervades the whole body of Christ. All the disciples of Christ are bound, according to their ability, to advance the cause of their Master, and labor for the illumination and salvation of men: and the diversity of talent among the ordinary disciples, may be compared to the diversity of hill and valley in the ordinary face of the country. But ministers are distinguished, by their superior qualifications for service, from the ordinary mass of Christians, like mountains rising above the common undulations of the surrounding landscape.

The special qualifications which the Holy Spirit bestows, bind him on whom they are bestowed to use them in the service of Christ. They are given to fit him for this service, and they constitute a divine call for him to engage in it. They are not given

---

[1] 2 Cor. iii. 6.   [2] 1 Tim. i. 12.   [3] Eph. iii. 8.
[4] 1 Cor. xii. 29.   [5] 1 John v. 19.

to confer a privilege merely, but they are a solemn call to duty—a call demanding the service of the whole life.

The apostles, when called by Christ, immediately left their secular employments, and gave themselves ever afterwards to the service of their Lord. Paul, when called, conferred not with flesh and blood. The work of the ministry did not cease, when these holy men left the earth; but other persons have been fitted to carry it on, by the same Spirit that qualified them for the peculiar service. He bestows his gifts " for the perfecting of the saints, for the work of the ministry, for the edifying of the body of Christ, till we all come in the unity of the faith, and of the knowledge of the Son of God, unto a perfect man, unto the measure of the stature of the fullness of Christ."[1]

The ministers of Christ are not a separate class of men in such a sense as to constitute them an organized society. They are fellow-laborers in the Lord's service, but have no power over one another; and have no authority from Christ to combine themselves into an ecclesiastical judicatory to exercise power in any manner. They are all on a level as brethren; are the servants of Christ, and the servants of the churches.

THEIR WORK.

The special service for which the ministry is designed is the preaching of the word. The obligation to spread the knowledge of Christ is shared, to some extent, by all Christians. The effectual call of the Holy Spirit, by which any man is brought to repentance and faith, imposes on him an obligation to show forth the praises of him who hath called him out of darkness into his marvellous light; to let his light shine before men, that they, seeing his good works, may glorify his Father in heaven; and to hold forth the word of life. Every Christian is bound to do what he can for the conversion of others, and for spreading the knowledge of the truth. But special gifts are conferred on some, accompanied with special obligations. These constitute a special call to the ministry of the word.

During the Saviour's personal ministry he made many disciples:

---

[1] Eph. iv. 12, 13.

but he did not intrust to them equally and indiscriminately the work of spreading the knowledge of his religion. He sent forth seventy with a special commission to preach the kingdom of God. He chose the apostles to be his immediate attendants and special witnesses, and gave them a commission—"Go preach the gospel to every creature. * * * Go make disciples, teaching them," &c. Preaching and teaching were prominent and important parts of the service required of them. When Paul was made an apostle, the commission to him, as explained by himself, was to preach the gospel: "Christ sent me, not to baptize, but to preach the gospel." The obligation which he felt to perform this service was beyond that imposed on ordinary Christians, and was exceedingly pressing: "Necessity is laid upon me; yea, wo is unto me if I preach not the gospel."[1] With him, to preach the gospel was not to utter a proclamation in a brief sentence; but at Troas he preached to a late hour of the night. In his ministry teaching was conjoined with preaching, and included in it: "Whereunto I am ordained a preacher and an apostle, a teacher of the Gentiles in faith and verity."[2]

The obligation of particular men to give themselves to the ministry of the word was intended to be a perpetual arrangement, and not confined to the ministers appointed by Christ in person. Timothy was specially appointed to this service, and was commanded, "Preach the word; be instant in season, out of season; reprove, rebuke, and exhort, with all long suffering and doctrine."[3] "Make full proof of thy ministry."[4] "Neglect not the gift that is in thee."[5] A special gift and a special obligation are here clearly recognised, and the duty to be performed is clearly preaching, in the comprehensive sense in which teaching is included. Paul had committed the gospel to Timothy; nor was the succession to cease in him. "The things which thou hast heard of me, the same commit thou to faithful men, who shall be able to teach others also."[6] Special ability and special obligation to preach and teach were to be perpetuated in men, separated to the service from the body of Christ's disciples.

---

[1] 1 Cor. ix. 16.
[2] 1 Tim. ii. 7.
[3] 2 Tim. iv. 2.
[4] 2 Tim. iv. 5.
[5] 1 Tim. iv. 14.
[6] 2 Tim. ii. 2.

THEIR CALL.

The ministers of the word receive a special call from God, directing them to the service. The Jewish priests were a separate class of people, distinguished from the rest of the nation by natural descent from Aaron. The Congregation of the Lord was perpetuated by natural descent; and if the Christian church had been a continuation of it, we might expect its ministry to be perpetuated in the same way. But the members of the church are separated from the rest of the world by a divine call; and it is suitable that the ministers of the church should be distinguished in the same manner; accordingly, their designation to office is ascribed to God. "God hath set some in the church, first apostles," &c., and the qualifications for the work are the special gift of the Spirit.[1]

The Holy Spirit calls to the ministry of the word none but true Christians, members of Christ's spiritual body. The apostles were chosen to be the personal attendants of the Saviour, and special witnesses of his daily life and ministry. Though he knew, from the beginning, the hypocrisy and treachery of Judas Iscariot, he chose to have a traitor among his witnesses. The blameless character of the Redeemer extorted, even from this man, the testimony, "I have sinned, in that I have betrayed the innocent blood." This testimony is of great value to Christianity. Had Christ been an impostor, had there been a scheme to deceive the people, Judas must have known it. His testimony, confirmed by his return of the money with which he had been bribed, and by his suicide, banishes every suspicion dishonorable to the Saviour. It was therefore wisely ordered that Judas should be among the apostles. But he was not among them when the last commission was given, under which we now act. When the Holy Spirit calls men to the ministry, he bestows on them qualifications for the work—qualifications both of head and heart. The qualifications of the heart include a sincere desire to glorify God, and save souls; a desire never felt by the unregenerate. Hence, the Holy Spirit never makes unregenerate ministers. When such men enter the sacred office, they, in the language of Paul, are "ministers of Satan."

---

[1] 1 Cor. xii. 11.

As true ministers are members of Christ's spiritual body, so their ministry is intended for its benefit:—"for the perfecting of the saints, for the work of the ministry, for the edifying of the body of Christ." Their office pertains to the spiritual, universal church, of which they are all members. The ministry of some of them may have a relation also to local churches, placed under their special charge; but they serve in these for the good of the whole body of Christ.

In Ephesians iv. 11, Paul enumerates the officers whom God set in the church: "Some apostles, some prophets, some evangelists," &c. Of these the first three are not confined to local churches, but are ministers of the church universal. This is apparent, from the words of Paul: "Who now rejoice in my sufferings for you, and fill up that which is behind of the afflictions of Christ, in my flesh, for his body's sake, which is the church, whereof I am made a minister."[1]

The apostles were, according to the import of the name, persons *sent forth*. The term is applied specially to those whom Christ sent forth in person, and who are called the apostles *of Christ*. Paul claimed to be an apostle in this sense: "Am I not an apostle? Have I not seen Jesus Christ our Lord?"[2] And again: "Paul, an apostle, not of men, neither by man, but by Jesus Christ."[3] Paul numbered himself among the witnesses of Christ's resurrection, and the apostles were chosen to be witnesses of this fact. Peter, when he proposed the election of one to take the place of Judas, stated the qualifications necessary for an apostle in this manner: "Wherefore of these men which have companied with us all the time that the Lord Jesus went in and out among us, beginning from the baptism of John, unto that same day that he was taken up from us, must one be ordained to be a witness with us of his resurrection."[4] These qualifications cannot now be found in any man living, and therefore the apostolic office has necessarily ceased.

The name apostle is applied, in another sense, to Barnabas,[5] the companion of Paul. These two ministers had been *sent forth* by the Holy Ghost, from Antioch, to a special work. Barnabas is probably called an apostle, with reference to this fact; and, in this

---

[1] Col. i. 24, 25. [2] 1 Cor. ix. 1. [3] Gal. i. 1.
[4] Acts i. 21, 22. [5] Acts xiv. 14.

sense, the term corresponds in signification to our modern name, *missionary*. Paul and Barnabas had been sent forth as missionaries, on a tour of missionary service.

Prophets were persons divinely inspired to make revelation from God, consisting sometimes in the foretelling of future events. This office was needed, before the volume of divine revelation was completed. The absence of the prophetic gift in modern times, demonstrates that the Holy Spirit, who imparts every needful gift, accounts further revelation unnecessary. The absence of the gift proves the sufficiency of the Scriptures, and the cessation of the prophetic office.

Evangelists were persons employed in the spread of the gospel. They appear to have labored in connection with the apostles, to extend the religion of Christ and plant new churches. They did not need miraculous endowments for their work; and therefore their office continues to the present time. Every minister of the word, when he labors, not for the special benefit of a local church, but for the spread of the gospel, is doing the work of an evangelist.[1] Timothy was required to do this, though remaining at Ephesus, and laboring for the interest of that particular church.

A knowledge of gospel truth, an aptness to teach, and a heart moved by the desire to glorify God in the salvation of souls, are the evidences of a divine call to the work of the ministry. All these qualifications may exist, in a measure, in ordinary Christians; and a proportionate obligation accompanies them, to use them in the Redeemer's service. No church, no minister of the gospel, can, under a proper influence, forbid the exercise of these gifts, where they exist. Moses repelled the suggestion to forbid some who prophesied; and said, "Would God that all the Lord's people were prophets."[2] An active, prudent employment of the gifts possessed by ordinary Christians, would promote incalculably the interests of religion; and the restriction of all labor for the spread of the gospel, and the promotion of piety, to a select few, is greatly detrimental to the cause of Christ.

But it is still true, that there are some whose gifts for public usefulness rise high above the rest; and, in bestowing superior qualifications, the Holy Spirit, who divides to every man severally as

---

[1] 2 Tim. iv. 5.   [2] Num. xi. 29.

he will, has indicated his will that the possessor of the qualifications should use them for the work of the ministry, for the edifying of the body of Christ.

The Holy Spirit works harmoniously in all the parts of his operation. He diffuses one sympathy through all the body of Christ, so that the eye cannot say to the hand, I have no need of thee. When qualifications for service are imparted by the Spirit to one member, other members, under the influence of the same Spirit, welcome its service. Hence, every man who believes alone, that he is called of God to the ministry, has reason to apprehend that he is under delusion. If he finds that those who give proof that they honor God and love the souls of men, do not discover his ministerial qualifications, he has reason to suspect that they do not exist. The Head of the church has graciously provided, that in the ordinary course of things, men are able to obtain counsel in this matter, and are not compelled to act on their individual responsibility. If, in some extraordinary case, he calls some men to stand alone, as Elijah did, in defence of the truth, this gives no just plea to others to isolate themselves, and act on their own responsibility, when circumstances do not demand it. Elijah's proof of a divine call to the prophetical office consisted wholly in his possession of the prophetical spirit; but Elisha had the additional proof, that he had been anointed to the office by Elijah. Such proof, in ordinary cases, the Holy Spirit has provided for the ministers of the word; and the use of it is necessary to the success of the ministry and the order of the churches.

When any one is introduced into the ministry, the highest responsibility, next to that which he himself sustains, devolves on the ministers with whom he is to associate as a fellow-laborer. On the ministers a peculiar responsibility rests, to pray that laborers may be sent into the harvest; and also to seek out and encourage gifts for the work, and thus continue the succession of laborers. It was made the special duty of Timothy, to look out faithful men, able to teach others, that he might commit the ministry of the word to them. It was to the ministers of the church at Antioch, that the Holy Ghost said, "Separate me Saul and Barnabas for the work whereunto I have called them;"[1] and the

---

[1] Acts xiii. 2.

public designation of them to the work, appears to have been made by these ministers, doubtless with the concurrence of the church. In this method of procedure, there is an obvious fitness. It was fit that Elisha should be anointed to the prophetical office by a prophet. Men whom the Spirit has filled with a burning desire to preach the gospel, and has qualified for the service, are the most suitable persons to look out aids in the service, and judge of their fitness. Hence the obligation was laid on Timothy, already a minister. Hence the duty imposed on Titus: "For this cause left I thee in Crete, that thou shouldst ordain elders in every city." Hence the instructions respecting the qualifications necessary for office, are given in the epistles to these ministers, rather than in those to the churches.

The propriety of ministerial concurrence, in public designation to the ministerial office, appears from the nature of the case apart from apostolic example. But we have apostolic example to assist our reasoning. Saul and Barnabas were solemnly set apart by their brethren in the ministry, with fasting, prayer, and imposition of hands. In this case, he who was not a whit behind the chief of the apostles, bent before those who had no pretensions to apostolic authority, that he might receive the imposition of hands. What a sanction did his act give to the solemn ceremony, and to the established church order, of which it was a part! If such solemn services are appropriate in public designation to a particular service in the ministry, much more are they appropriate when any one enters the ministry itself. We learn from other Scriptures that such services were performed. Paul mentions the appointment of Timothy to the ministerial office in these words: "Neglect not the gift that is in thee, which was given thee by prophecy, with the laying on of the hands of the presbytery."[1]

It has been a question whether the concurrence of a single minister is sufficient in ordination. We have no explicit instruction on this point. From the instruction to Titus, it appears that he alone was authorized to ordain elders in every city. Yet Paul, though a minister of superior authority, did not ordain Timothy alone. He was the chief agent in the work; and says, "By the putting on of my hands;"[2] but yet he chose not to act alone, and

---

[1] 1 Tim. iv. 14.   [2] 2 Tim. i. 6.

therefore he says in another place, "By the laying on of the hands of the presbytery." The concurrence of a presbytery might not be possible in every city of Crete, where the churches had been recently planted; but where it was possible, even Paul with his apostolic authority chose not to act without it. We have, therefore, apostolic example confirming our reasoning on the subject, that where a presbytery can be obtained, its concurrence ought to be procured. The minister, who, from the direction given to Titus, takes it upon himself alone to ordain to the sacred office, assumes a power which Paul himself did not assume.

The institution of local churches has divine authority, and ought to be respected by every disciple of Christ. It is the duty of every one to become a member of some local church, and walk with the other members in love and Christian obedience. Brethren so connected are bound to exhort one another to diligence in the duties for which they are severally qualified. The obligation of a member to labor in the ministry may be recognised by his church, and the church does not go out of its proper sphere when it exhorts to this duty. Paul directed the church at Colosse, "Say to Archippus, take heed to the ministry which thou hast received in the Lord, that thou fulfil it."[1] He did not send the message to Archippus as from himself, but instructed the church to perform this duty. Such exhortation to a minister is therefore proper to be given by a church; and it follows, that a church is not without responsibility as to the question whether its gifted members are using their gifts as they ought. This responsibility makes the church a party in ministerial ordination. We have no express declaration that the church at Antioch concurred in the setting apart of Saul and Barnabas; but it may be inferred, not only from the tenor of the narrative, but especially from the fact that these missionaries, on their return, reported their doings to the whole church.

All the parties concerned in ordination ought to seek the guidance of the Holy Spirit, and act under his influence. The highest responsibility rests on him who is entering the sacred office. He should act under a deep sense of his responsibility, and with a persuasion, the result of prayerful, heart-searching examination, that he is moved by the Holy Ghost. The presbytery have the next

---

[1] Col. iv. 17.

degree of responsibility. They should be persuaded that the Holy Spirit has called the candidate to the ministry; and be prepared, under this conviction, the result of due examination, to receive him as a fellow-laborer with them in the Lord's service. The lowest degree of responsibility rests on the church; but even this is solemn and important. The same Spirit dwells in the ministry and in the churches; and every member is concerned in whatever concerns the spiritual body of Christ. A hearty concurrence of the church is necessary in the ordination; and, without it, a presbytery should never act. When a candidate has the threefold testimony, of his own conscience, of the presbytery, and of the church, he may proceed to labor in the ministry, with an assurance that he is "sent forth by the Holy Ghost."

Every step in the process of ordination recognises the principle that a divine call is necessary to a proper entrance on the ministerial office. The candidate, the presbytery, the church, all admit it, and act on it. This principle is of great importance to the preservation of a spiritual and efficient ministry; and it cannot be neglected, without immense evil to the cause of pure religion. When a father chooses the ministry as a profession for his son, or when the son chooses it for himself, as he would choose any other profession, the authority of God is contemned, and the holy office profaned. If a church should think that they need a minister, and should conclude to appoint one without regard to a divine call; and if a presbytery should aid them in accomplishing their purpose; the church and presbytery together may make a minister; but he will be, if not a minister of Satan, at the best only a minister of men, and not a minister of Christ.

The divine call is not only indispensable, but it is also complete in itself. The presbytery do not assemble to complete it, but to signify their concurrence in the persuasion that it exists. The earliest and the least hurtful form which the pernicious doctrine of baptismal regeneration assumed, regarded baptism as the completion of regeneration. It did not make regeneration consist wholly in the outward ceremony; but it regarded no one, whatever the Holy Sprit may have effected within him, as fully regenerated, until he had gone through the outward ceremony. A similar mistake has been made respecting the Holy Spirit's call to the ministry. The call is supposed to be incomplete, until the outward ceremony of ordination has been performed. In both cases a distinction should be made, between what the Spirit does, and what it is the duty of him to do on whom the Spirit operates. The Spirit regenerates; and it is the duty of the regenerated man to be baptized. The Spirit calls to the ministry; and it is the duty of the man so called, to enter on the work of the ministry through all the forms which are prescribed in the word of God. Why the Holy Spirit permits one whom he has regenerated to err so far as to neglect baptism; and why he permits one whom he has called to the ministry to err so far as to neglect both baptism and regular ordination; I as little understand, as I understand why God permitted sin to enter the world. The proof of all these facts is irrefragable; and I am compelled to admit their existence, and believe that God will overrule them for his glory.

OBJECTIONS.

Objection 1.—The doctrine of a special divine call to the ministry, savors of fanaticism. Such a call was suitable to the day of miracles, but now the grace of God, like his providence, operates by ordinary means. The Spirit resides in the church and ministry; and what they do, the Spirit does. To expect any other call of the Holy Spirit is fanatical.

Had the objection simply maintained that the Holy Spirit uses means, in calling men to the ministry, the proposition would have been admitted. He uses the word as a means, in his call of men to repentance and faith; and he uses the same word in calling men to the work of the ministry. But the objection marks out another channel in which the spiritual influence is supposed to flow, namely, the church and the ministry; but how can the necessary qualifications for the ministry be derived through this channel? If the grace of God now operates by the use of ordinary means, we know that the word is the ordinary means which the Holy Spirit employs in illumination and sanctification; and the conclusion is rational, and not fanatical, that the superior illumination and sanctification necessary for the work of the ministry, are the effect of the same means more successfully employed, or more abundantly blessed. The laying on of apostolic hands could confer spiritual gifts in the day of miracles; but ordaining hands have now no gifts to confer.

It is the objection which carries us back to the day of miracles, and expects effects from causes inadequate to produce them. A ministry made by outward ordination, without a divine call, is a curse to the world.

Objection 2.—If a divine call is indispensable to constitute a minister of Christ, since the call is invisible, we can never know who are true ministers.

The supposed invisibility of religion is presented in various forms of objection. It makes the church invisible, and the ministry invisible. But in what sense is religion invisible? The power of gravity is invisible, but we see its effects everywhere; and we feel it binding us to the earth. The influence of the Spirit is invisible, but its effects are seen and felt as certainly as the effects of gravity. The Spirit's call to the ministry is unseen; but the effects of it have been displayed in the successful conflict which the ministry has waged with the powers of darkness, and in the victories which it has achieved. The history of the world testifies that a divine power has wrought in the ministry of the word; and, wherever the gospel has been faithfully preached, every one has had an opportunity to observe such effects as demonstrate that the ministry of the word is the ministry of the Spirit. Why, then, need we, to render the ministry visible, suppose it to consist in outward form? There is a proper form for the ministry to assume, but the form may be without the power; and the mere form does not constitute a minister of Christ. May we not be deceived in this matter? We may. Ministers of Satan have appeared as ministers of righteousness; and compliance with external forms is a method by which they recommend themselves. We are commanded to try the spirits; and this cannot be done by a mere examination of ordination credentials. An obligation to discriminate otherwise than by ordination certificate, devolves on every church in the choice of its pastor; and on every pastor in inviting a minister to preach to the people of his charge.

Objection 3.—If ordination does not make a minister of Christ, and does not prove a man to be a minister of Christ, it may be dispensed with as useless.

This does not follow. Though it may not accomplish either of these purposes, it may, nevertheless, be of great utility; and if we were wholly unable to see any utility in it, yet, as the will of

God, we ought to observe it. Men may be Christians without baptism; and may profess Christ without baptism; but it does not follow, that baptism is useless. The Head of the church has, in his wisdom, made it the appointed ceremony for the Christian profession, and so he has made ordination the appointed ceremony for a regular entrance into the ministerial office. As every converted man ought to profess Christ by baptism, so every one who has been called of God to the ministry, ought to enter on the work by ordination. The proof of the obligation in the latter case, is not so clear from the Holy Scriptures, as in the former, but it is sufficiently clear to guide our practice.

Section II.—ADMINISTRATION OF BAPTISM.

The apostles were commissioned to preach, to baptize, and to teach. If the office held by ordinary ministers were identical with that held by the apostles, there would be no difficulty in deciding, that it includes the administration of baptism. But the apostolic office has ceased, and the work assigned to the apostles has devolved on inferior officers. The apostles could not, in person, preach, baptize, and teach, in every country of the world, and in every age till the end of time; but the commission made it their duty to provide for the full performance of this work; and their apostolic authority, guided by the infallible direction of the Holy Spirit, enabled them to make all necessary arrangements for carrying it into effect. Now, we cannot determine, from the commission itself, whether to preach, to baptize, and to teach, would be assigned, as distinct duties, to three distinct classes of officers; or whether they would be committed, without separation, to one class. For information on this point, we are left to inquire into the instructions given by the apostles by precept and example.

Some have argued, that, because preaching is a more important work than baptizing, the authority to preach necessarily includes authority to baptize. The greater, say they, must include the less. But this mode of argument is fallacious. The whole includes its parts, but the greater does not always include the less. A high dignitary of the realm may be guilty of usurpation, if he assumes the functions of an humble official. So, though preaching is a higher office than baptizing, it does not necessarily include it.

We learn that the Holy Spirit has called men to preach the gospel, by the qualifications which he has conferred; but we can have no proof of this sort, that the Holy Spirit has called any one to the work of baptizing. Spiritual qualifications are not required; and, if we have no other means of knowing, it may remain doubtful, whether the work may not be done by any one whom the candidate may select.

Among those who have held that baptism possesses a saving efficacy, it has often been a matter of pressing importance, to obtain the administration of it, in case of sickness, when a priest was not at hand. It has been held, that, in case of necessity, the rite may be administered by laymen, and even by women. Some persons who are free from such superstitious reliance on the outward ceremony, have held that any one who makes a disciple, may baptize him. According to this interpretation of the commission, it would be proper for a mother, whose instructions have been blessed to the conversion of her son, to be the administrator of his baptism. But this interpretation is inadmissible. If some of the work to which the apostles were specially appointed, may, to some extent, be performed by other persons, it does not follow, that these persons are invested in full with the apostolic commission.

The commission specifies duties, for the performance of which the apostles were to provide. One of these was the administration of baptism. They were commanded, not to make disciples and teach them the duty of being baptized; but to make disciples and baptize them. The administration of the rite was to be their care; and, where they could not perform it in their own person, it was made their duty to provide for its performance. This reasoning proves satisfactorily, that the administration was not designed to be left to any one whom the candidate might select; and it is confirmed by the words of Paul: "Christ sent me not to baptize, but to preach the gospel." These words imply, that Christ had sent some persons to baptize. The duty was to be performed; and these words, taken in connection with the fact that John the Baptist and the other apostles were commanded to baptize, confirm the deduction that the work was to be done by agents provided.

On the question, whether the administration of baptism is necessarily included in the commission to preach, or necessarily connected with it, the words of Paul just quoted, throw some light.

The word translated "sent," is the verb from which the word *apostle* is derived; and, as used by Paul in this passage, it imports that Christ had not given to Paul an apostolic commission to baptize, but to preach the gospel. On comparing the commission given to him, with that given to the other apostles, the difference in this particular is apparent. This proves that the offices of preaching and baptizing were not inseparable. Had the greater included the less, the authority and obligation to baptize were included in Paul's commission, and he could not have said with literal truth, "Christ sent me not to baptize." To understand the passage to signify nothing more than that baptism was a less important part of the work which Paul was authorized to perform, does not satisfy the literal import of the words, and it is a departure, without necessity, from the literal interpretation, which is fully sustained by a comparison of Paul's commission with that of the other apostles. Moreover, the literal import best agrees with the context, since, according to it, the fact alleged by Paul cut off, from those whom he had baptized, all plea to claim him on that account as an apostle for their party leader. If in baptizing them, he had not acted as an apostle, the fact gave them no pretext to claim him as a party leader in that high character. Had Paul's state of mind permitted him to preach on the next day after Jesus appeared to him, and gave him his commission, he was authorized to preach; but not to administer baptism. Yet he did afterwards baptize Crispus, Gaius, and the household of Stephanas; and he must have obtained authority to do this in some way. In what way? If not by extraordinary commission, it must have been in the ordinary way, in which others received authority to baptize. He received the command to be baptized himself, in the ordinary way, and he honored and obeyed the command. In the same way, he must have received the authority under which he acted, in the administration of baptism.

Although baptizing is not necessarily connected with preaching and teaching; yet the manner in which it is conjoined with them in the commission, appears to indicate that the connection is suitable. No separate class of officers is anywhere provided in the New Testament, for administering the rite, and yet, if we have reasoned correctly, the apostles were under obligation to provide for it. We are led to the conclusion, that this provision was made, in the ordinary method instituted for transmitting the ministerial office. Paul had committed the office to Timothy, in the presence of many witnesses, by the laying on of his hands, and the hands of the presbytery. Timothy was, in like manner, to commit the office to others, and enjoin on them the same duties which Paul had enjoined on him. There was a fitness in the arrangement that this ceremonial induction into office, should add the ceremonial authority to baptize. It cannot be proved to be given, in the internal call of the Spirit. It was not given in the extraordinary commission of Paul. If Paul received it in the ordinary way, whether in his being set apart at Antioch, or in some similar service at some previous time, we have this point established :—the authority to administer baptism is conferred in the ordinary course of the ministerial succession, when an individual, called by the Holy Spirit to the ministry of the word, is publicly set apart to this service. The process of reasoning by which we reach this conclusion, is less clear and direct than that which many other subjects admit; but it is sufficiently clear to determine our practice, in the absence of explicit instruction from the holy oracles. We have, moreover, the satisfaction of knowing that this course of procedure has been generally adopted in the churches which have conformed in their order most nearly to the Scriptures.

Section III.—APOSTOLIC SUCCESSION.

We have seen that baptism ought to be administered by an ordained minister of the word. A question, then, arises before every believer who desires to receive baptism, "how shall he know who is authorized to administer it?" Some have thought, that the candidate may lawfully leave the whole responsibility of deciding this question with the administrator. But, if he knew the administrator not to be authorized, it would be wrong to receive baptism at his hands; and it cannot, therefore, be right, to be indifferent to the question whether he is authorized. Moreover, the conscientious administrator is deeply interested in the question. He ought not to act without divine authority, and deceive the confiding disciples, by giving to them for true Christian baptism, that which is but a human counterfeit. How does he know that he has been duly ordained to perform this work; that they who ordained him were duly ordained; and that the line of connection with those who originally received the commission from Christ, has been unbroken? Is there an obligation, binding on the conscience of every individual who seeks baptism, and still more binding on the conscience of him who administers it, to know that his right to administer has been derived by unbroken succession from the apostles?

There is an intrinsic improbability in the supposition, that the Scripture binds all who receive the gospel, in every country and every age of the world, to perform a specified duty; and yet leaves that duty in the dark, so that no one can know what it is, except by the light of tradition? In a former chapter we applied this consideration to the question, whether the consciences of men are bound by Scripture authority to receive the traditionary succession of the Sabbath, as of like authority with Scripture precepts. The examination then made, discovered that the divine precept is most wisely given, in a manner which secures all the ends of the observance, without binding the individual conscience with a responsibility to which it is unequal, and for which it has not the requisite knowledge. The precept does not bind men to observe the seventh day of an unknowable week; and it does not so bind them to the regular succession, that, if they have lost it by circumnavigating the globe, they can never regain it. If we find nothing in the Scriptures, when properly interpreted, binding our consciences to the tradition of the sabbatical observance, we may, from the analogy, expect to find nothing binding our consciences to the apostolic succession.

An humble disciple of Christ desirous to obey all his Lord's commands, learns his duty from the Holy Scriptures, and sees in them the order established in the primitive churches. He looks around him to discover whether there are churches like the primitive churches, and ministers preaching and baptizing, like the primitive ministers. He finds them. The beginning and the end of the succession appear. The middle of it he sees not; but he knows that the Head of the church has lived during all the intermediate time, and that he is the God of providence, and the giver of the Holy Spirit, by whose influence the chain of succession could be preserved. He feels assured, that, if an unbroken succession is necessary for any purpose which the Head of the church has in view, he has preserved it. With this assurance, he proceeds in what appears to him to be the plain path of duty, the same path in which the ancient saints walked; and he confidently expects that his obedience will receive his Lord's approbation. Is there anything in the Scriptures which can prove such reasoning fallacious?

Suppose that at some point in the line the apostolic succession was lost, was it impossible to re-establish the ancient order; or, in other words, was it impossible ever afterwards to obey Christ's commands? The Holy Spirit qualifies and calls persons to preach the gospel, and teach men to observe whatsoever Christ commanded, and we have seen that this call of the Spirit is complete in itself. In the case supposed, how could persons called by the Holy Spirit teach men to observe Christ's commands, if the observance had become impossible? Surely, the reasoning which infers the impossibility must be fallacious, or the failure of the succession has never taken place, to disturb the counsels of him who said, "Lo, I am with you alway, even to the end of the world." Now, whether it be that the chain has been throughout unbroken, or that the Head of the church has a method of restoring it, the effect is the same to us. It is ours to do our duty, according to the light which we possess. This mode of settling the question is sufficient for all practical purposes.

As a question of mere theory it may be asked, whether a breach in the succession would render a new revelation necessary. To set aside any command of Scripture would require a new revelation. But to depart from the order which Christ has instituted is one thing, and to return to it after having wandered from it is quite another thing. For the latter we need no new revelation. The wisdom from above, given by the ordinary influence of the Spirit, is sufficient for such an emergency, without a miraculous inspiration. If holy men of God have had the responsibility thrown upon them of returning to the good old path after it had been deserted, they doubtless sought wisdom from above to direct them, and the success of their efforts to regain the lost way, is a sufficient assurance to us that the Lord gave them the necessary wisdom.

But is there any wall built along the wayside to prevent the return of wanderers? So far as I can see, the whole difficulty is resolvable into the question whether ministers of the word, called to the work by the Holy Spirit, may, in any case, perform the full duties of the office without the regular ceremonial induction into it. According to the view which we have taken, the call of the Spirit is complete in itself; but the same Spirit teaches the called to respect the order instituted for ceremonial induction into office. An obligation to respect this order, when it exists, imposes on them the duty of deferring the exercise of the ceremonial functions until they have been ceremonially inducted; but in the case supposed the church order does not exist, and therefore the obligation to defer does not exist. Their duty is to respect the order when it exists, and to restore it when it does not. The Head of the church designed that the ministers of the word should make disciples, baptize them, and teach them to organize churches, to celebrate the Lord's supper, exercise discipline, and walk in all the commandments and ordinances of the Lord. The ministers of the word are officers of Christ's spiritual church, and derive their qualifications and call from the Holy Spirit. Like other men, they are bound to observe what Christ commanded, and therefore to regard established church order. But if church order has become prostrate, their call by the Holy Spirit requires them to restore it, and not to teach that it must now for ever be neglected.

In the regular course of things, ordination stands at the beginning of the ministry, as baptism stands at the beginning of the Christian life; but there are several important particulars in which the two observances differ.

Baptism is enjoined by express precept, ordination is not. Much of the order instituted by the apostles originated in expediency. The appointment of deacons, recorded in Acts, chapter vi., is manifestly a case of this kind. Expediency has its obligation, as well as positive precept; and a question of expediency, decided by apostolic wisdom, binds us in like circumstances. The community of goods in the first church does not bind us, because our circumstances are different. Ordination is expedient, and the observance of it obligatory in the regular order of things, instituted by the apostles; but it cannot be inferred that it is obligatory in all circumstances. Nothing in Scripture determines the number of the presbytery; and if this may be determined by considerations of expediency, the same expediency may determine that ordination by a presbytery may, in some extraordinary circumstances, be dispensed with.

All the disciples of Christ, in the primitive times, were required to be baptized; but all the ministers of Christ were not ceremonially ordained. We have no proof that the apostles, or the seventy whom Christ sent forth, were thus ordained. No presbytery was convened in their case, but they were ordained or appointed by Christ in person. When he baptized disciples, he put the work into the hands of those who were afterwards to perform it. But his direct call conferred the ministerial office without human ordination. We have in the New Testament a much larger number of unordained than of ordained ministers, if imposition of human hands is necessary to ordination. Saul and Barnabas were so ordained to a missionary service, and Timothy was so ordained to the work of the ministry, but who else?

Jesus honored the institution of baptism by receiving it from a human administrator, but he did not so honor ordination. Among the benefits resulting to ministers from ordination, an important one is, that they go forth into the work with the concurrent testimony of the presbytery and the church, recommending them to all as the ministers of Christ. Jesus was willing to receive the testimony of John, but of John as his baptizer, not as his ordainer. "That he should be made manifest," said John, "therefore am I come baptizing."[1] At the beginning of his ministry, Jesus received baptism from John in the Jordan; and when he had gone up from the water, and was standing on the bank, his august ordination took place. The Holy Spirit, by whom his human nature was qualified for the ministry on which he was entering, descended on him in visible form, and the voice of the Father audibly pronounced, "This is my beloved Son, in whom I am well pleased."[2]

From this comparison, it clearly appears that ordination does not come to us enforced by like obligations to those of baptism. If our doctrine of strict communion be correct, baptism is a prerequisite to membership in the local churches; and, since the administration of baptism properly belongs to the ministers of the word, the local churches are, in this particular, dependent for their existence on the ministry. Local churches cannot originate the minis-

---

[1] John i. 31. [2] Matt. iii. 17.

try on which their own existence is dependent. The ministry originated before the local churches, and might have been perpetuated without them, if the Lord had so willed. The power from which the ministry originates is not that of the churches, but of the Head of the Church; and his call to office is the highest authority. John was sent to preach and baptize, without being baptized or ordained; yet the evidence of his mission was clear, and the people believed it. Paul was commissioned to preach the gospel while he was unbaptized and unordained; and the call was not conditioned on his being afterwards baptized and ordained. The call was complete and unconditional. He was under obligation to be baptized, as all other converted persons are; and he discharged this obligation, as every called minister ought to do; but his call was complete while he was yet unbaptized and unordained.

In the view which we have taken, the Christian ministry is an institution of surpassing importance. It does not grow up from the churches, but comes down from heaven. It is a gift sent down to mankind from the ascended Saviour. After stating that the exalted Redeemer "gave gifts unto men," Paul proceeds to enumerate these gifts in the following words: "He gave some, apostles; and some, prophets; and some, evangelists; and some, pastors and teachers."[1] To these heaven-bestowed ministers, the Spirit, which qualifies them for their work, gives testimony. The churches receive the testimony of the Spirit, and, in their turn, add their testimony; and the ministry and the churches become joint witnesses for God to the world. Whether these two witnesses have lived during all the dark period of papal persecution, I leave for others to inquire; but if they were ever slain, I doubt not that the Spirit of God has reanimated them, and will enable them to continue their testimony to the end of the world.

---

[1] Eph. iv. 8, 11.

SECTION IV.—CHURCH OFFICERS.

BISHOPS.

THE CHURCHES SHOULD CHOOSE, FROM AMONG THE MINISTERS OF THE WORD, BISHOPS OR PASTORS TO TEACH AND RULE THEM.

Numerous passages of Scripture speak of persons who bore rule in the churches. "Obey them that have the rule over you."[1] "The elders that rule well."[2] The term bishop signifies overseer, and implies authority to rule. Among the qualifications necessary for a bishop, one was, that he ruleth well his own house; and the reason assigned is, "If a man know not how to rule his own house, how shall he take care of the church of God?"[3] It is clear, from this passage, that the bishops were invested with an authority bearing some analogy to the authority which the head of a family exercises over his household.

The question has been much discussed, whether the authority of a bishop is restricted to a single local church. Episcopalians maintain that it extends to the churches of a large district called a diocese; and that the Scriptural title for the ruler of a single church, is presbyter or elder. Against this opinion, the following arguments appear conclusive. The single church at Philippi contained more bishops than one.[4] The elders of the church at Ephesus are styled overseers or bishops.[5] Peter addresses elders as persons having the *oversight*[6] of the flock, that is, the authority of overseers or bishops. In Paul's epistle to Titus, after the ordination of elders is mentioned, the qualifications of a bishop[7] are enumerated; and the connection plainly indicates that elder and bishop were titles of the same office.

The bishops were the pastors or shepherds of the flock committed to their charge. The bishops or elders of the church at Ephesus were required to "feed the flock." The elders whom Peter addressed were commanded to "feed the flock;" and their office as shepherds is presented to view as subordinate to that of Christ, "the chief shepherd." Since the churches are to be fed, not with

---

[1] Heb. xiii. 17.   [2] 1 Tim. v. 17.   [3] 1 Tim. iii. 4, 5.
[4] Phil. i. 1.   [5] Acts xx. 28.   [6] 1 Peter v. 2.
[7] Titus i. 5, 7.

literal food, but with knowledge and understanding, the office of teaching is included in that of pastor. Hence a bishop was required to be "apt to teach." In enumerating church officers, Paul mentions both pastors and teachers. It appears from this that there were teachers in the primitive churches, who were not invested with pastoral authority. These were ministers of the word, authorized by the commission to teach the observance of all Christ's commands, but not authorized to rule. The ministers of the word are officers of the universal church, but, as such, they have no authority to rule in the local churches. This authority belongs to the pastors or bishops.

The ruling authority of a pastor is peculiar in its kind. Though bearing some analogy to that of a father in his family, or of a governor in civil society, it differs from these. Christ distinguished His rule from that of earthly kings by the absence of coercion: "If my kingdom were of this world, then would my servants fight."[1] So the spiritual rulers under Christ have no coercive power over the persons or property of those under their authority. A well marked distinction between their authority and that which is exercised by civil rulers, is drawn in these words of Christ: "Ye know that the princes of the gentiles exercise dominion over them, and they that are great exercise authority upon them. But it shall not be so among you: but whosoever will be great among you, let him be your minister; and whosoever will be chief among you, let him be your servant."[2] Another peculiarity of their rule is that they cannot govern at their own will. This would be to act as lords over God's heritage. Such power, if exercised by them, is a usurpation, and does not legitimately belong to their office. The only rule which they have a right to apply is that of God's word; and the only obedience which they have a right to exact, is voluntary. The civil ruler is armed with the sword, and coerces obedience. Zion's King has put no carnal weapons into the hands of church rulers, and all coercion is inconsistent with the nature of the authority intrusted to them. No submission to the Lord is acceptable but that which is voluntary; and the same kind of submission which the ancient Christians rendered to the Lord, they rendered to their

---

[1] John xviii. 36.   [2] Matt. xx. 25—27

spiritual rulers:—"They first gave their own selves unto the Lord and unto us by the will of God."[1]

The surrender of their property was voluntary. Peter's address to Ananias and Sapphira proves that this was true, even in the general surrender which was made by the first church; and it is clear that the contributions afterwards made by the churches, were made not of constraint but willingly. They who claim or indirectly exercise a coercive power over the property of church-members, are taking the oversight for filthy lucre's sake, and have no sanction from the authority of Christ, or the example of his apostles.

Since the obedience of churches cannot be coerced, no one can begin or continue the exercise of spiritual rule over them, but at their will. Hence their bishops must be persons of their own choice. The apostles, though all collected at Jerusalem, and invested with full power from on high to do all that appertained to their office, did not appoint even the inferior officers of the church until after they had been chosen by the whole multitude of the disciples. In this procedure they recognised and established the right of the churches to elect their own officers. Even the appointment of an apostle to take the place of Judas appears to have been made by popular vote: and much more ought that of bishops over the several churches. The Greek word rendered *ordain* in Acts xiii. 48, signifies to stretch out the hand, and is supposed to refer to the mode of popular election by the lifting up of the hand; but, whether this criticism be just or not, the proof that church officers were so elected is sufficient without the aid of this passage.

Because the bishops must labor in word and doctrine, as well as rule, the churches should elect them from the ministers of the word. As they have no right to coerce the churches, so the churches have no right to coerce their acceptance of office. The relation must be voluntarily entered into by both parties. This voluntariness on the part of ministers is necessary to the proper exercise of their office: "Not of constraint, but willingly; not for filthy lucre, but of a ready mind."[2] The minister cannot coerce a support from the church, but God has ordained that they who preach the gospel should live of the gospel.[3] The duty of a church to

---

[1] 2 Cor. viii. 5. [2] 1 Peter v. 2. [3] 1 Cor. ix. 14.

support its pastor is clearly taught in the word of God; and without the performance of this duty on their part, they have no right to expect his services; and they, in a manner, put it out of his power to render them.

DEACONS.

Deacons should be chosen by the churches, from among their members, to minister in secular affairs.

By apostolic direction, the church at Jerusalem chose from among themselves seven men, honest, and of good report, who were appointed to serve tables. This measure originated in the expediency, that the apostles might give themselves to the word of God and prayer. The same expediency requires that pastors should be relieved from secular burdens, and be left to the spiritual service of the church. We know that deacons existed in the church at Philippi;[1] and directions were given to Timothy respecting the qualifications necessary for the deacon's office. These facts authorize the conclusion, that the deacon's office was designed to be perpetual in the churches. The mode of appointment should conform to the example of the first church. The persons should be chosen by popular vote, and invested with office by ministerial ordination.

Some have thought that deacons, as well as bishops, are called elders in the Scripture. We read of bishops and deacons in connection, but never of elders and deacons;—of the ordination of elders,[2] without the mention of deacons, when deacons were needed as well as bishops; and of contributions sent to the elders at Jerusalem,[3] after the deacons had been appointed, who were the proper officers to receive and disburse them. It is argued, moreover, that the distinction which appears to be made, in 1 Tim. v. 17, between preaching and ruling elders, naturally suggests that the ruling elders were the deacons of the primitive churches.

In the Presbyterian church, a distinct class of officers exists, called ruling elders. The only Scripture authority claimed for this office, is the text last referred to. This text, however, does not distinguish between different classes of officers, but between different modes of exercising the same office. The word rendered

---

[1] Phil. i. 1.   [2] Acts xiv. 23.   [3] Acts xi. 30.

"labor," signifies to labor to exhaustion. Not the elder who merely rules, is accounted worthy of double honor, but the elder who rules well; and the special honor is not due to the elder, as merely invested with the office of ministering in word and doctrine, but as laboring therein—laboring to exhaustion. Thus interpreted, the text furnishes no authority for Presbyterian lay elders; and no argument for supposing that deacons are called elders.

The other arguments to prove that the deacons were included in the eldership of the primitive churches, are not without plausibility, but they are not conclusive; and they are opposed by the facts, that all the elders of the church at Ephesus are called bishops; that all the elders addressed by Peter are said to have the oversight or episcopal office; and that the elders whom Titus was to appoint appear to have been all bishops, inasmuch as the qualifications for the deacon's office are not subjoined to those which are described as necessary for the other office.

Among the qualifications of the deacons' office, it is not required that they should be apt to teach; and they are therefore not appointed to act as public teachers of the word: but other qualifications are mentioned, which indicate, that they are expected to be forward in promoting the spiritual interests of the church. An obligation to do this rests on every member; and deacons are not released from it by their appointment to minister in secular affairs. Instead of becoming immersed in secularity, they are expected, by the proper exercise of their office, to purchase to themselves a good degree, and great boldness in the faith.[1] If deacons were everywhere active in holding up the hands of the pastors, as Aaron and Hur held up the hands of Moses, the prosperity of the churches would be greatly advanced, and the success of the gospel far more abundant.

---

[1] 1 Tim. iii. 13.

CHAPTER IX.

DISCIPLINE.

Section I.—ADMISSION OF MEMBERS.

THE CHURCHES SHOULD ADMIT BAPTIZED BELIEVERS TO MEMBERSHIP.

A properly organized church consists of disciples who have professed their faith in Christ by baptism. Hence, such persons only should be admitted to membership. Unity and brotherly love require that all should be lovers of Christ; and love ought to be manifested by obedience: but Christ is not obeyed, if his command, directing the mode of Christian profession, is not obeyed.

Each church for itself has the responsibility of admitting to its own membership. A single church may exclude from its own fellowship, as in the case of the incestuous member excommunicated by the church at Corinth; and the power to exclude implies the power to admit. The pastor has not the power; nor is it possessed by any ecclesiastical judicatory except the church itself. The church is bound to exercise the power of admitting to membership, in subjection to the revealed will of Christ; and is, therefore, prohibited from receiving any who do not possess the requisite qualifications.

In order that the church may judge whether a candidate is duly qualified for membership, they should hear his profession of faith. He is bound to let his light shine before all men, to the glory of God; and it is specially needful that they should see it, with whom he is to be associated in fellowship as a child of light. He is bound to be ready always to give an answer to every one that asketh the reason of the hope that is in him;[1] and especially

---

[1] 1 Pet. iii. 15.

should he be ready to answer, on this point, those who are to receive him into their number, as called in one hope of their calling. He is bound to show forth the praise of him who has called him out of darkness into his marvellous light; and he should rejoice to say, "Come and hear, all ye that fear God, and I will declare what he hath done for my soul."[1]

The churches are not infallible judges, being unable to search the heart; but they owe it to the cause of Christ, and to the candidate himself, to exercise the best judgment of which they are capable. To receive any one on a mere profession of words, without any effort to ascertain whether he understands and feels what he professes, is unfaithfulness to his interests, and the interests of religion. In primitive times, when persecution deterred from profession, and when the Spirit operated in a more visible manner, the danger of mistake was less; but even then, all who professed were not received. John the Baptist rejected some from baptism, who did not bring forth fruits meet for repentance. They who are unfit for baptism, are unfit for church-membership.

To preserve unity in the church, the admission of a member should be by unanimous vote. Harmony and mutual confidence are necessary to the peace and prosperity of a church; and, if these are to be disturbed by the admission of a new member, it is far better, both for him and the church, that his admission should be deferred, until it can be effected without mischief.

Admission to membership belongs to churches; but admission to baptism belongs properly to the ministry. A single minister has the right to receive to baptism, on his own individual responsibility; as is clear from the baptism of the eunuch by Philip, when alone. But when a minister is officiating as pastor of a church, it is expedient that they should unite their counsels in judging of a candidate's qualifications; but the pastor ought to remember, that the responsibility of receiving to baptism is properly his. The superior knowledge which he is supposed to possess, and his office as the shepherd of the flock, and the priority of baptism to church-membership, all combine to render it necessary that he first and chiefly should meet this responsibility, and act upon it in the fear of the Lord.

---

[1] Ps. lxvi. 16.

Section II.—SPIRITUAL IMPROVEMENT.

THE CHURCHES SHOULD LABOR INCESSANTLY, TO PROMOTE BROTHERLY LOVE IN THEIR MEMBERS, AND INCREASED DEVOTION TO THE SERVICE OF GOD.

The spirit of unity pervades Christianity, and tends to bring the disciples of Christ into association with one another. Under the influence of this tendency, churches are formed; and in them an opportunity is given for the display of brotherly love. By the display, Christ is honored, and the world become convinced that his religion is divine. For the sake of Christ, therefore, and for the sake of the world, every church should labor to promote brotherly love.

The churches are the glory of Christ, not only in the brotherly love which they exhibit, but in their purity and devotion to the service of God. They are but small and temporary associations; yet they may reflect the glory of Christ to the view of an admiring world, as pure dew-drops reflect the brightness of the sun. So to honor Christ, should be the constant effort of the churches; and to effect this, care should be exercised over the spirituality of every member. The pastor should devote himself, with incessant toil and prayer, to the spiritual good of his flock; the deacons should unite their efforts with his for the attainment of the great end; and the members should watch over one another, exhort one another, and provoke one another to love and good works.

God has given the Christian ministry for the edification of his people; and every church ought to avail itself of this divine gift, and use it to the best advantage. For this purpose, the minister should be supported by cheerful contributions from the members of the church, that he may devote himself to the promotion of their spiritual interests. He should be encouraged in every possible way to diligence and fidelity in his duties. His imperfections should be treated with tenderness; and if, at any time, he should become remiss in his work, or turn aside from it to secular pursuits, the church ought, in gentleness and love, to address him with such language as Paul directed to be used to Archippus.[1]

---

[1] Col. iv. 17.

But such an address cannot be made with good effect by a church which does not sustain its minister, and free him from the necessity of worldly care.

Punctual attendance on the ministrations of the word, is necessary to the spiritual improvement of the church. It is necessary to encourage the heart of the minister. He cannot be expected to preach with earnestness and persevering zeal, if his people manifest no pleasure in listening to the truth which he proclaims. Let him know that they drink in the word with delight, that their souls are refreshed by it, and that it greatly increases their fruitfulness in holiness; with this knowledge, he will be stimulated to go forward in his work with boldness, and to endure all his toils with the sustaining assurance that his labor is not in vain in the Lord.

Regular attendance on the ministrations of the word is necessary, that the hearers may grow in grace and in the knowledge of Christ. Food is not more necessary to the body, than spiritual nourishment is to the soul; and the word is the appointed means of spiritual nourishment. It is the sincere milk, which babes in Christ desire, and by which they are nourished; and it is the strong meat, which they can use profitably who have attained to mature age in the divine life. Nor can spiritual health be expected, if the spiritual nourishment which God has provided, be received at far distant and irregular intervals. A regular return of one day in seven has been wisely appointed by the great Author of our being, who knows our frame, and perfectly understands what is best for the promotion of our highest interests. They who neglect this provision of his benevolence, reject the counsel of God against themselves, and bring spiritual leanness on their souls.

It is not enough to receive the spiritual food, but it ought to be inwardly digested. The truth which is heard on the sabbath, ought to be a subject of meditation through the week; and its influence should bring the actions, the words, the thoughts, even the very imaginations into obedience to the gospel of Christ. Thus the process of spiritual nutrition will be carried on, until the next sabbath brings another supply of the heavenly food. Thus the soul will grow in strength, and attain the stature of spiritual manhood.

Besides the public ministrations of the word, other means of promoting religious knowledge ought to receive the attention and support of the churches. The study of the Bible ought to be encouraged, whether by individuals, by Bible classes, or by Sunday schools. It is a great fault if the work of instructing is entirely given up to the young. Let the heads which have grown gray in the service of the Lord, bow with pleasure to impart instruction to the opening minds of the rising generation, and sow in this promising soil the seed which will produce a rich harvest, when the gray-haired instructor shall have gone to his eternal reward. Let the circulation of good religious books and periodical publications be promoted, and a spirit of religious inquiry be fostered in every proper way. Let men be taught, both by the words and the deeds of those who claim to be Christ's, that religion is the chief concern.

The health of the body requires exercise as well as food; so spiritual action is necessary for the health of the soul. Churches should exhort their members to be diligent in every good work, not only for the benefit of those around them, but also for their own spiritual improvement. In this course of active service, their own souls will become strong in the Lord, and their personal experience will verify the words of Christ, "It is more blessed to give than to receive." The great work which demands the energy of all God's people, is the spread of religion. Every church-member should labor for this by his personal efforts within the sphere of his individual influence, and, by co-operating with others, to extend the blessings of the gospel to every part of the earth. The precise mode of co-operating, the word of God does not prescribe; as it does not prescribe the precise mode in which the church-members shall travel to their place of public worship. But the thing to be done is prescribed; and, if the heart is in the Lord's work, it will employ its energies in devising the best method of accomplishing it, and in laboring to effect the object with prayerful reliance on the divine blessing. The gospel is to be preached to every creature; and he who loves Christ ought to feel a holy pleasure in helping those to execute the will of Christ who are willing, at his command, to bear the word of salvation to the perishing. Union in religious effort, not only promotes the spiritual growth of individual Christians, but it also conduces greatly to the harmony of churches. When coldness in religion prevails, the members of a church are like pieces of metal, which are not only separate from each other, but may be employed to inflict blows on each other; but when spiritual warmth has melted them, they flow together and become one. Feuds and unprofitable controversies cease when men are actively engaged in the service of God, and when they strive to provoke one another to nothing but love and good works.

Prayer meetings are an important means of spiritual improvement. It has been said that the prayer meeting of a church is the thermometer by which its spiritual temperature may be known. When Christians love to meet, that they may pour forth their united supplications to the throne of grace, the Saviour, in fulfilment of his promise, meets with them, and bestows blessings which infinitely transcend all earthly good, and are a beginning of heavenly bliss.

Section III.—EXCOMMUNICATION.

The right to excommunicate belongs to the church, without any appeal.

This is clear from the words of Christ: "If he will not hear the church, let him be to thee as an heathen man and a publican." That it is not the province of a minister to excommunicate is clear from the instructions of Paul to the church at Corinth.[1] If ministers had a right to excommunicate, Paul, with his high apostolic authority, would have exercised the right himself, or would have directed to the clerical tribunal by which the right was to be exercised. But he instructed the church to do the work, and, therefore, to the church it properly belonged. The punishment was to be inflicted, not by the officers of the church, but by the whole church assembled together with the power and presence of Christ, and the act performed is called the punishment inflicted by many.[2] Some, because the word rendered "many" in the passage is in the comparative degree, have interpreted it *by the majority;* but whether this be its import or not, it seems to imply that the sentence was passed by popular vote.

The obligation to exclude unworthy persons from church-fellowship, is taught in various passages of Scripture. "Therefore put

---

[1] 1 Cor. v. 4, 5.   [2] 2 Cor. ii. 6.

away from among yourselves that wicked person."[1] "A man that is a heretic, after the first and second admonition, reject."[2] "Now we command you, brethren, in the name of our Lord Jesus Christ, that ye withdraw yourselves from every brother that walketh disorderly, and not after the tradition which he received of us."[3] "If any man obey not our word by this epistle, note that man, and have no company with him, that he may be ashamed."[4] "Now, I beseech you, brethren, mark them which cause divisions and offences, contrary to the doctrine which ye have learned; and avoid them."[5]

In excommunication, regard should be had, not only to the glory of God, but to the good of the offender. This appears from the words of Paul: "For the destruction of the flesh, that the spirit may be saved."[6] The happy result of this excommunication, the only one which is particularly recorded in the history of the New Testament churches, is a strong encouragement to the exercise of faithful discipline. It has been remarked, that when discipline leaves a church, Christ goes with it.

---

[1] 1 Cor. v. 13. [2] Titus iii. 10. [3] 2 Thes. iii. 6.
[4] 2 Thes. iii. 14. [5] Rom. xvi. 17. [6] 1 Cor. v. 5.

CHAPTER X.

MISCELLANEOUS TOPICS.

SECTION I.—EXPEDIENCE OF THE SCRIPTURAL CHURCH ORDER.

OUR obligation to observe the positive precepts of religion is dependent entirely on the revealed will of the Lawgiver. It does not follow, however, that they are without reason, but only that the reason for them is beyond the discovery of human wisdom. After the divine wisdom has instituted them, we may be able to discover their fitness to accomplish the purpose for which they were designed, and may become sensible that they are necessary to the order and harmony of God's arrangements. In this manner the expedience of obeying positive precepts may sometimes be clearly seen by the intelligent student of God's will; but where we are unable to walk by sight, we ought to walk by faith in the way of God's commandments, and to feel assured, in every instance, that to obey God in all things is always most expedient.

Throughout the preceding discussions, we have endeavored to fix our eyes steadily on the divine precepts, and to strengthen ourselves in the purpose of obeying implicitly, even when no reason for the requirement is discoverable; but now, at the close of our investigations, it will be profitable to take another view of the church order which we have deduced from the Holy Scriptures in respect of its expedience.

A fundamental doctrine, in the system of church order which we have deduced from the Scriptures, is, that genuine piety is necessary to church-membership. If this doctrine had been steadfastly maintained from the times of the apostles, the corruption which overspread the churches would have been prevented, and the papal apostasy would never have occurred. The admission of unconverted members opened the door to every evil, and ultimately subjected the churches to the spirit that worketh in the children of disobedience. The reformation by Luther corrected many abuses, but this chief inlet of mischief it did not close. Hence the reformed churches do not exhibit the purity, devotion, and zeal which characterized the churches of primitive times. We need a more thorough reformation. We need to have the axe laid at the root of the trees, and this is done when none are admitted to church-membership but persons truly converted. The doctrine which excludes all others establishes the value and necessity of vital religion, and it is therefore of the utmost importance to the interests of the church, and of the world.

Immense mischief has resulted from the ambition of the clergy. This raised the Roman pontiff to his high seat of power, and his adherents are actuated by the same spirit. To counteract its influence, Christ commanded his disciples, "Be ye not called Rabbi, for one is your Master, even Christ, and all ye are brethren."[1] The doctrine of equality among the ministers of Christ is at war with clerical ambition, and a steadfast maintenance of it would have effectually barred out the Man of Sin, and it would now demolish the Roman hierarchy, and teach haughty prelates the need of Christian humility.

The ambition of the clergy needs a combination of the churches to sustain it. The doctrine that every church is an independent body, and that no combination of the churches is authorized by Christ, opposes their schemes for ecclesiastical preferment. It makes the pastors or bishops equal, and allows no other preference than that which is due to superior piety and usefulness.

The independence of the churches, and the democratic form of church government, appeal strongly to individual responsibility, and have, therefore, a powerful tendency to promote holiness among the lay members. Every man feels that the cause of Christ is in some measure committed to him. The church is not a body intermediate between him and Christ, and charged with the exclusive responsibility of glorifying Christ; but he himself is in part the church, and to him belongs the obligation of honoring his divine Master. This doctrine of individual responsibility unites

---

[1] Matt. xxiii. 8.

with the doctrine of a converted church-membership, to render the churches the glory of Christ.

Enough has been said to direct the view of the thoughtful reader to the excellence of the Scriptural church order. In what remains of this section we shall consider some objections against the doctrine of church independence.

Objection 1.—The independent form of church government does not allow sufficient influence to the ministerial office. Learned divines may be outvoted by ignorant laymen; and pastors, who ought to rule their flocks, may have their peace and reputation destroyed by their churches, without any right of appeal.

The objection supposes some other than moral power to be needful for ministers. A man whose piety and call of God to the ministry are unquestionable; who gives full proof to those among whom he ministers that he seeks their highest good, and who serves a people that esteem him highly for his work sake; has an influence over them which is almost unbounded. He comes to them in the name of God, and they perceive that his instruction and precepts are drawn from the word of God. He addresses them with reference to the eternal world; and they realize that he and they are soon to stand together before God. The authority of God, and the momentous interests of the eternal world, give weight to every word which he utters; the powers of their minds bend under its influence. Such a minister as this has so swayed the hearts of Christian men, that martyrdom has had no terrors for them. They have defied the cruel rage of tyrants; and have faced popular fury undaunted. Is not this influence great enough for any minister to wield? Would the objection substitute for it a part of the tyrant's power which it has overcome? The apostles, on the day of Pentecost, were endued with power from on high; but it was not the power of coercion. God's truth, and a holy life, have rendered the ministry invincible; and the minister who asks for other power, mistakes the nature of his office.

It is alleged, that a learned divine may be outvoted by ignorant laymen; and what then? Do truth and holiness lose their power, by being outvoted? The learned divine may be in the wrong; or he may arrogantly claim a deference to which he is not entitled. In this case, to give him governing power would be a sad remedy for the supposed evil. Perhaps he is in the right, and possesses the meekness and gentleness of Christ. In this case, he will teach us how to answer the objection now before us. He will choose in meekness to instruct those that oppose themselves, rather than prevail over them by authority. It may be that they mean well, but need information. The remedy is, to give them the information needed. This is far better, than to deny them the power of thinking and acting. Possibly they may be evil and designing men. If so, they ought not to be in the church. It is certainly not wise to retain them in the church, and seek to render them harmless by depriving them of influence in the church; especially if we are obliged, at the same time, to make all the good lay members of the church equally powerless.

Among the relations in human society, that of a godly pastor to the flock of his charge, is one of the most prolific in blessings. While he points to heaven in his instructions, and leads them in the way by his example, they listen with reverence, and imitate with the affection of children. It is not enough to say, that his happiness and reputation are safe in their hands. They are a wall of defence around him; and a source of purest and sweetest enjoyment. But the benefits of this relation result from the moral tie that binds the parties. They spring out of brotherly love, which flows spontaneously from renewed hearts, and unites them in the service of their common Lord. Substitute for this the mere tie of official relation, and the garden of the Lord becomes a parched desert. When a pastor seeks defence from his people, by entrenching himself in official authority, or appealing to a higher tribunal, there is a radical evil which needs some other remedy.

We concede that the independent form of church government is not adapted to ungodly pastors, and unconverted church-members. It is suited to those only, who are bound together in brotherly love, and are striving together to glorify God, and advance the cause of truth and righteousness. For such persons Christ instituted it; and all the objections to which it is liable, find their occasion in the depravity of men. Church government was never designed to be a remedy for human depravity. It was designed for men whom the Holy Spirit has sanctified; and the wisdom which would adapt it to men of a different character, is not from above.

Objection 2.—Designing men have it in their power to mislead the people; and the evil which results cannot be prevented, if there is no high tribunal to which demagogues are amenable.

The prevention and cure of this evil are not to be sought in the establishment of a high ecclesiastical court; but in the illumination and sanctification of the people. Wisdom and benevolence unite in recommending, that men's minds be fortified against seducers, by being well instructed in the truth; and the expedient of restraining the seducer by high ecclesiastical authority, does not secure the highest possible good. Besides, we have no assurance that the tribunal will be uncorrupt. The same power that claims to restrain a seducer, may restrain a reformer whom God has raised up to bring men back to the right way. It is far better to oppose error with the truth and the demonstration of the Spirit, than with ecclesiastical authority.

Objection 3.—The independent churches have no bond of union and strength; and no means of preventing division.

Love is the bond of perfectness, which unites true members of Christ. When this golden bond is wanting, a band of iron, forged by ecclesiastical authority, may fasten men to each other; but it will not be in the fellowship of the gospel. A want of fellowship in a church, is a disease preying on the spiritual strength of the body; and it is better that it should be seen and felt, until the proper remedy is applied, than that it should be concealed by an outward covering of ecclesiastical forms. When mere organization supplies the union and strength on which we rely, we shall cease to cultivate the unity of the Spirit, and to trust the power of truth. The objection, therefore, is unfounded. What it accounts a fault, is in reality a high excellence of the church order taught in the Scripture, and demonstrates that it originated in the wisdom of God.

Section II.—FELLOWSHIP BETWEEN CHURCHES.

A happy intercourse might subsist between the churches, if they were all walking in the Spirit, sound in faith, correct in order, and careful in discipline. Such a state of things existed, to a great extent, in apostolic times. Christian men passed from one country to another, and found, in every place, that those who professed the name of Christ were of one heart and one soul.

The members of one local church were, in general, welcomed to the fellowship of every other church.

But the relation between different local churches, is not such as to bind each church to receive the ministers and members of every other church. This obligation was not felt even in the days of the apostles. John commanded, "If there come any unto you, and bring not this doctrine, receive him not into your house; neither bid him God speed."[1] These teachers of false doctrine were probably members of some local church, which, like the church at Pergamos, tolerated error;[2] but their membership did not entitle them to universal respect and confidence. Some have regarded each local church, as acting for the whole body of the faithful; and have inferred that its acts are binding on every other church. But this opinion is inconsistent with the true doctrine of church independence, and with the separate responsibility of individuals and churches. When churches do their duty, the recommendation of a minister or member from one church will, like the recommendation given to Apollos,[3] introduce him to the affections and confidence of other churches; but no recommendation of an unworthy person can bind the consciences of those who know his true character. Free intercourse and mutual confidence between the churches is very desirable, and every one should labor to promote it; but purity of doctrine and practice should never be sacrificed to effect it.

For the promotion of Christian fellowship, every one should require more of himself than of his brother. We may lawfully tolerate in others what we cannot tolerate in ourselves, or cannot approve. Some degree of toleration must be exercised, if imperfect Christians dwell together harmoniously in the fellowship of a local church. Such toleration the local churches are bound to exercise towards each other. Some things in the discipline of one church may not be approved by a neighboring church; but it does not follow, that their kind intercourse with each other must be disturbed. Each must act for itself, and not claim to bind the other. But when a church becomes corrupt in faith or practice, neighboring churches are bound to withdraw their fellowship.

---

[1] 2 John 10.   [2] Rev. ii. 14, 15.   [3] Acts xviii. 27.

Section III.—IMPOSITION OF HANDS.

The laying on of hands is sometimes mentioned in Scripture, when something is intended different from mere form or ceremony. Hands were laid on Queen Athaliah, that she might be put to death.[1] Nehemiah threatened to lay hands on those who violated the sabbath;[2] and in the same sense, it is said when they sought to lay hands on Jesus, they feared the multitude.[3] But imposition of hands is also mentioned as a significant form or ceremony. It was used: 1. To represent the transfer of guilt to the victims which were offered in sacrifice.[4] 2. To represent the transfer of authority, as from Moses to Joshua.[5] 3. As a form of benediction, sometimes accompanied with prayer.[6] 4. To confer the Holy Spirit;[7] and 5. To ordain to the ministerial office.[8]

The practice has prevailed in many churches, for the pastor to lay his hands on those who have been recently baptized, accompanying the act with prayer to God on their behalf. No command of Scripture enjoins this ceremony. Hands were laid on those who had been baptized in the times of the apostles, to impart the Holy Spirit; but this was done by the apostles only; and when Cornelius, and they who were with him, had received the Holy Spirit previous to their baptism, the apostle Peter omitted to lay hands on them afterwards.

In solemn consecration to ministerial service, other hands than those of apostles were sometimes laid on the persons ordained. In the case which occurred at Antioch,[9] the only apostle present was one of the persons on whom hands were laid. It follows that this was not done to impart the gift of the Holy Spirit, which appears to have been conferred by the apostles only. In the ordination of Timothy, other persons besides Paul, who are called "the presbytery," were concerned in the imposition of hands. These facts justify the conclusion, that the imposition of hands by ordinary ministers is, according to primitive usage, a proper ceremony in ordination to the ministerial office.

---

[1] 2 Chron. xxiii. 15.   [2] Neh. xiii. 21.   [3] Matt. xxi. 46.
[4] Lev. iv. 4; xvi. 21.   [5] Num. xxvii. 18—20;   [8] Acts xiii. 3.
[6] Gen. xlviii. 14; Mark x. 16.   [7] Acts xix. 6.
[9] Acts xiii. 1, 2.

The meaning of the injunction to Timothy, "Lay hands suddenly on no man,"[1] is not perfectly clear. It is not probable that it refers to literal force. As directing the use of a significant form, its most probable reference is to ministerial ordination. So understood, the injunction furnishes strongly corroborative proof, that imposition of hands was the proper ceremony for setting apart to the sacred office.

Section IV.—REBAPTISM.

MAY BE NECESSARY.

A believer who has, at some time, received sprinkling for baptism, is not freed from the obligation to be immersed, in obedience to Christ's command. In this case the immersion cannot, with propriety, be called rebaptism. But if an individual should be immersed in infancy, according to the usage of the Greek Church, this fact would not release him from the obligation to be re-immersed, on his becoming a believer in Christ. On the cases which have been mentioned, no doubt or diversity of practice exists, among those who adhere strictly to the precepts of Christ.

But other cases occasionally present themselves, the decision of which is attended with difficulty. The most common are the following: 1. Men who were once baptized on profession of faith, and afterwards turned away from Christ, sometimes return with proofs of recent conversion. 2. Men who have been immersed by Pedobaptist ministers, or by unworthy Baptist ministers, sometimes present themselves for rebaptism, or for admission into a church. On these two cases, the question arises, is rebaptism necessary, according to the Holy Scriptures?

WHO MUST DECIDE.

In deciding the question, the first responsibility devolves on the candidate. He is bound to make a baptismal profession of faith, according to the revealed will of Christ; and if he has not properly complied with his duty, the obligation to obey rests on him.

---

[1] 1 Tim. v. 22.

A responsibility is brought on the administrator, to whom the candidate may apply for rebaptism. It is clear from the Scriptures, that, in ordinary cases, baptism was designed to be administered but once; and the administrator, as a servant of Christ, is bound to decide, in the fear of God, whether the case before him justifies a repetition of the rite.

Besides the two parties that have been named, and that have the immediate responsibility in the case, the church to which an individual of doubtful baptism may apply for membership, has the responsibility of judging whether his baptism has fulfilled the divine command. If baptism is a prerequisite to membership, the church is not at liberty to throw the entire responsibility of the question on the candidate or the administrator.

It has sometimes happened, that ministers have differed in their views; and a candidate, whom one minister has refused to rebaptize, has been rebaptized by another. In such cases, no breach of fellowship between the ministers occurs; nor ought it to be allowed. In like manner, a difference of opinion may exist between churches; and one church may admit without rebaptism, when another church would require it. This difference should not disturb the kind intercourse between the churches. But if the individual who has been received without rebaptism, should seek to remove his membership to the church that deems rebaptism necessary, the latter church has authority, as an independent body, to reject him.

Though some difference of opinion on these questions does exist, and ought to be tolerated, yet every one should strive to learn his duty respecting them, by a diligent study of the Holy Scriptures. The directions of the inspired word are clear, so long as men keep in the prescribed way; but when they have wandered from it, no surprise should be felt if the method of return is not so clearly pointed out. Hence it arises that men who interpret the express precepts of Christ alike, may, in applying them to perplexing cases, differ in their judgment. In what follows I shall give my views, with deference to those whose investigations have led them to a different conclusion.

FIRST CASE.

The first case supposes that there was in the previous baptism a mistake respecting the qualifications of the candidate.

Baptism was designed to be the ceremony of Christian profession. If, in the first baptism, the candidate believed himself to be a Christian, and received baptism on a credible profession of faith in Christ, no higher qualification can be obtained for a second baptism. They to whom the administration of the rite has been committed, do not possess the power to search the heart. A credible profession of faith, sincerely made, is all that fallible men can expect; and, since the ordinance has been committed to fallible men, it is duly administered on sincere and credible profession.

Some confirmation of this view may be derived from the case of Simon the sorcerer. Though baptized on profession of faith, it was afterwards discovered that his heart was not right in the sight of God. On making the discovery, Peter did not command him to repent and be baptized, as he commanded the unbaptized on the day of Pentecost: but his address was, "Repent, and pray God, if perhaps the thought of thine heart may be forgiven thee."[1] This address, by containing no command respecting baptism, favors the opinion that rebaptism in this case would not have been required.

SECOND CASE.

The second case supposes that there was in the first baptism a want of due qualification in the administrator.

In the discussion of this question we should guard against improper notions respecting the validity of baptism. The rite has no sacramental efficacy, dependent on its validity, as the possession of an estate depends on the validity of the title. Were it so, it might be a matter of great importance to be able to trace the flow of the mysterious virtue through a continuous line of authorized administrators from the days of the apostles. But the validity of baptism means nothing more than that the duty has been performed. If performed, there is no necessity of repeating it.

The question, then, is whether the candidate has done his duty. The responsibility of deciding this question begins with him; but it does not end with him. The church of which he wishes to become a member, must exercise judgment on the case. If the candidate's satisfaction with his baptism would suffice, persons baptized in

---

[1] Acts viii. 22.

infancy might obtain admission into our churches without other baptism. The church is bound to judge, and to regulate its judgment by the will of God.

From the investigations in the preceding part of this work, we have learned that a candidate has no right to baptize himself, or select his own administrator, without regard to his being duly qualified according to the divine will. The proper administrators are persons called of God to the ministerial office, and introduced into it according to the order established by the apostles. To such persons the candidate was bound to apply; and, if he received the ordinance from any other, it was as if he had selected the administrator at his own will, or had immersed himself.

The possibility that a state of things may have at some time existed, in which a regular administrator could not be obtained, does not militate against the conclusion just drawn. This subject has been considered in Chap. VIII. § 3. Because when church order has been destroyed, something unusual may be done to restore it, we are not, on this account, justified in neglecting the regular order when it does exist. Every church is bound to respect this order, and a candidate who has failed to respect it in a former baptism, may, with a good conscience, proceed anew to obey the Lord's command, in exact conformity to the divine requirement.

In order to the proper performance of baptism, a willing candidate and a willing administrator are necessary, both of whom should render the service in obedience to Christ. By a wise provision the social tendency of Christianity is shown at the very beginning of the Christian profession. The candidate cannot obey alone, but he must seek an administrator to unite with him in the act of obedience, and by this arrangement Christian fellowship begins with Christian profession. But that two may walk together in this act of obedience, it is necessary that they should be agreed. If the administrator and candidate differ widely in their views respecting the nature and design of the ordinance, they cannot have fellowship with each other in the service. Some Pedobaptist ministers will administer immersion reluctantly, believing it to be an ineligible mode of baptism, scarcely consistent with refinement and decency. How can a candidate, who conscientiously believes that there is no other baptism, have fellowship in the service with such an administrator? But this is not all. Pedobaptist ministers do not, in general, administer the rite as an emblem of Christ's burial and resurrection. This important part of its design they entirely overlook. If an administrator of the Lord's supper, mistaking the design of the ceremony, should break bread and distribute wine in commemoration, not of Christ, but of the deliverance from Egyptian bondage under Moses, what Christian could receive the elements at his hands? So, when an administrator mistakes the design of baptism, and overlooks its chief symbolical signification, every enlightened and conscientious candidate, who understands the nature and design of the ceremony, may well doubt the propriety of uniting with such a minister in a service about which they are so little agreed.

The odium which has been attached to anabaptism deters many from a repetition of the ceremony; but the Scriptures nowhere brand it with reproach. He who would find an anathema against it, need not search for it in the Bible. The holy book furnishes satisfactory proof that when the rite has been once duly performed, there is no necessity to repeat it; but it furnishes no proof that God will be displeased, if one who has failed to come up to the full measure of his duty, should seek another opportunity to obey the livine command with scrupulous exactness.

SECTION V.—TREATMENT OF UNBAPTIZED MINISTERS.

In a tract, "An Old Landmark Reset. By Elder J. M. Pendleton, A. M., Union University, Murfreesboro, Tennessee," the author maintains that Baptists ought not to recognise Pedobaptist preachers as gospel ministers. This tract has been circulated extensively, and its doctrine is embraced by many. The discussions on the subject may sometimes have produced temporary evil, but where the parties have a sincere desire to know the truth, and a willingness to follow wherever it may lead, the final result must be good. Parties who agree with each other in their views of Christian doctrine and ordinances, and whose only difference respects the mode of treating those who are in error, ought not to fall out with each other on this question. Each one must act in the matter on his own responsibility; and discussions to ascertain the right mode of acting ought to be conducted in the spirit of kindness, meekness, and gentleness. Discussions so conducted will tend to develop truth; and if they do not bring us to the conclusions of the Landmark, may enable us to correct the premises from which those conclusions are drawn.

The question is not one of mere taste, about which persons may innocently differ; but it involves moral obligation. This is implied in the word *ought*. "Baptists *ought* not," &c. Whatever is morally wrong ought to be avoided as offensive to God. If we have sinned in this matter, through ignorance and unbelief, though God may have graciously pardoned our sin, we should not persevere in the wrong. Our attention is now called to the subject as a question of duty, and we are bound to examine it in the fear of God, and so act hereafter as God will approve.

Baptists are not the only persons concerned to know what duty is. If Baptists ought not to recognise Pedobaptist preachers as gospel ministers, can other persons recognise them blamelessly? If the thing is right for others, why not for Baptists? If the act is wrong in itself, no one can perform it without some degree of guilt. For Baptists to practise it may involve peculiar inconsistency, and a higher degree of guilt. But if the act is in itself one which God disapproves, all men should be warned not to commit it.

On searching the Landmark to find why *Baptists* ought not to recognise Pedobaptist preachers as gospel ministers, we soon discover that the reason has no exclusive relation to Baptists. The doctrine is, that Pedobaptist preachers are not gospel ministers; and, if this doctrine is true, other persons are bound to receive it, and act on it, as well as Baptists. Nor does the doctrine refer to a few Pedobaptist ministers only, who may be less worthy of esteem and confidence than the rest; but it refers to all. Not one of them is a gospel minister; and not one of them ought to be recognised as such.

The honor of Christ is deeply concerned in his ministry. If some messengers sent by the churches were called by Paul "the glory of Christ,"[1] the same may be affirmed emphatically of the messengers sent by Christ himself into the world, to preach his gospel to mankind. He has promised to be with them, they speak by his authority, and in his stead. They bear in earthen vessels

---

[1] 2 Cor. viii. 23.

an inestimable treasure which he has committed to them; and with which he designs to enrich the world. For men whom Christ has never sent to claim that they bear this treasure, and are authorized to dispense it; that they have a commission from him to address mankind in his name, and have his presence with them, and his approbation of their labors;—for men whom Christ has not sent to claim all this, is an evil of no small magnitude. Their presumption must be highly offensive to him; and all who recognise them as his ministers must oppose his will in a matter which he has greatly at heart. The question, therefore, is one of tremendous magnitude. Have all those offended Christ who have recognised as his ministers, Whitfield, Edwards, Davies, Payson, and other such men from whom they have supposed that they received the word of Christ, and by whose ministry they have thought that they were brought to know Christ? If Baptists ought not to recognise such men as gospel ministers, no one ought; and the respect which they have received from men as ministers of the gospel, must be offensive to Christ.

We do not affirm that all these consequences are stated in the Landmark. But if the doctrine of the tract has not led the author thus far, will it not legitimately conduct us to these conclusions, if we adopt and consistently maintain it? But we seem to have the author's approbation in making this application of his principles. He says, "If it is not too absurd to suppose such a thing, let it be supposed that there were persons in apostolic times corresponding to modern Pedobaptists. Can any Baptist believe that Paul, beholding the practices of such persons—seeing the sprinkling of infants substituted for the immersion of believers—would have recognised the ministers of such sects as ministers of Christ, acting according to the gospel? Surely not. Paul would have protested against such a caricature of the Christian system. He would have said to such ministers, 'Will ye not cease to pervert the right ways of the Lord?'"[1]

Conclusions so unfavorable to the entire Pedobaptist ministry are revolting to the minds of multitudes. They see in many of these ministers proofs of humble piety, sincere devotion to the cause of Christ, and deep concern for the salvation of souls. To

---

[1] P. 14.

these manifestations of the proper spirit for the gospel ministry, are added a high degree of Scripture knowledge, and a talent for imparting instruction. When such men are seen devoting their lives to arduous toil for the conversion of souls, and when God appears to crown their labors with abundant success, it is difficult to resist the conviction that they are truly ministers of the gospel, acting with Divine authority and approbation. But the Landmark teaches that these men are not gospel ministers; and its arguments in support of this opinion need a careful examination.

From what premises does the Landmark draw its conclusion? The author informs us in his letter to Dr. Hill. He says, "By a reference to what I have written you will see that Dr. Griffin, a celebrated Pedobaptist, has furnished the premises from which my conclusion is drawn."[1]

He does not profess to have derived them directly from the Scriptures. The tract does not contain a single quotation from the Scriptures, designed to sustain them. Whatever may be the weight of Pedobaptist authority in an argument with Pedobaptists, when Baptists are laboring in the fear of God to ascertain their duty, they ought to seek information from a higher source.

In the quotations made from Dr. Griffin we find the following statements: "Baptism is the initiatory ordinance which introduces us into the visible church; of course, where there is no baptism, there are no visible churches. * * We ought not to commune with those who are not baptized, and, of course, are not church-members, even if we regard them as Christians. * * * I have no right to send the sacred elements out of the church."[2]

These are the premises from which the Landmark draws its conclusion. Is the principle here laid down a doctrine of the Holy Scriptures? If so, we are bound to receive it with every consequence which can be legitimately drawn from it.

In Chapter III. we have investigated the Scripture doctrine concerning the church universal. If we have not mistaken the divine teaching on the subject, every man who is born of the Spirit is a member of this church. Regeneration, not baptism, introduces him into it. The dogma that baptism initiates into the church, and that those who are not baptized are not church-members, even

---

[1] P. 53.   [2] P. 4.

if they are Christians, denies the existence of this spiritual church, and substitutes for it the visible church catholic of theologians. The evils resulting from this unscriptural substitution, have been shown on pp. 132, 133. They are sufficient to deter us from an inconsiderate admission of the dogma from which they proceed.

Dr. Gill called infant baptism "a part and pillar of popery," and we may justly call the dogma of Dr. Griffin a part and pillar of infant baptism. If the true universal church is spiritual, comprising all the regenerate and no others; and if local churches are temporary associations of persons belonging to the universal church, no place is found in either for unregenerate infants. But when baptism is made the door of entrance, instead of regeneration, a way of entrance is opened for infants. Pedobaptism began in the doctrine of baptismal regeneration, and this doctrine, in some form, is necessary to its support. The regenerating power first attributed to baptism; appears to have been understood to be the conferring of the new relation constituting membership in the church. A spiritual church, with a spiritual door of entrance, did not suit the carnal tendency which was rapidly leading men to Romanism. The substitution of the visible church catholic for the spiritual church of Christ, and of baptism for regeneration, led to infant baptism, a corrupt church-membership, and all the evils of popery.

This dogma now efficiently sustains the cause of Pedobaptism. That Dr. Mason considered it a chief pillar of infant baptism, fully appears in his Essays on the Church. Its practical effect is clearly exemplified in the case of the late Dr. Alexander. That excellent man, with two other distinguished Presbyterian ministers of Virginia, became dissatisfied with the proofs of infant baptism on which they had relied. One of them for a time became a Baptist, and the others were strongly inclined to follow him. But all these men settled down at last in the belief of Pedobaptism: and the process of reasoning which satisfied Dr. Alexander's mind, and probably the minds of the rest, is given in his biography. Two considerations kept him back from joining the Baptists. The first was, that the prevalence of infant baptism as early as the fourth and fifth centuries, appeared to him unaccountable on the supposition that no such practice existed in the time of the apostles. The other was his inference that if the Baptists are right, they are the only Christian church on earth, and all other denominations are out of the visible church. He had perceived the corrupting tendency of infant baptism : but the dogma of a visible church catholic with a baptismal boundary, assisted to hold his noble mind fast fettered in error. Shall Baptists receive this dogma with all its consequences?

How thoroughly this Pedobaptist doctrine enters into the reasonings of the Landmark, appears in such passages as the following: "Who can be a minister of Christ according to the gospel, without belonging to the church?"[1] "Now, if Pedobaptist preachers do not belong to the church of Christ, they ought not to be recognised as ministers of Christ."[2] "Our refusal to commune with the Pedobaptists grows out of the fact that they are unbaptized, and out of the church."[3] In these passages, the Landmark uses the phrase, "the church," in apparent conformity to the common doctrine of the visible church catholic; since none are members of it, but baptized persons. But another passage in the pamphlet sets forth a different doctrine: "There is no universal visible church; and if the universal invisible church, composed of all the saved, has what Dr. E. calls 'form,' it is impossible to know what it is. We have no idea of 'form' apart from visibility."[4] According to this, the true and only universal church is "composed of all the saved." How can this be reconciled with the preceding quotations, which represent all unbaptized persons as out of "the church?" How can it be reconciled with the premises adopted from Dr. Griffin, that "those who are not baptized are not church-members, even if we regard them as Christians?" A church composed of "*all* the saved," must contain some unbaptized persons, unless all the unbaptized are unsaved; and if we may account any unbaptized persons members of "the church," we abandon the premises of the Landmark. I do not find evidence, that the pamphlet adopts Mr. Courtney's theory of the church generic; but whether it uses the phrase "the church" generically or collectively, the result is the same. In some way, its signification extends beyond the bounds of a single local church; and yet it is not the true universal church, "composed of all the saved." But "the church" which appears in the premises and reasonings of the Landmark is, at best, only a Baptist modification of the visible church catholic, the church that has given Pedobap-

---

[1] P. 12.   [2] P. 13.   [3] P. 16.   [4] P. 42.

tism and Popery to the world. Many able Baptist writers have fallen into this Pedobaptist error respecting the church; but the discussions to which the Landmark has given occasion, will tend, we may hope, to establish a sounder theology.

The Landmark inquires for the authority on which Pedobaptist preachers act. "If Pedobaptist societies are not churches of Christ, whence do their ministers derive their authority to preach? Is there any scriptural authority to preach which does not come through a church of Christ? And if Pedobaptist ministers are not in Christian churches, have they any right to preach? that is to say, have they any authority *according to the gospel?* They are doubtless authorized by the forms and regulations of their respective societies. But do they act under evangelical authority? It is perfectly evident to the writer, that they do not."[1] We answer, that, if the Holy Spirit has qualified men to preach the gospel, they preach it with divine authority. The Holy Spirit, who divides to every man severally as he will, does not give the necessary qualifications for the gospel ministry, without designing that they shall be used; and since he only can give these qualifications, we are sure that every man who possesses them, is bound, by the authority of God, to use them to the end for which they are bestowed. We arrive at this conclusion, aside from all reasoning about ceremonies and churches; and the proof brings irresistible conviction. Here is a landmark of truth, which must not be deserted, however much we may be perplexed with reasonings about outward forms.

We have maintained, in Chapter VIII., that ministers of the word, as such, are officers of the universal church; and that their call to the ministry by the Holy Spirit, is complete in itself, without the addition of outward ceremony. The person called fails to do his duty, if he neglects the divinely appointed method by which he should enter on the work to which he is called; and this failure tends to obscure the evidence of his divine call. But when, through the obscurity, evidence of his call presents itself with convincing force, we act against reason and against Scripture if we reject it. The seal of divine authority is affixed to that minister who brings into his work qualifications which God only can bestow.

---

[1] P. 11.

While we maintain that Pedobaptist preachers, who give proof that they have been called to their work by the Holy Spirit, ought to be regarded as gospel ministers, we do not insist that Baptists ought to invite all such to occupy their pulpits. This is a different matter. When the Holy Spirit calls, he makes it the duty of the called to study the Holy Scriptures, and to preach what is there taught. His call does not render ministers infallible, or pledge the divine approbation to whatever they may teach; and it therefore does not bind any one to surrender the right of private judgment, and receive with implicit faith whatever may be preached. Much error is sometimes inculcated by preachers, whose divine call to the ministry we cannot question. Even baptism and ordination, however regular, do not make a minister sound in doctrine, and worthy to occupy any and every pulpit. The responsibility of inviting ministers into the pulpit, ought to be exercised with a conscientious regard to the glory of God, and the interests of souls.

An argument for excluding Pedobaptist preachers from our pulpits is drawn by the Landmark from our close communion:—"It is often said by Pedobaptists that Baptists act inconsistently in inviting their ministers to preach with them, while they fail to bid them welcome at the Lord's table. I acknowledge the inconsistency. It is a flagrant inconsistency. No one ought to deny it."[1]

This Pedobaptist objection is endorsed not only by the Landmark, but also by Baptists who practise open communion. All these maintain that we are inconsistent in admitting ministers into the pulpit, when we deny them a seat at the communion table. But a charge of inconsistency made against us by persons who are in error on the very point, ought not to surprise or disquiet us. Let our procedure, in each case, be regulated by the word of God, and we may be sure that, in the end, we shall be found consistent, even if we cannot at once make our consistency apparent to all. The insidious tendency to substitute ceremony for spirituality meets us everywhere, and lies, I apprehend, at the foundation of this charge. If communion at the Lord's table is "a principal spiritual function," as affirmed by Mr. Hall, and if, as is done in this objection of the Landmark, it may be classed with the preaching of the word, as a thing of like character, the charge of incon-

---

[1] P. 16.

sistency in requiring a ceremonial qualification for one, and not for the other, will have a show of justness. But if the Lord's supper is a ceremony, a ceremonial qualification for it may be necessary, which may not be indispensable to the ministry of the word. And it may be the duty of Baptists, both by theory and practice, to teach their erring brethren the important distinction, too often overlooked, between spiritual service to God and that which is ceremonial.

The lawfulness of inviting Pedobaptist preachers into the pulpit, has been defended on the ground that any Christian has the right to talk of Christ and his great salvation. Our Landmark brethren admit that all have a right to make known the gospel privately, but deny that any have the right to proclaim it publicly, except those who have been regularly inducted into the ministerial office. The distinction between talking of Christ privately and proclaiming his gospel publicly, appears to me to respect obligation rather than right. If a Christian has a right to tell of Christ to a fellow man who sits by his side, or walks in the highway with him, he has the same right to address two in like manner, and, so far as I can see, he has an equal right to address ten, a hundred, or a thousand. The obligation to exercise this right is limited only by his ability to do good, and the opportunity which Providence presents of using such talents as he possesses to the glory of God and the benefit of immortal souls. A divine call to the work of the ministry being always accompanied with qualifications for public usefulness, creates obligation rather than confers right, as wealth creates obligation rather than confers right, to relieve the poor. Now, to defend the lawfulness of inviting a Pedobaptist preacher into the pulpit, it has been deemed sufficient to maintain that the person so invited has a *right* to talk of Christ to perishing men, and recommend his salvation to their acceptance. The argument appears to me to be valid; but I have chosen to take higher ground, and to maintain that many Pedobaptist ministers give convincing proof that the Holy Spirit has called and qualified them to preach the gospel, and that it is therefore not only their right, but their duty, to fulfil the ministry which God has committed to them.

We have supposed that an undoubted divine call of any one to the gospel ministry, would command the respect of all who revere the authority of the Most High; but on this point the Landmark holds the following remarkable language :—" I go farther and say, that if God were, with an audible voice, as loud as heaven's mightiest thunder, to call a Pedobaptist to preach, we would not be justified in departing from the Scriptures, unless we were divinely told the utterances of that voice were intended to supersede the teachings of the New Testament. Such information would intimate the beginning of a new economy, and I am writing of the present dispensation."[1]

To this we know not what to say. We have no argument to offer. If God's voice from heaven cannot prevail, all our arguments must be ineffectual, for we have nothing more forcible to urge than the word of the King Supreme. For ourselves, were the undoubted voice of God from heaven to fall on our ears, we have nothing to oppose to his authority. We reverence the Scriptures, but all our reasonings from the Scriptures are as nothing when God speaks. We claim no right to demand explanations respecting his dispensations as a condition of receiving his word. What if God's voice from heaven ushers in a new economy, we want no higher authority than his mere announcement, even if unaccompanied with any explanation; and we may be well assured that all our reasonings about economies, church order, and similar topics, are erroneous, if they lead us to reject the voice of God speaking from heaven.

But how does a divine call of the unbaptized to preach the gospel, constitute a new economy ? John the Baptist, who preached by divine authority, at the beginning of the present dispensation, was unbaptized; and, after the dispensation had been established by the exaltation of Christ, and the gift of the Holy Spirit, Saul of Tarsus was called to preach the gospel while unbaptized. Cases now occur in which persons who undergo examination in order to ordination, refer their convictions of duty with reference to the ministry, to a period anterior to their baptism; and no ordaining presbytery would be justified in denying the possibility of a call by the Holy Spirit, while the subject of it was unbaptized. He who calls the unbaptized to repentance and faith, has the power and right to call them to the ministry also, if it is his pleasure. God has never bound himself in any manner to require none but

[1] P. 48.

baptized persons to preach his word; and we have no right to limit the Holy One of Israel. In our view, the bestowment of ministerial grace and qualifications by the Holy Spirit, indicates the divine will: if not as certainly as it would be indicated by a voice from heaven, yet we cannot resist the conviction which it brings to our minds. When God speaks from heaven, or otherwise clearly indicates his will, we know nothing but reverence and submission.

It has been argued that Baptists ought not to invite Pedobaptist ministers into their pulpits, while they would exclude, both from their communion and their pulpits, a Baptist minister who should inculcate Pedobaptist doctrine. This argument also is a mere appeal to consistency. Such argument ought never to be used when better can be had. If there is any established usage among Baptists with which the invitation of Pedobaptist ministers is inconsistent, the usage may need to be changed. Then the present argument will fall to the ground. But, so far as I know, men who have left the Baptist ministry for the ministry in a Pedobaptist denomination, are, other things being equal, regarded and treated like other Pedobaptist ministers, each case being judged according to its merit. If a false-hearted Baptist minister should retain his connection with a Baptist church, and avail himself of it to disseminate Pedobaptist error, he would deserve to be excluded both from the communion and the pulpit. But if a Baptist minister should become a Pedobaptist, and leave behind him, in the minds of his Baptist brethren, a full conviction that in so doing he acted honestly and conscientiously, I am not aware that he would be viewed less favorably than other Pedobaptist ministers. I remember a case which will illustrate this point. A young Baptist brother, of fervent piety and distinguished talent, was licensed by his church and entered on a course of study to prepare himself for usefulness in the ministry. In prosecuting his studies, his mind came under Pedobaptist influence, and he announced to his church a change of his views, and a desire to connect himself with Pedobaptists. The church separated him from their communion; but the very men who voted this separation, invited him afterwards into their pulpit. They had licensed him because they believed him called of God to the work of the ministry. Their full belief of this remained; and they invited him to preach, not as a Pedobaptist, but as a minister of Christ, whom, as such, they loved. In their view, it was improper for him to remain in a Baptist church and partake of its communion; but they believed it to be right for him to fulfil the ministry to which he had been divinely called. In their view, the exclusion from the communion, and the admission to the pulpit, were perfectly consistent. If others think differently, they will still admit that there was no principle violated in this case, merely because of his having been once a Baptist. This admission will nullify the present argument, and leave the question to be settled on other grounds.

If we admit a Pedobaptist minister into our pulpits, do we not countenance his errors? We do, if we expect him to inculcate these errors, or if we permit him to inculcate them without correction. But this is equally true with respect to Baptist ministers. The responsibility of inviting generally devolves on the pastor of a church, who is bound to instruct the people of his charge in truth and righteousness, and to guard them, as much as possible, from all error. He is, therefore, under obligation, when he invites others to occupy his pulpit, to exercise prudent caution; and this caution is needed with respect to Baptists as well as Pedobaptists. On various occasions I have invited Pedobaptist ministers to preach, where I have been accustomed to officiate; and, in every case, I have been able to approve the doctrine which they preached. In a single case, it happened, that a minister invited to occupy the pulpit, preached doctrine so erroneous, that I deemed it my duty to correct it in a discourse subsequently delivered; but the preacher of this error was a Baptist. If this experience is of any practical value, I would infer from it, not that the Baptist ministry is less orthodox than the Pedobaptist, but that caution is needed where we least suspect danger; and that the inviting of Pedobaptist ministers does not necessarily introduce unsound preaching. If a pastor invites into his pulpit a Pedobaptist minister, whom he sincerely believes to be called of God to the ministry, and who, he believes, will, in his preaching, know nothing but Christ, and him crucified; that pastor may enjoy a pure conscience towards God, undisturbed by any errors of his Pedobaptist brother which he has never approved.

But it will be said, that, although the pastor does not design his invitation of the Pedobaptist minister to be an approval of his errors, it will be so understood by the minister himself, and by others. This, I think, is a mistake. If the pastor has taken due pains to make the truth known, and has clearly defined his own position, and maintained it with firmness and consistency, there will be little danger that his act, in this case, will be misconstrued. What we have maintained is, that the invitation of a Pedobaptist minister to preach in a Baptist pulpit, is not in itself unlawful; but whether it is expedient in any particular case, must depend on the circumstances of the case. If a Baptist pastor is conscious that he has failed to set forth the truth clearly and fully, the objection which we are considering may justly embarrass him; but the proper mode of escape from it, is, to declare the whole counsel of God habitually and unreservedly.

If we were under no obligation with respect to Pedobaptist ministers, we might, as a safe course, decline to have any connection with them. But our Divine Master has commanded us to love all who are born of God. Many of these men manifest strong love to Christ; and we are bound to love them for Christ's sake. They are laboring zealously and faithfully, to honor Christ, and save the souls of men; and the proof that they are called of God to this work, compels us to admit, that they are fellow-laborers with us in the glorious cause, notwithstanding the irregularity of their entrance into it. Can we turn away from such men; and proclaim to the world, that they are not God's ministers? It is surely not necessary, in discountenancing their irregularities, to discountenance their entire ministry. We may approve all that they do right, and rejoice in it, without approving the wrong. This is the simple mode of solving the whole difficulty; and, if people do not at once understand the solution, let us act upon it, conscientiously, and in the fear of God, till men do understand it. In this way we shall give the most effectual recommendation of the truth.

CONCLUSION.

DUTY OF BAPTISTS.

The church order which this treatise claims to have adduced from the Holy Scriptures, could not rely for support on human authority. The sect that maintains it, makes no imposing figure on the pages of ecclesiastical history, and does not hold such rank among the Christian denominations, as to recommend its peculiarities to the general acceptance of mankind. When the gospel was first introduced into the world, but few of the wise, the mighty, and the noble, appeared in its defence. God was pleased, with the weak things of the world, to confound the mighty, that no flesh should glory in his presence. The gospel is not a system of human devising; and true faith receives it as the wisdom of God, however weak and contemptible the instruments of its promulgation may appear. The true disciple of Christ ought not to permit the odium of the anabaptist name to deter him from strict obedience to all his Lord's commands.

Although the truth of God does not need human authority, or the patronage of great names, it is nevertheless the Divine pleasure to make it known to the world by human instrumentality; and this instrumentality needs to be adapted to the purpose for which it is employed. If God has commissioned a sect everywhere spoken against, to make known truth which the wise and learned have overlooked, that sect ought to understand the service to which they have been appointed, and ought to fulfil the prescribed duty firmly, faithfully, and in the fear of the Lord. As men designed for a peculiar service, let us, by earnest and constant endeavor, seek to ascertain the will of him to whose supreme authority we yield all our powers, and let us diligently and perseveringly obey that will, whether men revile or praise.

1. It is our duty to maintain the ordinances of Christ, and the church order which he has instituted, in strict and scrupulous conformity to the Holy Scriptures.

If the investigations of the sacred volume, which have been attempted in this work, have not been unsuccessful, the great body of Christ's professed followers have wandered from the right way. They have established ecclesiastical organizations which are not in accordance with his will; and have corrupted the ceremonies of worship which he instituted. These errors have the sanction of age, and of men venerable for their wisdom. To maintain our peculiarities in opposition to such influences has the appearance of bigotry and narrow-mindedness; and, if they are peculiarities which God's word does not require, we ought to relinquish them. But if we have attained to a knowledge of the Divine will, on points where the great mass of our fellow Christians have mistaken it, a duty of solemn responsibility is imposed on us, to hold fast what we have received, and defend the truth specially committed to our charge.

The plea is often urged that there are good men in all the denominations, and that the various forms of religion, being alike consistent with piety, are matters of minor importance, and ought to be left to the preferences of individuals. If we do not readily admit this plea in its full extent, we are perhaps understood to deny that piety can be found out of our own party, or to claim undue deference to our judgment in religious matters. But whether men understand us or not, we are bound to obey God in everything. No command which he has given can be so unimportant that we are at liberty to disobey it at our pleasure. When the finger of God points out the way, no place is left to us for human preferences. And when we know the will of God, we are not only bound to obey for ourselves, but also to teach others to obey, so far as they are brought under the influence of our instruction. We may, without arrogant assumption, declare what we are firmly persuaded to be the will of God; and we must then leave every one to the judgment of him to whom all must give account. The man who can disobey God, because the thing commanded is of minor importance, has not the spirit of obedience in his heart; and the man who, knowing the will of God, forbears to declare it, because the weight of human authority is against him, fears men more than God.

2. It is our duty, while rendering punctilious obedience to all the commands of God, to regard the forms and ceremonies of religion as of far less importance than its moral truths and precepts.

One of the earliest corruptions of Christianity consisted in magnifying the importance of its ceremonies, and ascribing to them a saving efficacy. With this superstitious reverence of outward forms, a tendency was introduced to corrupt these forms, and substitute ceremonies of human invention for the ordinances of God. To restore these ordinances to their original purity, and, at the same time, to understand and teach that outward rites have no saving efficacy, appears to be a service to which God has specially called the Baptists. We are often charged with attaching too much importance to immersion; but the notion that baptism possesses a sacramental efficacy finds no advocates in our ranks. It introduced infant baptism, and prevailed with it; and it still lingers among those by whom infant baptism is practised. Our principles, by restricting baptism to those who are already regenerate, subvert the doctrine of baptismal regeneration, and exhibit the ceremony in its proper relation to experimental religion. To give due prominence to spirituality above all outward ceremony, is an important service to which God has called our denomination.

3. It is our duty to hold and exhibit the entire system of Christian doctrine in all its just proportions.

An important advance is made in the proper exhibition of Christian truth, when ceremony is rendered duly subordinate to spirituality. This gives an opportunity to adjust the parts of the system in their proper harmony. An additional security for the preservation of sound doctrine, is found in the converted church-membership which our principles require. The church universal is the pillar and ground of the truth, because it consists of those who love the truth; and in proportion as local churches are formed of the same materials, they are prepared to stand as bulwarks against heresy. This service Baptist churches have been known to render to the cause of truth. The general agreement of Baptist churches, in doctrine as well as church order, is a fact which gives occasion for devout gratitude to God. Let it be our continued care never to distort the beautiful system of divine truth by magnifying any part of it beyond its just proportion, or suppressing any part of the harmonious whole.

Because we differ from other professors of religion in our faith and practice respecting the externals of religion, we are under a constant temptation to make too much account of these external peculiarities. Against this temptation we should ever struggle. If we magnify ceremony unduly, we abandon our principles, and cease to fulfil the mission to which the Head of the church has assigned us.

4. It is our duty to maintain lives of holy obedience in all things.

Many persons have the form of godliness who are strangers to its power. They render obedience to ceremonial precepts, while they neglect weightier matters of moral obligation. But a punctilious observance of ceremonies has no necessary connexion with remissness in more important duties. In an affectionate family, the children who strive to please their parents, and gratify their wishes in the most trivial concerns, are expected to be most dutiful in things of greatest moment. Such children of our heavenly Father ought Baptists to be. We claim to obey his will more fully in the outward forms of religion than any other people. Consistency requires that we should be more obedient also in matters of highest importance. It is highly offensive to God, if, while we neglect his most important commands, we attempt to please him with mere outward service. His omniscient eye detects the attempted fraud, and his holiness detests it. Even short-sighted men discover the cheat, and contemn our hypocrisy. The reputation of religion suffers by our unfaithfulness, and men, who observe our conduct, become confirmed in unbelief, to their everlasting ruin. Persons who do not profess to obey God in all things, may, with less pernicious effect, neglect his holy precepts; but Baptists ought to be holy in all things. Our profession requires us to be the best people in the world; and it should be our constant effort to walk according to this profession.

5. It is our duty to labor faithfully and perseveringly to bring all men to the knowledge of the truth.

We claim that we execute the commission which Christ gave to his apostles more fully than other Christian denominations. This commission requires us to preach the gospel to every creature; and we ought to be foremost in obeying it. This obligation has been felt by some of our faith and order, and all of us ought to feel it. The English Baptists have the honor of being foremost in the work of modern missions; and the names of Carey, and his fellow-laborers, who were the pioneers in this difficult service, deserve to be had in lasting remembrance. The names of Judson and Rice appear among the foremost in the history of American missions; and the conversion of these men to the Baptist faith may be regarded as a special call of God on American Baptists to labor for the spread of the gospel throughout the earth. On the Continent of Europe, Oncken and his noble band of associates, are, by their laborious and successful efforts in the Redeemer's cause, but fulfilling the obligations which every Baptist should feel. Voluntary devotion to Christ, and immediate responsibility to him, are conspicuous in our distinguishing peculiarities; and we ought to be conspicuous among the followers of Christ, by our labors or sufferings in his cause.

6. It is our duty to promote the spiritual unity of the universal church, by the exercise of brotherly love to all who bear the image of Christ.

Various schemes have been proposed by the wisdom of men for amalgamating the different Christian denominations. All these originate in the erroneous conception that the unity of the universal church must be found in external organization. To effect the union sought for, compromises are required of the several parties, and the individual conscience must yield to the judgment of the many. All these schemes of amalgamation are inconsistent with the Baptist faith. We seek spiritual unity. We would have every individual to stand on Bible ground, and to take his position there, in the unbiassed exercise of his own judgment and conscience. There we strive to take our position; and there, and there only, we invite our brethren of all denominations to meet us. We yield everything which is not required by the word of God; but in what this word requires, we have no compromise to make. We rejoice to see, in many who do not take our views of divine truth, bright evidence of love to Christ and his cause. We love them for Christ's sake; and we expect to unite with them in his praise through eternal ages. We are one with them in spirit, though we cannot conform to their usages in any particular in which they deviate from the Bible. The more abundantly we love them, the more carefully we strive to walk before them in strict obedience to the commands of our common Lord. And if they sometimes misunderstand our motives, and misjudge our actions, it is our consolation that our divine Master approves; and that they also will approve, when we shall hereafter meet them in his presence.

APPENDIX.

SITUATION OF ENON.

Since *to baptize* is *to immerse,* the declaration of Scripture that "John was *baptizing* in Enon," is proof that the place afforded water in sufficient quantity for the purpose of immersion. Additional proof is furnished in the statement of the inspired writer, that John selected this place of baptizing, "because there was much water there." In the remarks made on this subject in p. 60, I did not think it necessary to enter into any inquiry respecting the geographical situation of Enon. This subject has been considered by the Rev. G. W. Samson, in the tract referred to on p. 63, and he arrives at the following conclusion:—"It was at the point upon the Jordan where the great thoroughfare from Western Galilee and Samaria crosses it, that John selected his favorable location for baptizing." "The permanent record of the early Christians, sanctioned by the New Testament writers, and confirmed by all subsequent observations, leaves no doubt that Enon was at a passage of the Jordan." In this part of the river, its course is very winding, its average width forty-five yards, and its average depth four feet.

The tract of Mr. Samson has been published, in connection with several other valuable tracts, in a duodecimo of 194 pages, entitled "Baptismal Tracts for the Times." The reader who desires to understand the baptismal controversy, will find some important topics discussed in this little volume with much ability.

A different situation has been assigned to Enon, in a work which has just issued from the press—"The City of the Great King; or Jerusalem as it was, as it is, and as it is to be." The author of this work, Dr. Barclay, a resident missionary in Jerusalem for three years and a half, thinks he has found the ancient baptizing-place within a few miles of the Holy City. He describes it thus:— "Returning by a circuitous route to the place whence we had started, from the brow of Wady Farah, we descended with some difficulty into that 'valley of delight'—for such is the literal signification of its name—and truly I have seen nothing so delightful in the way of natural scenery, nor inviting in point of resources, &c., in all Palestine. Ascending its bold stream from this point, we passed some half dozen expansions of the stream, constituting the most beautiful natural natatoria I have ever seen; the water, rivalling the atmosphere itself in transparency, of depths varying from a few inches to a fathom and more, shaded on one or both sides by umbrageous fig trees, and sometimes contained in naturally excavated basins of red mottled marble—an occasional variegation of the common limestone of the country. These pools are supplied by some half dozen springs of the purest and coldest water, bursting from rocky crevices at various intervals. Verily, thought I, we have stumbled upon Enon." * * * "Although this *conjecture*—that Ain Farah was Ænon—must be set down to the account of a mere random suggestion of the moment, yet a more intimate acquaintance with the geography of the neighborhood has brought me to an assured conviction that this place is indeed no other than the 'Enon near to Salim, where John was baptizing, because there was much water there.'"

PLACE OF THE EUNUCH'S BAPTISM.

The sacred writer who has recorded the Acts of the Apostles, has informed us that the Eunuch was baptized in "the way that goeth down from Jerusalem unto Gaza, which is desert."[1] The word "desert" seems to have suggested to some minds the idea, that the baptism occurred in an arid region, in which water of sufficient depth for immersion could not be found. Gaza, though once

---

[1] Acts viii. 26.

a populous city with massy gates,[1] was now almost without inhabitants, according to the prediction of the prophets, "Baldness is come upon Gaza:"[2] I will send a fire on the wall of Gaza, which shall devour the palaces thereof."[3] In Scripture language, the name *desert* or *wilderness*, is applied to a thinly inhabited country, even though including cities or towns distant from each other. It was, therefore, applicable to the region in which Gaza was situated, and into which the road of the Eunuch's descent from Jerusalem penetrated.

Dr. Barclay describes a journey which he took from Jerusalem to Gaza. He found the way passing through a fertile country, well supplied with water. He sought for the place of the Eunuch's baptism; but the disquieted condition of the country stopped his prosecution of the search. He says: "We were the more anxious to visit El-Hassy, on account of information received recently from Sheikh of Felluge, and abundantly confirmed at Burrier, that in Wady-el-Hassy about two or three hours distant, at Ras Kussahbeh and at Moyat es-Sid, in the same wady, the stream of water is as broad as our tent (twelve feet), and varies in depth from a span to six or seven feet—occasionally sinking and reappearing. This was, doubtless (Moyat es-Sid), the certain water of which we were in quest; but we were constrained, however reluctantly, to abandon the idea of seeing it."

Mr. Samson's description of the country through which the Eunuch journeyed, agrees with that of Dr. Barclay. Several places are noticed on the way, in which immersion may have been performed. Concerning one of these, he thus writes: "In front of the fortress by us is a fine gushing fountain of sweet water, and broad stone troughs in which we water our horses. This spot has been fixed on by Dr. Robinson as the *Bethsur* mentioned by Eusebius and Jerome as the place where the Eunuch was baptized. The ground in front of the fountain, and of the structure behind it, is so broken up and covered with stones, that it is difficult to determine what was once here. There is now a slightly depressed hollow, with a sandy or gravelly bottom. It is hardly conceivable that, in the days of Herod, the fountain-builder, this most favorable spring should not have been made to supply a pool in this

---

[1] Judges xvi. 1—3.   [2] Jer. xlvii. 5.   [3] Amos i. 7.

land of such structures; and even now water sufficient to supply such a reservoir flows from the troughs, and soaks into the soil; as, according to Jerome's mention, in his day it seems also to have been absorbed. That an ancient '*chariot*' road passed this way, the observant traveller will often perceive on his journey. Dr. Robinson twice between Hebron and Jerusalem, notices this; and we have traced even plainer evidences."

IMMERSION IN COLD CLIMATES.

To the objection stated on p. 67, that immersion is not suited to cold climates, I have not attempted a formal reply. It gives me pleasure to present to the reader the following remarks on this subject, which have been written at my special request, by the Rev. Mr. Samson:

The idea that immersion, as an ordinance of Christ's church, is incompatible with his design that his religion should spread to all nations and climates, is alike disproved by Scripture, and by the facts of history in the spread of Christianity.

When Jesus said "Go teach," or make disciples of "all nations," he added, "baptizing them in the name of the Father, and of the Son, and of the Holy Ghost." The word *baptize* in the language in which Christ spoke, as every Greek scholar allows, meant nothing else than immerse. It is impossible to reconcile it with the supreme wisdom of Jesus, that without qualification of language, he commanded this ordinance in this form to be performed among the nations of every clime, if there really were anything in immersion inconsistent with health in any latitude, or with propriety in any age of refinement.

Early in the apostolic history this was tested. The apostle was accustomed to baptism at first in the neighborhood of Jerusalem, among the "common people" that bathed in Jordan, and the pools of the Holy City. He writes a letter to Rome, the centre of refinement and luxury, where some members of "Cæsar's household" had joined the Christian church, in a region *ten degrees* north of Jerusalem, where the cold of winter compelled the self-denying martyr to send as far as Old Troy for a Roman coat he had left there; yet there had not been, either on account of the peculiar refinement and delicacy of the people of Rome, or on account of the rigor of their winter, any change in the mode of baptism, if we may draw an inference from the apostle's words: "Therefore we are buried with him by baptism into death."[1] It ought to be remembered that summer is warm in every climate; that bathing is often practised, as it was in Rome, and as it is in our country, more by people in northern than in southern latitudes; and that the winter of the southern climate, in the latitude of Jerusalem, where the snow thaws almost immediately on its fall, is more trying than in far northern regions, the air being chillier, and the water more icy-cold.

Subsequent history is more convincing than even these facts of the apostolic age in this regard. The Eastern or Greek Church (by the side of which the Western or Roman Church, occupying three or four little countries of Southern Europe, is a speck on the map), embraces every variety of climate and class of people. Beginning with Abyssinia, in the hot regions of Central Africa, extending through Egypt in Northern Africa, it spreads along all Western Asia, takes in half of Europe, and embraces especially all Siberia and Northern Russia; thus comprising the very coldest regions, as well as the hottest, in which man can live. In all these climates, among all these people, baptism is administered by triple immersion. If it be an infant that is brought, despite his struggles and cries, he is three times plunged in the broad baptismal font. In mid April, while the Jordan's waters are yet chilly with the melting snows that cover the top of Hermon and all the Lebanon range (from which that stream flows), every year from 5000 to 6000 persons of every age, sex, climate, and condition in life, go down into the chilling stream, and either bury themselves or are buried by others beneath its waters. At St. Petersburgh a stranger expression still is given, at midwinter, in reply to the objection that climate renders immersion impracticable. The chosen day for immersion is at Christmas, near New Year's; and that through the ice of the Neva. A temporary chapel is erected on the ice, a large hole is cut, and with a round of ceremonies the water is consecrated by the priest; when mothers bring their infants and plunge them, and people of mature age come and dip themselves there. Moreover, at any time in the winter, when proselytes in the most

---

[1] Rom. vi. 4.

northern regions of the Russian possessions are made, they are baptized through the ice. Any one wishing to verify these statements, may consult such a work as William Burder's Religious Ceremonies, published at London, 1841; or he may perhaps be personally an eye-witness.

It is the Western, especially the Roman church, that has departed from the original mode of baptism; and that not from reasons connected with climate. All the Northern portion (not the Southern) of Western Europe, which originally was converted to pure Christianity and denied the authority of the Roman church, which in the age of subsequent corruption departed least from the faith as it is in Jesus, and only nominally became allied to the Roman church, and which was the first to hail and to embrace the call for the reformation,—all the coldest regions of Western Europe received and maintained the longest the rite of immersion. It was the warm latitudes that departed from it.

To verify this, one needs but turn to the Latin chronicles of Alcuin and others of those Judson-like missionaries, who, during the reign of Alfred of England and Charlemagne of France, carried pure Christianity into the heart of Germany, and won all the rude tribes of those lands, from which our ancestry sprung, to Christianity. It impresses the thoughtful mind with gratitude, that the truth as it was in Jesus was preached and embraced by the rude men from whom our strong race has come, as we read Alcuin's letters to Charlemagne, rather commanding than entreating his sovereign to be true to Christ's appointment; charging him not to *force* these people by the sword, which he never could do, to receive Christian baptism; and quoting Jerome's Commentary on Matt. xxviii. 19, 20: " Primum eos doceant, deinde doctas intinquant aquâ," to show that the fathers of the church taught that missionaries "*must first teach their people, and then immerse them in water.*" And in the cold northern Vistula, thousands on thousands, the records of the times tell us, were, in the heat of summer, and in the cold of winter, baptized on sincere personal profession of faith in Christ.

If farther confirmation of this fact be desired, that the people of *cold* countries have preferred immersion, it may be found in the work of "*Wheatly on the Book of Common Prayer of England,*" Bohn's edition, pp. 337—350. Of the fonts now found in the old English churches, he says, "So called, I suppose, because baptism in the beginning of Christianity was performed in springs or fountains. * * In the primitive times we meet with them very large and capacious, not only that they might comport with the general customs of those times, viz.: of persons being immersed or put under water, but also because the stated times of baptism returning so seldom, great numbers were usually baptized at the same time. In the middle of them was always a partition, the one part for men, the other for women; that so by being baptized asunder they might avoid giving offence and scandal." The author here cites the orders of Edward, when the crowd was so great they could not be gathered around the church door; all of which shows that baptism was often administered to adults, that it was by immersion, and that a very large number could be baptized on one occasion in the ordinary font. Again the author says, "Except upon extraordinary occasions, baptism was seldom, or perhaps never, administered for the first four centuries but by immersion or dipping. Nor is aspersion or sprinkling ordinarily used, to this day, in any country that was never subject to the Pope; and among those that submitted to his authority, England was the last place where it was received; though it has never obtained so far as to be enjoined, *dipping* having been always prescribed by the rubric. The Salisbury Missal, printed in 1530 (the last that was in force before the Reformation), expressly requires and orders dipping. And in the first Common Prayer Book of King Edward VI., the priest's general order is to dip it in water." Here we see that it was not on account of climate any change grew up; the people in the extreme north were the last to surrender the original mode; and not even the Pope's authority could compel them to strike out of their Missal the form received in the simplicity of their early reception of Christianity. Farther, we read that from love for the primitive ordinance, "fonts were in times of popery unfitly and surreptitiously placed near the churches." The author states the alleged, and then the real cause why affusion took the place of immersion, as follows:—"Many fond ladies at first, and then by degrees the common people, would persuade the minister that their children were too tender for dipping. But what principally tended to confirm this practice, was that several of our English divines flying to Germany, Switzerland, &c., during the bloody reign of Queen Mary, and returning home when Queen Elizabeth came to the crown, brought back with them a great love and zeal for the customs of those churches beyond sea, where they had been sheltered and received. And consequently having observed that in Geneva and some other places, baptism was ordered to be performed by affusion, they thought they could not do the church of England a greater service, than to introduce a practice dictated by so great an oracle as Calvin. So that in the times of Queen Elizabeth, and during the reigns of King James and King Charles I., there were but very few children dipped in the font." So it appears it was not on the score of health (which down to 1500 years after Christianity had existed in England never had been thought of), but it was *fashion* which led to the change. Of subsequent times, and the folly of the Reformers of Elizabeth's and of James' day, the author adds, "These reformers, it seems, could not recollect that fonts to baptize in had been long used before the times of popery, and that they had nowhere been discontinued from the beginning of Christianity, but in such places where the Pope had gained authority. But our divines at the Restoration, understanding a little better the sense of scripture and antiquity, again restored the order for immersion." Yet though this is still the order of the Book of Common Prayer, the author regrets that it is ineffective. Custom, fashion triumphs, even over a statute of the realm of England.

The struggle of his own mind to be satisfied with the appeal to climate as an argument for sprinkling, speaks out in these two sentences of the author. The present Order of the Prayer Book as to baptism is he says "keeping as close to the primitive rule for baptism as the coldness of our region, and the tenderness wherewith infants are now used, will sometimes admit. Though Sir John Floyer, in a discourse on cold baths, hath shown from the nature of our bodies, from the rules of medicine, from modern experience, and from ancient history, that nothing could tend more to the preservation of a child's health than dipping it in baptism."

THE END.

A BIOGRAPHICAL SKETCH OF JOHN LEADLEY DAGG
(1794-1884)

BY

JOHN FRANKLIN JONES

A Biographical Sketch of John Leadley Dagg (1794-1884)

John Leadley Dagg was born at Middleburg, Loudoun County, Virginia, February 13, 1794 (*ESB*), the eldest of eight children (*DCA*). He worked as saddler (his father's trade), taught school, and studied medicine. A soldier in the War of 1812, he witnessed the bombardment of Fort McHenry at Baltimore (*ESB*).

Largely self-taught in his mastery of Latin, Greek, Hebrews, and higher mathematics, he only had six or seven years of formal schooling (*DCA*). Pursuing his studies by candlelight left his eyesight permanently impaired, and in later life, he mostly wrote and read assisted by others (*ESB*).

In 1812 he was baptized into the Ebenezer Baptist Church (*DCA*). He began preaching in 1816 (*ESB*), and was ordained to preach in 1817 (*DCA*). He served churches in Loudoun, Fairfax, and Fauquier counties. Financial necessity compelled his employment conducting a school for girls at Middleburn and later, as principal of the Upperville Academy (*ESB*).

Dagg was pastor of the Fifth Baptist Church of Philadelphia 1825-1834 (*DCA*). In that position, he advocated temperance, missions, and benevolence. He founded the Pennsylvania Missionary Association (later, the Pennsylvania Baptist Convention), was prominent in Triennial Convention and served that body as vice president and as a member of the board of managers. He was also a trustee at Columbian College, a leader in the American Baptist Home Mission

Society, the American and Foreign Bible Society, and the Baptist General Tract Society (became the American Baptist Publication Society (*ESB*).

Difficulties with his throat required his withdrawal from preaching. Thereafter, he devoted himself to teaching, administering educational programs, and writing. He headed the Haddington institution near Haddington (*DCA*). Hadding College was a manual labor school near Philadelphia and was devoted to educating Baptist ministers. At Hadding, he began his career teaching theology (*ESB*).

He moved to Tuscaloosa in 1836 to the Alabama Female Athenaeum, (*DCA*), becoming its president in 1836. At AFA, he associated with Basil Manly, then president of the University of Alabama. Manly conferred the D.D. degree upon Dagg in 1843. Manly recommended Dagg to be appointed as president and professor of theology Mercer in 1844 (*ESB*).

Dagg was president of Mercer University in Penfield, Georgia 1844 to 1854 and professor of theology at Mercer until 1856 (*DCA*). Patrick Hues Mell was his colleague at Mercer and testified to Dagg's being the most successful college president he knew. Dagg helped build Mercer's theological seminary to a position unequaled in the pre-Civil War South (*ESB*).

Upon retirement from the Mercer faculty in 1856, Dagg lived with relatives at Madison, Cuthbert, and Forsyth, Georga until 1870. In that year, he moved to Hayneville, Alabama until his death June 11, 1884 (Ibid.).

His *An Essay in Defence of Strict Communion* (1845), *A Decisive Argument against Infant Baptism* (1849), and *Origin and Authority of the Bible* (1853) dealt with the ordinances and Scripture (*DCA*).

After retiring, he wrote his most famous theological books: *A Manual of Theology* (1857), *A Treatise on Church Order* (1858), *The Elements of Moral Science* (1860); and *The Evidences of Christianity* (1869) (*DCA*).

Dagg was devoted to preparing ministers for service. His theology was biblical and "moderately Calvinistic" and he was reputed a pioneer Baptist theologian in America (*DCA*). In the South, Dagg's books replaced Northerner texts by men such as Francis Wayland (*ESB*).

He was married twice. His first wife was Fannie H. Thornton of Virginia. This first marriage birthed a son, John Francis Dagg, also a minister, college president, and the editor of the *Christian Index*. Dagg's second wife was Mary Young Davis, the mother of Noah K. Davis, the philosopher (*ESB*).

BIBLIOGRAPHY

[Boykin, Samuel]. *History of the Baptist Denomination in Georgia and Biographical Compendium*. 1881.

Dagg, J. L. "Autobiography of John L. Dagg." Manuscript. Mercer University, Atlanta, GA.

Dagg, John L. *A Treatise on Church Order* (1858).

Dictionary of American Biography. S.v. "John Leadley Dagg," by F. G. Lewis.

Dictionary of Christianity in America. S.v. "Dagg, John Leadley (1794-1884)," by W. M. Patterson. (Cited as *DCA*).

Encyclopedia of Southern Baptists. S.v. "Dagg, John Leadley," by Malcolm Lester.

Gardner, R. G. "John Leadley Dagg." *Review and Expositor* 54 (1957): 246-63.

Straton, H. H. "John Leadley Dagg" (1926).

By John Franklin Jones
Cordova, Tennessee
July 2006

THE BAPTIST STANDARD BEARER, INC.

a non-profit, tax-exempt corporation
committed to the Publication & Preservation
of the Baptist Heritage.

CURRENT TITLES AVAILABLE IN
THE BAPTIST *DISTINCTIVES* SERIES

KIFFIN, WILLIAM — A Sober Discourse of Right to Church-Communion. Wherein is proved by Scripture, the Example of the Primitive Times, and the Practice of All that have Professed the Christian Religion: That no Unbaptized person may be Regularly admitted to the Lord's Supper. (London: George Larkin, 1681).

KINGHORN, JOSEPH — Baptism, A Term of Communion. (Norwich: Bacon, Kinnebrook, and Co., 1816)

KINGHORN, JOSEPH — A Defense of "Baptism, A Term of Communion". In Answer To Robert Hall's Reply. (Norwich: Wilkin and Youngman, 1820).

GILL, JOHN — Gospel Baptism. A Collection of Sermons, Tracts, etc., on Scriptural Authority, the Nature of the New Testament Church and the Ordinance of Baptism by John Gill. (Paris, AR: The Baptist Standard Bearer, Inc., 2006).

CARSON, ALEXANDER	Ecclesiastical Polity of the New Testament. (Dublin: William Carson, 1856).
BOOTH, ABRAHAM	A Defense of the Baptists. A Declaration and Vindication of Three Historically Distinctive Baptist Principles. Compiled and Set Forth in the Republication of Three Books. Revised edition. (Paris, AR: The Baptist Standard Bearer, Inc., 2006).
BOOTH, ABRAHAM	Paedobaptism Examined on the Principles, Concessions, and Reasonings of the Most Learned Paedobaptists. With Replies to the Arguments and Objections of Dr. Williams and Mr. Peter Edwards. 3 volumes. (London: Ebenezer Palmer, 1829).
CARROLL, B. H.	*Ecclesia* - The Church. With an Appendix. (Louisville: Baptist Book Concern, 1903).
CHRISTIAN, JOHN T.	Immersion, The Act of Christian Baptism. (Louisville: Baptist Book Concern, 1891).
FROST, J. M.	Pedobaptism: Is It From Heaven Or Of Men? (Philadelphia: American Baptist Publication Society, 1875).
FULLER, RICHARD	Baptism, and the Terms of Communion; An Argument. (Charleston, SC: Southern Baptist Publication Society, 1854).
GRAVES, J. R.	Tri-Lemma: or, Death By Three Horns. The Presbyterian General Assembly Not Able To Decide This Question: "Is Baptism In The Romish Church Valid?" 1st Edition.

	(Nashville: Southwestern Publishing House, 1861).
MELL, P.H.	Baptism In Its Mode and Subjects. (Charleston, SC: Southern Baptist Publications Society, 1853).
JETER, JEREMIAH B.	Baptist Principles Reset. Consisting of Articles on Distinctive Baptist Principles by Various Authors. With an Appendix. (Richmond: The Religious Herald Co., 1902).
PENDLETON, J.M.	Distinctive Principles of Baptists. (Philadelphia: American Baptist Publication Society, 1882).
THOMAS, JESSE B.	The Church and the Kingdom. A New Testament Study. (Louisville: Baptist Book Concern, 1914).
WALLER, JOHN L.	Open Communion Shown to be Unscriptural & Deleterious. With an introductory essay by Dr. D. R. Campbell and an Appendix. (Louisville: Baptist Book Concern, 1859).

For a complete list of current authors/titles, visit our internet site at:
www.standardbearer.org
or write us at:

he Baptist Standard Bearer, Inc.
NUMBER ONE IRON OAKS DRIVE • PARIS, ARKANSAS 72855
TEL # 479-963-3831   *FAX # 479-963-8083*
EMAIL: Baptist@centurytel.net   *http://www.standardbearer.org*

Thou hast given a standard to them that fear thee; that it may be displayed because of the truth. — Psalm 60:4

www.ingramcontent.com/pod-product-compliance
Lightning Source LLC
Chambersburg PA
CBHW021753230426
43669CB00006B/73